PENGUIN BOOKS

THERE WAS A TIME

THERE WAS
A TIME

Dorothy Butler

PENGUIN BOOKS

PENGUIN BOOKS

Penguin Books (NZ) Ltd, cnr Airborne and Rosedale Roads, Albany,
Auckland 1310, New Zealand
Penguin Books Ltd, 27 Wrights Lane, London W8 5TZ, England
Penguin USA, 375 Hudson Street, New York, NY 10014, United States
Penguin Books Australia Ltd, 487 Maroondah Highway, Ringwood, Australia 3134
Penguin Books Canada Ltd, 10 Alcorn Avenue, Toronto, Ontario, Canada M4V 3B2
Penguin Books (South Africa) Pty Ltd, 4 Pallinghurst Road, Parktown,
Johannesburg 2193, South Africa

Penguin Books Ltd, Registered Offices: Harmondsworth, Middlesex, England

First published by Penguin Books (NZ) Ltd, 1999

1 3 5 7 9 10 8 6 4 2

Designed by Mary Egan
Typeset by Egan-Reid Ltd
Printed in Australia by Australian Print Group, Maryborough

There was a time when meadow, grove, and stream,
The earth, and every common sight,
To me did seem
Apparell'd in celestial light,
The glory and the freshness of a dream.

From *Ode on Intimations of Immortality from Recollections of Early Childhood*,
by William Wordsworth.

Acknowledgments

My deepest thanks go to my friend and son-in-law David Munro, who, with never-flagging patience and good cheer not only transformed my handwritten scrawl into neat pages of word-processed script, but more than once made sensible suggestions.

The rest of my large family, particularly my husband Roy, have been, as ever, considerate and supportive. They all have my love and thanks.

I must express gratitude also to Creative New Zealand, whose grant for the writing of this book helped in practical ways, and ensured its completion in reasonable time.

PROLOGUE

I am sitting in Ross's wheelchair, the best place to sit for a chat with him when he is at his desk. There is a splendid leather armchair for more formal visitors on the other side of the room, but the two computer screens and sundry paraphernalia which help my brother get words on to paper tend to create a barrier. I prefer the wheelchair. It must not be moved, of course, even an inch, if he is to manoeuvre himself unaided into it when he wants to; but I know this, and check that the brake is on before I take possession.

Just beyond the windows, which are wooden-slatted, unglazed apertures, the Francis Drake Channel reflects the startling blue of the West Indian sky. The background sound is of soft, swishing waves on the shingled beach on the other side of the low rock 'hurricane' wall. An occasional yacht turns the prospect into a tourist brochure.

More than sixty years have passed since the water we gazed at from our front window in Devonport, Auckland, New Zealand was the Waitemata Harbour: blue in some of its moods, but never as blue as this. Ross's laugh hasn't changed much over the years, and he is laughing now.

'Remember,' he says, 'I must have been eight, so you'll have been seven and we went over the cliff to Dockie Beach at dawn on a Sunday morning, and the old man came after us?' Our father must have been thirty-one at the time of this incident, but he was always 'the old man' to Ross.

Yes, I remember. We shared a bedroom in those days and we had planned the expedition the night before. We assured one another that Mum and Dad would be delighted at our decision to start collecting driftwood for winter fires. We had heard that other kids were doing it. Why not us?

Our house was on one side of Calliope Road, the cliff on the other. It was just light as we slid out of the house, each equipped with a sack: 'sugarbags' they were, in those days. The cliff looked, and was, precipitous, but we were not worried. It was not *really* sheer; there would be plenty of handholds, and we were both used to cliffs, even if we had never braved this one before. Down we went.

'Dockie Beach' was the name used by local people for the short stretch of sand just around the cliff from Stanley Bay, our beach, in the direction of the Calliope Dock. Here 'warships', as we called them, were tied up and serviced.

The tide was conveniently out. Ross may have anticipated this but I hadn't given it a thought. Sea and air were utterly still. We seemed to be the only people in the world, and there was, indeed, plenty of wood for the gathering. Filling the sacks was easy.

Getting up the cliff with our booty was another matter altogether. (We found out later that the 'other kids' were all much older than us, and were in the habit of tying their sugarbags with rope and slinging them on their backs.) Reluctantly, we reduced the amount of wood in each bag and tried again. No good; even Ross could manage only a short ascent with one hand entirely devoted to clutching a half-filled bag of wood. Philosophically, we gave up.

Neither of us had emerged from that stage of early childhood that easily transfers its attention to alternative occupations if the first becomes unrewarding, so we played one of our favourite games for a while, identifying pieces of driftwood as alligators, tigers, snakes, or monkeys, floating them in the shallows, endowing them with personalities, assigning to them kindly or malevolent intentions. We might have kept this up for hours, but the sun was well up and we had had no breakfast.

We had better go home.

Leaving the wood — and the sugarbags — was a wrench, but had to be done. Up the cliff we went, Ross, as usual, first. He was, I suppose, three-quarters of the way up, I, just behind, copying his hand and foot grips, when our father's head appeared over the top of the cliff.

'Christ!'

He said years later that the sight of our two blond heads with, as background, a far-below beach embellished with vicious rocks almost sent him over the edge. (He was never very steady on Sunday mornings anyway. Saturday afternoons in the pub ensured that.)

Our panted, cheerful shouts had no effect. Lying with half his torso over the cliff edge, Dad began giving us quite unnecessary — even dangerous, had we heeded them — instructions.

'Move your left foot, Ross! Dorothy, *stay where you are*!'

Our father, Bill Norgrove, had been an inner-city boy, and a frail one at that. He had probably never gone up a cliff in his life. Ross and I took no notice, and kept climbing. The only frightening bit was the wild yank Dad gave each of us as, one after the other, we came within his reach.

All three of us collapsed on the grass.

'Christ!' Dad seemed incapable of saying anything else. The arm he placed round each of us was shaking; we could feel his heart pounding. Our cheerful reassurances, our explanations of the failure of the mission and the loss of the sacks went unheeded. He seemed to be in a world of his own, a world, no doubt, in which two of his precious children lay broken and bleeding on the rocks of Dockie Beach.

The reality of two red-faced, noisy, *live* children registered ultimately, and he made some effort at fatherly behaviour. But he kept an arm round each of us still, as we crossed the road. When he managed his usual 'You two!' with a laugh and a shake of his head, we knew he would be all right. 'You both deserve a damn good hiding' — and we knew he was himself again. (This was a statement of opinion, not of intention.)

In the kitchen, our mother was pouring boiling water into mugs, which clearly contained cocoa. The usual porridge was bubbling on the coal range. Mum had got up to attend to our little sister, Val, and, finding our beds empty, suspected that we might have embarked on this particular exercise. She had no doubt heard mutterings. Now she looked as if she might laugh. Mum's reaction to my father's Sunday morning hangover was always a mixture of amusement and exasperation. Nothing could have got him out of bed at such an unpalatable hour, on his only day of rest, but a real or imagined threat to the safety of one or more of his children. Implicit in my mother's amusement was a 'you got more than you bargained for this time' element. He was probably still shaking.

'You'd better go back to bed, Bill,' she said. 'I'll make a cup of tea.' You could count on Mum to be kind, however blunt. To us she said, 'That was a silly thing to do,' but without any real conviction. Her stories about her own and her sister's and brothers' escapades as children in Thames eclipsed anything we might come up with. She couldn't have it both ways.

❃

Later, I took Dad his cup of tea, gripping the handle of the cup with one hand, the saucer with the other, and watching my feet all the way. (There had been a recent incident when Ross had sprung out on me from behind the heavy, looped-back curtains in the hall. He claimed that he didn't know I was carrying a cup of tea, but I never believed him.) Dad had gone back to bed in his clothes, and appeared to be asleep. He had black hair, curly like ours, and thick dark eyelashes. Everyone remarked on his good looks. Other people's fathers paled by comparison.

I put the tea on the bedside table. Dad's eyes opened, and he put out a hand to take mine briefly.

'Thanks love,' he said.

I loved him, utterly.

ONE

I imagine I share the frustration of the rest of humanity when I try to penetrate the fog that surrounds my earliest impressions of life. Wafting sensations, snatches of awareness . . . Do I really remember *that* event, or have I been told so often that it has become embedded in a kind of pseudo-memory which is a pastiche of the truly remembered and the acquired? No one could have had a mother who related the events of one's earliest days more persistently, and in such detail. Perhaps most of my memories are not memories at all.

'You roared so loudly I thought you were another boy,' my mother told me a hundred times. She didn't exactly *say* 'feared' but I was left in no doubt that this had been her emotion. Ross was already established as the idol of the large, sprawling household I was to join. In no time at all he was to become my idol too. But, if they had wanted another child at all only sixteen months after his triumphant arrival, they had wanted a girl. I was engulfed in ecstatic approval, from all quarters. The curls my mother and aunt proposed to tie up in bows were already apparent, I have been told, and I was a large healthy child, as Ross had been.

The noted bellows, which were my first comment on a world I have enjoyed but not always agreed with, might have taken the edge off my parents' rapture had they thought about it. For this, their daughter, was to be if nothing else, outspoken. 'Dorothy would argue that black was white,' my mother would say serenely, once this propensity had surfaced. Serenely, because she had an unusual acceptance of the way people 'were'. 'Well, that's the way Val *is*,' she would say to me years later when I complained about some aspect of my younger sister's behaviour. This tolerance was a feature of my mother's nature, which was to gratify but also annoy me in the years to come, depending on its object. It was, of course, a welcome attitude as applied to me, but it rankled that she never tried to modify the unacceptable behaviour of certain other people. A deep sigh was the closest my mother ever came to criticism, and even that had a philosophical flavour.

Well then. In the autumn of 1925 I was borne home from a small nursing home in Grey Lynn (conducted, I have been told, by one Nurse Porteous) to my maternal grandparents' home on the corner of Surrey Crescent and Richmond Avenue (now Road), in the same suburb. There I was to be loved, indulged, given mother's milk and anything else anyone could think of that I might like, and invariably snatched up by a hovering adult before any squeak could develop into a cry proper. I was presented to my brother as the finest gift anyone could have devised for him and surprisingly, he seemed to believe this. Clearly, he did not expect any reduction in the adulation and indulgence to which he had become accustomed and, just as clearly, none occurred.

My mother had firm opinions about what babies and children needed, though one should perhaps not call them 'opinions'. Rather, they were tenets of faith. If questioned she would rest her case on 'common sense'. Babies only cried, she claimed, if they were hungry, frightened, uncomfortable or bored. In all of these circumstances, the remedy was the same. Pick the child up, feed it or comfort it or change it or play with it — or all four, if diagnosis was unclear. She was certain that these simple procedures would produce happy children, seemingly her only intention, and in our case she was right. Ross and I were reputed to be sublimely happy children. Certainly, all my memories of that old house, shadowy as they are of the two years I lived there, clearer of the subsequent visits and overnight stays, are of a warm, accepting place, full of noise and laughter.

For this was a large household, comprising a set of grandparents, our own family of four, a younger aunt (whose name, Muriel Dorothy, I was given in its entirety) and sundry boarders who had replaced two older sons, now independent: one married, one vaguely 'in Australia'. Some of the boarders were transient friends, but several others were almost 'family'. I recall Jack, who worked in the 'Dress Materials' department of George Courts in Karangahape Road. Unmarried and about fifty, he was a quiet, kindly man, dapper in appearance and sober in habits. Jack was a foundation member of the baby-and-toddler support club: always good for a game, with a strongly developed leg for Ride-a-Cock-Horse, and a good voice for song and story. My mother described him years later as having been 'a clean, steady man', qualities much valued in these days. (My father, while certainly 'clean' was later revealed as not 'steady', a fact my mother almost certainly knew when she married him. But he was charming, and lovable. I recall many deep sighs, but also much laughter, in those early days.)

The old house is still there, but no longer on the corner, for its large garden has been usurped by an unlovely panelbeating establishment. My grandmother was a good gardener, and grew fine crops of vegetables for the family table. For the rest, the front lawn was mowed regularly (probably by Jack) and the remainder of the property, which was peppered with fruit trees, planted haphazardly with shrubs and 'slips' from other people's gardens. A rough order was the flavour, the result an idyllic playground for children. Alas, all that has gone. No one so far has restored the old house, though it is far from derelict. Perhaps someone, someday, will move it bodily, as happened in Virginia Lee Burton's book *The Little House* so loved by generations of children. Perhaps someone will 'look her all over' and say, 'Sure, this house is as good as ever. She's built so well we could move her anywhere . . .' and they will jack her up and put her on wheels. Then, just as the Little House 'rolled along the big roads and rolled along little roads until they were way out in the country . . .' so will she, and the echoes of seventy-year-old laughter and song will be heard eerily from within.

I drive past the house often, on my way to a daughter's home in Grey Lynn, and once, a few months ago, I parked my car and walked along the sadly foreshortened front fence. The house seemed deserted, so I stood and stared for a long time. Surely, in my grandparents' time, it was bigger? Certainly the jumble of outbuildings behind has gone; and my grandfather's shed, built especially to house the secondhand printing press he bought on his retirement from the *Thames Star* was obviously a casualty of the panelbeating enterprise, or some earlier desecration. Was the press with all its appurtenances dumped or sold as scrap — or preserved by some unknown devotee . . . could it still be in existence?

My grandfather, who had taught my mother to set type, used to say that she was one of the best typesetters he had ever known, and, to the end of her long life, she was an impeccable speller. She had left school at twelve as had my father. In those days, clever working-class children in New Zealand usually had fewer years at school than slower pupils, as they passed the Proficiency Examination earlier and simply 'went out to work'. I recall my mother's description of the typesetting process; and surely I *remember* seeing the oblong boxes, and the tiny type, which one had to set, letter by letter and line by line, with punctuation, *backwards*, so that, once inked, inserted in the press and printed, it all emerged as readable text?

I stand at the fence, and see thin, tall Emily, 'the clever one', feeding print with lightning speed into the boxes, totally occupied with the task in hand, as she was always. Alas, no 'great-great-great-granddaughter' of the man who built *this* house 'so well' will ever come upon it unexpectedly as in the children's book, and start repossession and removal proceedings . . . and I, the granddaughter of the man who acquired it for his family in the years before the First World War, struggled to keep up mortgage payments in the Depression and finally lost it in the early thirties, can now only stand and stare and 'pine for what is not'.

I recall a large kitchen in which we all ate, its coal range sporting a steaming black kettle which facilitated tea and hospitality at any hour of the day or night, and a big round flat girdle iron, which hung by its semi-circular handle from a hook by the stove. Onto this utensil, pre-heated, Grandma would slap a huge thick scone mixture, shaping it to fit exactly. Then she would cut the dough into a dozen or more wedges, and cook the delectable whole on the stove top, turning the pieces separately, and serving them, as 'done' straight to the waiting eaters. Cut open, smothered with butter and jam, honey or golden syrup, Grandma's girdle scones made a heavenly repast. We enjoyed them well into our childhood. When Grandma came to live with us years later, she proved to have retained the old iron, and would produce girdle scones on whatever cooking appliance the current house offered.

Most family homes at this time in New Zealand had a 'front room' or 'sitting room'; never 'parlour' or 'drawing room' in my experience. These may have featured, of course, in the houses of the rich and cultured, but, as a child, I was unaware of the existence of such people, or their houses. In many working-class houses the 'front room' was virtually out of bounds to the family (Roy, my husband, has described his family's example to me often). This chamber would be furnished with sofas and chairs which no one sat in, a multitude of draped small tables supporting ornaments which were usually hideous, curtains which were always drawn to keep out the sun — even, in some homes, a piano that was never played. Not so in my grandparents' house. Furniture in this 'front room' was minimal, and pushed back against the walls. Though the room would occasionally be used for more formal dining than was possible in the homely, cluttered kitchen, its *real* use was as a dancing studio. Mats were kept rolled and dining chairs lined the walls. The piano was the most important piece of furniture in the house. In my earliest memories there is always someone playing the piano, always someone singing. At regular intervals there would be dancing too. The floors would shake, and there would be laughter. Flushed faces and merriment were the order of the day. At the centre of it all was 'Auntie', younger than our mother by seven years, and quite different from her. Where our mother was quiet, Auntie was boisterous. Our mother enjoyed solitude, sewing and reading, but Auntie loved company and noise. And she loved us. Simply 'Auntie', as against more formal aunts with names appended, she seemed determined to extract fun from our very existence. Outings and presents abounded.

Auntie was aided and abetted in her indulgent propensities by 'Ockie' (who later became our Uncle Oscar), an Australian of impressive corpulence and undoubted charm who knew all the words of all the Gilbert and Sullivan operas and sang them with magnificent tunelessness, to everyone's delight. Ross and I loved him from the start, and indeed, to the end of his long life. Ockie became, simply, one more adult to love and indulge us; he had 'taken us on', with his beloved Muriel (or 'Mick' as he always called her) and he never deserted us.

TWO

*O*ur Aunt Muriel Brown's success on the New Zealand stage was legendary in our family, and among old friends. We knew that she had performed during and just after the First World War with both the Fuller and J. C. Williamson theatre companies, who regularly brought opera, vaudeville and pantomime to the main New Zealand cities. What had it been like, to be a girl from Grey Lynn who found herself, at sixteen, touring the country with some of the great names in Australasian entertainment?

I am probably not alone in wishing that I had spent more time encouraging a relative to reminisce in his or her extreme old age. But somehow . . . well, Auntie was never the storyteller that my mother was and I was always busy. And then, suddenly, it was too late. Auntie died on the sixteenth of May 1997. She was ninety-nine, and had been part of my life for more than seventy years. I was given her name, but was in almost all ways quite unlike her. I never shared her passion for the stage, and I doubt she read more than a handful of books in her life. But from the start we were totally committed to one another. About three years before she died, Auntie had told us that she was 'writing it all down'. There had never been any evidence that she had done so; but Pat, her daughter, found three notebooks among her mother's effects when she came to sort them. They seemed to contain a hotch-potch of notes about her early life and subsequent career, Pat told me. I was stunned. Just what I wanted, when I wanted it.

Fragmented, incomplete and in no particular order, Auntie's notes were nonetheless a joy to me. They occupied three small school notebooks, only one of which was full. Her small handwriting was neat and legible, and her punctuation and spelling extraordinarily correct. Obviously, teachers set store by such things in 1910, when twelve-year-old Muriel left school to face the world ('My mother's friend's little boy', impeccably apostrophied, 'millinery and drapery' with no confusion over doubling or not doubling consonants — even 'La Belle Parisienne', though she had certainly learned no French at school. One suspects that Muriel, along with the rest, was taught that such precision *mattered*).

One of the notebooks was obviously intended to be a final copy, as she had used her 'best' handwriting. She had even given it a title: 'Spotlight'. Clearly, Auntie was intending to write a book! She had told both Pat and me that her proposed 'notes' were 'for Dorothy'. We both assumed at the time that, as I was the one who 'wrote', she thought I would be most appreciative of her efforts. Or perhaps, in Muriel-style, she merely wanted to show that she could do it, too. Well, she could, and did!

Auntie's journal begins:

'I am writing this book in loving memory of my sister Emily. From the time I was born, her young life was centred around me . . .' (Her older life, too, I thought. We three children always claimed that Mum would rush off to Auntie and even leave *us*, if she felt that her beloved young sister needed her.) This third notebook petered out after three pages, but not before Auntie had reported that 'My sister had three lovely children who were all adored. Her eldest was Ross, a good-looking boy with a smile from ear to ear. Dorothy arrived on the scene next, a lovely golden-haired girl with bunches of lovely curls . . . Then Valerie arrived, another adorable little girl . . .' There is no doubt at all that Auntie saw us through similar rose-coloured spectacles to those worn by our mother. But I had always known this. What I wanted was details of her own early life, and stage career.

I was not disappointed. It was all there.

Auntie's 'theatrical' life began at the age of three, 'at the Thames' as the family always phrased it. Her parents held musical evenings at least once a month and, announced as 'Bubba Brown', Muriel would appear in a frilly dress and knickers and sing 'in a loud voice' the heart-rending ballad 'The Luggage Van Ahead' (which, in the song, contains the coffin of the child's little brother). The fact that the artiste, who could not yet manage her 'l's, called it the 'Juggage Van' would produce a predictable response from the audience, one imagines. The journal records that 'everyone used to laugh'. It notes further that 'Bubba' was always bribed to perform with 'lollies' and that she had usually to be bodily removed from the limelight!

All the Browns were musical. My grandfather and grandmother both played the mandolin and the banjo, and my grandfather had a fine singing voice. My mother, from her early adolescence, played the piano for concerts and the home entertainments so popular in those days, and both brothers sang and performed. (Young George, the second son, later became involved in the professional show world in Sydney, and several times brought a touring company to New Zealand — once, including the famous soprano Gladys Moncrieff.)

After the move to Auckland when Muriel was five, the horizons for her talents expanded rapidly. She was able to join a dancing class, and soon rose from the ranks. My mother, seven years older, was already an accomplished dressmaker, and took great delight in dressing her little sister for the many engagements that came her way. By the time she was eight Muriel was a polished and versatile performer.

> I was eight years old when I was in a concert in the Orange Ballroom in Newton. I sang a song, and for an encore I did fancy swinging of clubs. My brother [George] had taught me as he used to teach at the Leys Institute Gym in St Marys Road in Ponsonby. For the occasion my sister Emily made me a lovely royal blue satin dress that had silver stars printed all over it. The clubs were painted blue with silver stars on them all covered in glitter, and my ankle-strap shoes were blue with silver stars on them too. I swung the clubs with great vitality to the tune of *Camptown Races*. I used to get great applause as it was a very uncommon item for a child of my age.

She had also lost none of her early spirit:

> When I lived in Surrey Crescent Grey Lynn, I was nine years old and I took up skating, and so did my mother's friend's little boy the same age. His name was Jack Hastings. Every Saturday morning

the pair of us would be given our fares on the two buses we had to catch to get there, but I'm afraid we never used the pennies for rides. The skating was at the Britannia in Ponsonby Road, near the Three Lamps Corner, and sometimes at the Princes Rink in Victoria Street. We always set off walking and bought lollies at Rush Munro's in Ponsonby Road, then we would go cross-country to Victoria Street.

In this sphere, also, Muriel quickly outclassed those child skaters who simply enjoyed the fun:

> . . . I often gave displays with the manager of the rink consisting of tapping [tap-dancing] on skates, and acrobatic figure skating. I remember a professional skater arriving here to give displays. Her name was Gertie Campion. She had only been here a couple of days when she fell and broke her leg, and young as I was, I was called on to take her place. I must have had plenty of cheek in those days as I took all these experiences without turning a hair. I think I had nerves of steel. I loved every minute of performing.

Small Jack Hastings was clearly determined to keep his end up in the face of skating-companion and partner-in-parental-deception Muriel Brown's talent. Auntie notes that they both became 'very professional skaters. Our names were on big bills at carnivals.' Such enthusiasm, backed by undeniable talent, paid off:

> I was twelve years old when I travelled round with the Commercial Travellers' Concert Company. I was put in [the] charge of a chaperone by the name of Miss Eva Sharpe. She was a lovely singer with a deep contralto voice. I had to share a room with her everywhere we performed. I remember quite well that after every show several of the travellers were plonked on the end of our double bed talking over everything that happened in the show.

This seems to have been an innocent pleasure, but one wonders how young Muriel's trusting parents would have viewed it had they known. Visions of stricken Edwardian maidens in floating nightgowns being pursued around bedrooms by twirling-moustached commercial travellers in tight trousers, high collars and bowler hats are irresistible. One can only assume — or hope — that Miss Eva Sharpe, she of the 'deep contralto voice', had made it clear that nonsense of this kind was not to be entertained. At sixteen, Muriel was chosen as one of eight New Zealand dancers to augment an Australian touring company, dancing first at Fuller's theatre in Wellesley Street, Auckland, and then, over a period of twelve weeks, in every major town in New Zealand. Before long she was dancing important roles at His Majesty's Theatre, and travelling throughout the country with the Australian company J. C. Williamson. It was by now wartime, and patriotic concerts constantly offered opportunities, which seem to have been eagerly taken up.

Even more interesting from my point of view was Auntie's account of the setting up, in the early years of the war, of 'The Juvenile Players', a Grey Lynn based group that arose from the Brown family's by-now-famous musical evenings. Organised by 'Miss Emily and Mr Raymond Brown' (my mother's eldest brother) and at first performing locally, this group before long was giving performances 'in aid of King and Country' all over Auckland, and finally as far north as Kaitaia. My mother, choosing the bits that she knew would captivate her children, had told us of arriving a day late in Kaitaia, as their 'motor-bus' had sunk up to its axles in custard-like mud. This seemed like fun to begin with (the 'company' was aged from eight to sixteen) but an hour or so of cheerful patter and singing finally gave way to apprehension and some gloom. It was, after all, mid-winter. The arrival of a local farmer with ropes, carthorses and assurances of waiting warmth and hospitality back at the farmhouse turned it all into a wonderful adventure. 'We all slept in the big farm kitchen, with mattresses, pillows, rugs, and a blazing fire — and the farmer's wife made hot scones to fill us all up,' our mother had told us. We were achingly envious.

My father, William Norgrove, was one of these 'Players' and at that time was Muriel's constant dancing partner. A Kaitaia revue of the visit described him as having 'a rich and musical voice'. Astonishingly long and detailed, this same review (preserved for eighty years!) spoke of audience enthusiasm which must have gladdened the 'Players' young hearts.

Each and every item of the long and varied programme was greeted with rounds of applause, and the encores were so numerous that it was 11 o'clock before the performance terminated. The enthusiasm of the audience reached its culminating point when . . . Colonel Allen Bell presented to the audience Miss Emily and Mr Ray Brown, the organisers and trainers of the Company. Then the

large audience rose and cheered them and their Company again
and again . . .

The 'Juvenile Players' were talented children and teenagers; the 'Company'
by this time attracted large numbers of aspiring performers, and only the
best were chosen to go 'on tour'. The present company numbered no more
than twenty, including several supervising adults, and the pianist (my
mother, 'Miss Emily'). I inherited from her a small, suede-leather bound
copy of Fitzgerald's translation of the *Rubáiyát of Omar Khayyám*, inscribed
on its fly-leaf: 'To Miss Emily Brown. An appreciation of your talent so
ably conveyed to others and in memory of a great tour.' It is signed 'E. J.
Samuel' and dated 28.8.17. My mother was always heartfelt in her praise
of the performers; but I think her quiet skills were noted. She knew verse
after verse of the *Rubáiyát* by heart, and would repeat them to us. I think
its wanton advocacy of pleasure *now* escaped me, but I loved to hear it:

> Ah, fill the Cup: what boots it to repeat
> How time is slipping underneath our feet . . .

My aunt had recorded details about my father, and I found these, somehow,
touching. (He must have been about fourteen at the time.) 'We were always
taken for brother and sister as we were both dark and had very curly hair.
We used to go on the stage and smile at each other, but argue like mad in
the dressing room.'

They were, in fact, very much alike. Both 'showy' with plenty of social
confidence and charm, they also had matching quick tempers, but no
capacity at all to bear a grudge. Muriel added: 'Bill had a lovely nature, and
was always inclined to get the giggles . . .' as was she. They were friends
— though often sparring partners — for years; but it was Emily, seven years
older than Muriel, whom Will Norgrove married. He was twenty-one, and
she thirty-one. Perhaps she had waited for him; no one ever discussed the
subject with us as children and no personal detail emerged from the journal.
But Muriel noted: 'The Brown family were delighted . . . Bill had, a short
time before, left home and come to live with us in Surrey Crescent. On
the other hand the Norgroves weren't so happy. Bill's sister Maud thought
he should have looked higher than being hitched to a Brown. The only one
of the Norgroves who took the wedding well was Bill's mother. She was
the nicest woman you could ever meet, but his father was a real b......'
Auntie was always a straight speaker.

THREE

I have always felt closer to my mother's family than my father's. This is not only because we lived with my maternal grandparents when I was very young; it stems, I think, from my father's unconcealed dislike of his father. Dad made no attempt to hide this from us as children, though for his mother's sake he continued to take us on irregular visits to his parents' home, usually on a Sunday. These were formal affairs. The older Norgroves' home was ordered, polished and run in a manner quite unfamiliar to the three of us, and we were always warned to be on our best behaviour when visiting. According to Auntie, the Norgroves had always 'given themselves airs'.

The Norgrove name was originally Northgrove, the family owning a manor house and sizeable estates near Bromsgrove in Worcestershire. Apparently, the house is still there; one of my father's older brothers, Harold, wrote to the Bailiff of Bromsgrove in the early seventies, and received in reply an assurance of this, and also the startling fact that the Northgroves who were, presumably, Royalists, had been (all but one) killed by Cromwell's army after the Battle of Naseby, in 1645. There is a typically romantic story about Prince Charles having been hidden in a room in the manor, before his escape to France. The sole Northgrove survivor 'escaped to Oxford', according to the received account. Certainly, my father's father

Charles and his brother David emigrated to New Zealand from Oxford two hundred years later, but this is doubtless coincidental.

I could have visited, or at least checked some of these details on one of my sorties to England (one of my cousins, Iris Norgrove, did, and says that the story is true) but I have little interest in remote ancestors. On the other hand, I felt I was keeping faith with my grandmother, Emily Stewart, when I wandered around her village of Ightham, in Kent. But then, Grandma, whom I had loved, had actually lived there as a child. I had a vision of her, long dark curly hair flying as she played with her brothers on the green, as she had remembered, and told us . . .

If the Norgroves, or Northgroves, really had had these highborn origins, they had come down in the world. Charles Norgrove arrived in New Zealand as a young man in the late nineteenth century and had entered the butchery trade. He was said to have been both clever and ambitious, and in time owned his own flourishing business in that part of Richmond Road that used to be known as 'the Richmond Terminus'. It is now in its new, rather upmarket guise called 'West Lynn'.

The shop Charles Norgrove built is still standing, on the corner of Richmond Road and Hakanoa Street. The name, etched in concrete high up on the corner face, is still discernible as C. Norgrove, with the date 1905 beneath it. Surprisingly, it is still a butcher's shop. Even more surprisingly, many features of the original interior have been retained, and are in excellent order. The tiles on the wall behind the counter are original and have never been broken. One large tile set among the smaller, plainer variety depicts a bull's head, and has been the object of many offers, the current butcher told me. The 'cooler' is also authentic, though doubtless powered by modern machinery, and there are photos of the Norgrove butchers — Charles and sons — framed and hanging on the wall, just inside the shop door. Charles could not have foreseen that his shop would survive the twentieth century, and certainly could never have suspected that it would become, as it has, a well-known *organic* butchery!

Charles built a house for his rapidly expanding family in nearby Tutanekai Street. More than eighty years later our youngest daughter, Josephine, was to build a small house on a cross-leased section in what was once the back garden of the oldest house (she was told) in the same street. As Uncle Norman, my father's brother, had also built in Tutanekai Street after his return from the First World War, I feel as I drive down the increasingly 'gentrified' road that I am in family territory. (Like other parts of inner-city Auckland, Grey Lynn has both declined and begun to rise again, socially, since those days.)

The sight of my Norgrove grandparents' old home does not move me as does the old Brown house, only a short walk away in Surrey Crescent. But Uncle Norman and Auntie Maggie's house brings a warm glow. For, of all the 'ordinary' aunts (as against 'Auntie'), Uncle Norman's wife, Maggie, was my favourite. My mother had added the story of Norman and Maggie to her vast repertoire of anecdotes from both sides and several generations of the family, and we loved to hear it. They had been engaged when Norman went away to war. He had been left for dead in the 'no-man's-land' between opposing British and German trenches in France, but a heroic doctor, determined (literally) to leave no apparent corpse unturned, had found a flicker of life in the young soldier, cut off his right leg there and then without anaesthetic, and managed to drag him to shelter. Norman hovered between life and death for weeks; almost all of one hip had gone along with his leg, and internal organs had been damaged. Months later he returned to New Zealand on crutches looking twice his age, dispirited and ill. Naturally, he told Maggie, they could not now marry. Maggie would have none of this. She had intended to marry Norman Norgrove, and marry him she would. With brisk determination and irrepressible good humour she ran the whole show. Uncle Norman, swinging his new leg with do-or-die spirit, was wed to Auntie Maggie, installed in a job at the Bank of New Zealand, and fathering a family of fine children 'before you could turn round twice' according to my mother.

We children liked Uncle Norman. He was 'funny' like our father, though rather more staid. He used to demonstrate, on request, how he kept his right sock up with drawing pins. (As a party trick, this defied competition.) The stumps of his missing fingers looked as if they had been tied off roughly with string and allowed to heal, before the string was removed. They had. Auntie Maggie would never allow him to undergo further surgery to 'tidy them up'. 'He's had quite enough,' she said.

I suspect that Norman Norgrove had always been quieter than his brothers. His wife, Margaret Ness, came from a staunch Scottish Presbyterian family, ran her house and family with calm efficiency and was, to quote my mother, 'the kindest woman in the world'. Under her influence, Norman became a regular church-goer. (My father eyed this development with deep suspicion. 'Christ!' he would say. 'Imagine old Norm turning into a Bible-banger!') But Uncle Norman shared my father's gift for making us laugh, and we loved him. His son, Freddy, who was my age, was my favourite cousin. He had been named Frederick Charles after the eldest Norgrove son, who had died on the first stage of *his* journey to the trenches of France, in Trentham Camp, New Zealand, of meningitis. This had 'broken his mother's heart', we were told. His father had maintained a stiff upper lip. Our father, with a cynicism he reserved for his father, told us that 'old Charlie would rather Fred had been killed *at* the war; it would have seemed to him more honourable, less ignominious — something to boast about'. 'Oh Bill,' said my mother, who had known Fred, and liked him. ('He was the best of all the Norgroves,' said Auntie, who had known them all too. But then, of course, poor Fred had never had to defend this reputation . . .)

There can be no doubt that my grandfather, Charles Norgrove, treated his children harshly, even, on occasion, brutally. It is certain, also, that his wife, Alice — 'Grandma Norgrove' — did her best to soften the effects of this harshness. But she, like so many women of her generation, was almost powerless in the face of a husband who presented a respectable, even charming face to the world outside (he became, ultimately, a Justice of the Peace) and behind the scenes bullied and oppressed both his wife and his children. Alice's subjection was certainly complete. A family joke had it that Charles was so outraged when she produced a daughter as their first child that she never did it again. In fact, she fell into line immediately, and produced six sons in a row. My father, born in 1901, was the fifth of these boys.

My mother was the real storyteller in our family, but my father had a few tales that he savoured. Significantly they all involved his father's loss of dignity or 'face'. On one notable occasion — the *only* occasion she ever truly stood up to him — my grandmother Alice, before the delighted, if astonished eyes of her assembled children, threw a whole pot of porridge at her husband, with an almost gleeful shout of, 'Well, take the lot!' (He was complaining, apparently, at her lack of speed in meeting *his* needs as she served the youngest children.) Bully that he was, Charles must have sensed that the opposing forces had suddenly become insuperable. He withdrew with what little dignity he could muster, his wing-collared shirt and waistcoat, elegantly draped with gold watch and chain, now engulfed in a glutinous, slithering mass of oatmeal porridge.

Yet more dramatic — but even more satisfying — was the account, passed down the family from Maud, the eldest, of the last time her father had attempted to chastise her physically. Maud was sixteen, and Charles was already equipped with the belt he used for beating his children, when Fred, his eldest son, appeared. Fred was fifteen, and already taller than his father. He was holding a loaded rifle. 'If you touch Maud now, or ever again, I'll kill you,' he told his father. Neither Maud (nor, presumably, Fred) was ever beaten again.

Dad's third saga was the best of all. Harold, aged twelve, the second of the six brothers, was about to be caned by the headmaster of his school (Grey Lynn Primary). On the desk that separated the terrified child from the fearful figure of his oppressor was a whole tray of filled inkwells. At his side, a large wide-open window offered a vision of freedom. As the headmaster moved, so did Harold. Snatching up the tray of inkwells, he hurled it at the advancing man, leapt out the window and ran. Somewhere in the playground he encountered a younger brother — Norman, probably — and he, perceiving his brother in flight, went too. Harold's astonishing crime so completely claimed the attention of all the teachers (no doubt filled with outrage) and all the pupils (certainly filled with delight) that it was some time before the absence of the perpetrator and his younger brother was discovered. Parents and the police were summoned, and a chase was mounted.

But of course there were no patrolling police cars, no radio to alert the populace, inadequate, if any, telephone services — and the boys had had a good start and were fleet of foot. According to my father, Charles was murderously furious, Alice and Maud frantic with anxiety, and the rest of the family enchanted. (Nothing in the past had even approached this for fun.) The day wore on, and there was still no sign of the runaways. No one in the playground had noted the direction they had taken; the bellows from the headmaster's study, and his subsequent electrifying appearance, looking for all the world like one of the golliwogs the little ones played with in those days of racial nonchalance, ensured *that*. Alice was rigid with fear by nightfall as she supervised the little boys' bedtime. Charles was off somewhere with the police, Maud was in tears, and the boys themselves, frightened at last, were unaccustomedly subdued. (They usually enjoyed their father's absence.)

As dawn broke over the hills and fields of Glen Eden, a farmer found two dirty but obviously well-dressed children asleep against his haystack. He roused them, intending to help, but they ran off immediately and he could not catch them. But the slow wheels of official pursuit now had a direction, and within a few hours a posse of police and farmworkers — and Charles — were on the spot. The boys were flushed out like a pair of grouse, but they were not beaten yet. Surrounded, they retreated into a swamp, which came up to Harold's waist and the little brother's armpits. Neither inducement nor threat could move them. (The sight of their father would certainly have struck fear to the very marrow of their bones, even without a bevy of uniformed 'coppers') and two policemen were obliged, ultimately, to wade in and 'collar them'.

My father was never clear on the subject of subsequent retribution, but the boys became heroes to the young of Grey Lynn. The escapade occupied the local gossips for weeks, and was reported in the newspapers. Charles's shame (obviously, Harold was a criminal in the making) seems to have eclipsed his fury. Perhaps he really had been shaken, for once, or perhaps he believed that the blaze of unwelcome publicity would fade fastest if ignored. What the school did about the incident is not on family record, either. Perhaps the headmaster shared Charles's fear of yet more publicity. Life returned to normal.

But Charles did not forget. Years later, when Harold married a Catholic, his father made this an excuse to ostracise him; and many more years later, on my grandmother's death several years after her husband's, it was discovered that he had cut Harold out of his will. Alice, who, my father told me, had always covertly kept in touch with her handsome, genial second son and his likeable wife, would have been horrified; but the old villain had not told her, and she had not thought to examine the will after his death. She believed that everything had been left to her, thereafter to be shared among the surviving children. My father, joined by his brother Norman, made a great fuss about this injustice and insisted that all shares be pooled and redivided to include Harold. Not that there was much to *be* divided by this time — but the unfairness shocked them all, and the adjustment was made.

I was in my mid-teens when my mother told me that Uncle Harold and Auntie Min had had a son who was older than Ross, and would thus have been the eldest Norgrove grandson. Mum and Dad must have visited

Harold and his wife, because Mum said, 'He was a beautiful baby, but he died unexpectedly when he was only a few weeks old.' She sighed as she said, 'They never had another child.' If anything were needed to confirm my father's disgust with his own father, this was it. Alice never saw this little boy, and was not allowed to go to his funeral.

Why didn't the Norgrove sons defy their father on their mother's account? My own mother said that they were utterly cowed as children, and later believed it would 'only make things worse' for their mother. And of course, through all the bitter, early years, Alice would have had no claim to any money, nor even to a roof over her head — nor to her children, come to that — if she had left him. And where could she have gone? Her situation was no different from that of many women in those days; in fact it was infinitely better. She was well housed, dressed and fed, had daily household help, was accorded public respect, and was not physically abused. Her reward was her children's love, which did not fail; but their lives must have brought times of sadness, too.

It was everyone's good fortune that a stroke in early old age — brought on, it was said, by a fit of rage at the loss of a substantial amount of money in 'the slump' — robbed Charles of much of his venom, and indeed, engendered a degree of rather pathetic good humour. I recall him in my middle childhood as a kindly, though still pompous old man. My father didn't trust him. Once, when I was about thirteen, Grandfather (who fancied himself as a debater) asked me if I knew what 'perogative' meant. I said that yes, I did, but it was actually *pre*rogative (I, also, fancied myself in the field of verbal disputation). My father turned quite pale, hustled me off and hissed, 'For God's sake don't cross the old devil — he'll have another stroke!' I was in no doubt that Grandfather did not approve of girls at all; and *clever* girls ran terrible risks.

One of my father's most endearing qualities was that he treated his children as people. Ross and I dared not catch his eye when, on Sunday visits to our Norgrove grandparents, the whole company was obliged to rise and stand to attention for the eight o'clock radio broadcast of 'God Save the King'. (My grandmother and Maud were required to plan the evening meal so that it finished *exactly* in time for this ritual, my mother told me.) Our father's expression of passionate patriotism, assumed for his children's delectation, led almost to their undoing, on numerous occasions.

How different had been the cheerful, informal meals round the big kitchen table in the Brown household just up the road in Surrey Crescent! Alas, by the times I have just written of, this house had been surrendered to the mortgagee, and Grandfather George Brown had died.

FOUR

Grandma Brown was to support and comfort and occasionally astonish us (she was a 'character', my maternal grandmother) for many years after her husband died, living with her children's families in turn, according to their and her need. She died at ninety-three in my mother's home, in the January of 1953.

On Christmas morning, less than a month earlier, Roy had driven from our little house in Birkenhead to my mother's home in John Street, Ponsonby, to bring my mother and grandmother, via the vehicular ferry, to share our Christmas. Grandma Brown — Emily, like her daughter, my mother — spent the day tucked up on our sofa, and would not be banished to the bedroom for 'a rest'. I remember her shaking with laughter at the bossiness of our youngest child, Patricia, then aged eighteen months, refusing to have the little girl removed when she climbed without ceremony on to the sofa and tucked herself under the rug with her great-grandmother. Vivien, our fourth child, was born in early March, only six weeks after Grandma's death, and I remember cradling her and thinking with a pang, 'Grandma will never see her.'

Grandma Brown had been born Emily Stewart, the fourth of her parents'

twelve children in Kent, England, in 1860. The family had lived in the village of Ightham, and Grandma's tales brought her birthplace alive for us. Her father, Edwin Stewart, had started his working life as a carpenter, but had been able in due course to set himself up as a cabinetmaker who employed other men. But Edwin was restless; surely there was somewhere in the world where his children could be freer than in overcrowded England? Tales abounded of opportunities on the other side of the world, places where men and women of vigour and vision could make their own way, buy their own land . . . He had always fancied farming, and had boundless confidence in his own capacities. He had been successful against odds in stifling England. What might he not accomplish in the green Antipodes? Edwin Stewart sold his business in Kent and booked passages for himself, his wife Ellen, and their large family on the *Cospatrick* bound for New Zealand. It was 1874.

Collecting and verifying early facts about these forebears has been fascinating. It has also revealed that a vaguely held belief that the Stewarts narrowly evaded disaster on their trip to New Zealand was true.

My grandmother's brother, Horace Stewart, in a letter dated 22nd October 1948, at which time he was eighty-three, produced the following details:

> There were such glowing accounts about New Zealand in those years that my father decided to give up his job, and booked a passage on a very large sailing ship called the *Cospatrick* in 1874. One of my elder sisters got the measles and we had to wait for the next boat. The *Cospatrick* was burnt in mid-ocean, between four and five-hundred souls perished. My dear Father and Mother, and nine children, came a month later on a vessel called the *Invererne*, landed in Auckland on 29th January . . .

Sir Henry Brett, in *White Wings Volume I* (Brett Printing Company, Auckland, 1924) tells the story of 'The *Cospatrick* Tragedy'.

> A terrible disaster that caused a thrill of horror throughout the Empire and particularly Auckland for which port the vessel was bound, was the burning of the emigrant ship *Cospatrick*, 1220 tons, west by south of Cape of Good Hope on November 17, 1874. There were 473 souls aboard, and only three survived . . .

The account speaks of the horror experienced by the occupants of a lifeboat, as they watched the end of the tragedy. The mate, Mr Henry McDonald, one of the three survivors, is quoted as saying:

> The main mizzen masts fell and many of those who crowded aft were crushed to death. Then the stern was blown out. That was the end, and the shrieks of the survivors were silenced suddenly in the flames.

Stories abound about near misses; this one was true. Edwin and Ellen and their children might well have shared that terrible fate, had not one of their children caught the measles in time to delay their departure for a month. The *Invererne*, a smaller but still comfortable ship, made a safe journey to Auckland with my grandmother and family aboard.

But tragedy was not avoided altogether. Horace Stewart's letter mentioned nine children as embarking with their parents, but there were actually ten: three-year-old Effie, the youngest, died on the voyage. There was nothing unusual about shipboard death of course. Water was necessarily rationed, and fresh food was the exception. The very young, and the old and frail, went first when sickness ravaged the passenger ranks. But, I suppose then as now, such tragedies were thought likely to happen to other people's families, not one's own. The Stewarts were devastated. An earlier daughter had already died, in infancy, in England. Harry, the last child, was born in New Zealand a year after the family's arrival.

But my Grandmother Emily had happy as well as sad memories of the voyage, and exciting ones, too. Her tales, willingly repeated during my childhood, were engrossing. In the Bay of Biscay, for example, the trip only just begun, young Emily had sneaked up on deck when she should have been below. A huge wave hit the plunging ship, and swept her off her feet. She survived only because an alert adjacent sailor caught her at the last minute and held her outside the rail until the danger was past and he could haul her aboard. 'Strong as a lion, he was,' said Grandma. 'Everyone praised him, but *I* was punished!' Rightly so, thought her listening grandchildren. Think of it! We might never have been born.

On the day following their arrival in Auckland, a Sunday, my great-grandmother Ellen Stewart insisted that the family don its long packed-away 'best' and stroll through the centre of the town. Queen Street was officially 'metalled' but drainage was poor. Dust in summer and mud in

winter — with horse traffic to stir it all up and add its own mess — made
sedate walking difficult. Emily's younger brothers, Herbert, Francis and
Horace, reluctantly donned their Eton-style suits with stiff collars and top
hats and the family set off — to be met with jeers and even a few hurled
missiles. They retreated as fast as dignity allowed, and the little boys'
jackets, collars and hats never again saw the light of day.

My mother told us that her grandfather had been noted for his bright
blue twinkling eyes. He had 'laughed a lot, and been a man that children
liked'. Alas, he proved to be no farmer. Edwin Stewart might well have
established a flourishing business making furniture in raw, burgeoning
Auckland, but his eyes were on open fields. He spent all his money buying
land 'around Cambridge', the story has it, farmed it unsuccessfully, and lost
it. Thereafter, the family lived successively — and precariously, it seems —
in Thames, Te Awamutu, and finally Auckland. Here the parents
established a small book and stationery shop in Victoria Street West, and
lived in rooms above, until their death.

The Stewart children, by now grown, all became solid New Zealand
citizens, being each obliged to make his or her own way in life. There was
certainly no material inheritance. In varying proportions, fortunately, they
all developed their parents' qualities of energy and good humour. My
Grandmother Emily had a lavish share of both.

During the period they lived in Thames, Emily went into service 'in
a fine big house'. Many years later she was to conjure up visions for us of a
short, dark young woman, hardly more than a child, enveloped in an
overlong apron, her thick curly hair crammed under a cap, polishing
hundreds — thousands! — of silver knives, forks and spoons in a small,
cold pantry. Not for long. In the bustling, gold-mining town of Thames,
she met young George Brown, printer at the *Star*, and married him, when
she was eighteen and he twenty-one.

At this point in the annals of my antecedents, mystery and romance
enter. For my Grandfather George Brown's father, John Brown, was a
mystery man; and the mystery was never solved. The known facts about
that great-grandfather — so different from honest, idealistic Edwin
Stewart, foolishly and fondly wasting his talents and resources on a madcap
scheme for which he was totally unsuited — are few. John Brown (*was* that
his real name? — it seems unlikely) was described by a colleague in Thames
as a 'gentleman and a scoundrel'. As far as one can tell, this was a fair

assessment. The facts certainly confirm the scoundrelly charge; we are obliged to rely on hearsay to verify 'the manners and the bearing of an English gentleman'. Alas, the integrity was sadly absent.

John Brown had arrived in Thames about the year 1857 with a young wife and a very young baby (my grandfather, George) from Bendigo in Australia. Legend has it that his wife was 'the daughter of a publican' and that she had 'run off' with the dashing and gentlemanly John Brown. Poor girl, she seems to have been dispossessed by her family in the wake of this scandal. During the whole of their childhood, my mother told us, she and her sisters and brothers were told nothing of this grandmother's story, before her arrival in Thames — and that little only much later, when my mother was herself adult.

Two more children, Katherine and Anne, were born to John Brown and his wife (also Katherine) in Thames. Life, apparently, proceeded calmly. The family was not rich, but was obviously provided for in some way. John certainly never soiled his hands at any menial task, and my mother had it that her Grandmother Brown, when she knew her years later, 'gave herself airs, and was a bit stand-offish — but kind to us children'. And then, when George was twelve and his sisters about ten and eight, John Brown disappeared. There were no warning signs. One day he was simply not there.

One can only speculate on the consternation this occasioned in the small town. It would naturally be thought that an accident had overtaken him; but where was the body? Possibly borne away by the sea or river? But drowned corpses, on the whole, turn up, unless lost in mid-ocean. Did his wife really have *no* idea, never suspect him of the potential to desert or deceive? Katherine seems to have maintained a tragic, dignified silence. Speculation was rife, but ultimately fruitless. How *could* one disappear from Thames? Barring collusion with the crew, secret passage to Auckland on the steamer would have been impossible. Everyone knew everyone else at least by sight and strangers were inspected closely.

George's childhood was over. He was now the breadwinner, with a mother and two sisters to support. A job at the *Thames Star* was arranged, and he was to work there for years. He was a clever, spirited boy and grew into a capable man. His skill with machinery became quickly apparent, and over the years he was regularly dispatched as far away as the South Island to supervise the setting up of new printing presses, which arrived in those

days from England or America in a disassembled state. As well as having
natural musical ability, George painted creditably in oils, was an avid reader,
and built with his own hands the house in which he and Emily brought
up their family.

He was a calm, kind man, my mother's father, who 'never raised a
hand to any of his children, boy or girl'. It was left to his wife to discipline
the children 'and she was not very good at it', according to my mother. Life
was good for the four Brown children of Thames. Much more exciting than
his faithfully described virtues from his grandchildren's point of view was
Grandfather's ownership of a penny-farthing bicycle. My mother, on
demand, would tell us how, before the admiring eyes of his wife and
children, her father had climbed proudly *on* and fallen spectacularly *off* this
miraculous machine at his first practice run. 'Tell us again Mum,' we would
say. Knowing the climax ahead of time never seemed to lessen the effect.
Grandfather, with quiet pride, mounting the huge iron contraption from
the front fence (the main wheel of the penny-farthing was about six feet
in diameter, and one sat directly on top of it) . . . wobbling uncertainly but
with increasing speed down the hill . . . the wobble increasing . . . Disaster!
Two outraged housewives on opposite sides of the narrow road, their front
gardens all but destroyed by the separate components of the accident as
Grandpa and his mount parted company . . . Grandma, still aproned, and
all the children, fleeing down the hill to retrieve their dazed Papa and
search for his bowler hat . . . How my mother could tell a story!

There must have been a lingering sadness in the hearts of both Emily
and George, however, despite their good humour. Their first child, 'the first
George' (a later son was given this name) died at the age of four during a
bout of croup, and twin girls, born prematurely during a hard winter, lived
for only a few days.

My grandmother told me of this latter tragedy years later, when I was
having my own children. Her eyes filled with tears; the healthy baby girl
on her knee obviously sparked memories of a loss that was sixty years old,
but still recalled with anguish.

George Brown was in his early twenties when a letter arrived for him from
America. It was from his father, John Brown, now resident in Salt Lake
City, Utah. No explanation or excuse for past conduct was given (let alone

elucidation of the disappearing act) but an offer was made: John Brown had won in America the fortune that had eluded him in the Antipodes, and now wished his son to join him and become his heir. Neither mention nor enquiry was made of his wife, Katherine, nor of his daughters. It was his son he wanted. George is reputed to have replied immediately. With honest economy he informed his father that he despised him for his deception and desertion, and wished to have no dealings with him, ever. And that was that.

Did my great-grandfather pass as John Brown in Salt Lake City? And where did he come from in the first place? By accent and manner he was an English gentleman. Perhaps a 'remittance man', one of that breed of 'black sheep' from the English gentry who was actually *paid* to stay away from England to preserve the family from shame? (So much more acceptable to talk of 'Dear Henry who's gone out to the Colonies', than to be obliged to explain or justify Henry's scoundrelly behaviour on one's own doorstep.) Of course, John Brown may have stayed away from England for the simple reason that he would have been clapped in irons had he attempted to return; there was no evidence that he was receiving regular payments from an apprehensive family. We shall never know the truth — and strangely, not one of us has ever been more than mildly curious. I do remember romanticising him in my teens, though. Clark Gable as the charming, ruthless gambler in the film *San Francisco* epitomised my vision of John Brown. (I was disgusted when my film hero capitulated at the end of the film and knelt down to pray with the spotless maiden [Jeanette McDonald?] instead of seducing her. At least my rascally great-grandfather was consistent.)

Curiously, my Grandmother Brown's sister Kate ('Aunt Kate' to my mother) *did* marry a bona fide 'remittance man' — one Harry Tanner, whose father was alleged to have been Lord Mayor of London at one time. Some of my mother's best tales involved Uncle Tanner, as he was always called. He and his wife farmed not far north of Auckland, and he was known and liked as an expansive, jovial man and a hard worker. He had one fault. Whenever notice came that his money 'from Home' had arrived, he would disappear to Auckland City, draw the whole sum from his bank, and embark upon a drunken spree which would last as long as the current remittance held out. Then he would come home. My great-aunt (who aspired to gentility — and doubtless, poor woman, imagined that she had attained it when she married the high-born Tanner) would hear him 'coming roaring over the fields' according to my mother — 'all strung about with presents for Aunt Kate and their daughter' — and quake in her genteel shoes.

Obviously, this periodic descent into dissolution was a quality that had not appealed to Uncle Tanner's English family, and one could hardly expect it to appeal to his unfortunate New Zealand wife. But it certainly appealed to his low-born New Zealand connections. Outrage after outrage was reported by the — understandably — affronted Kate to her sister Emily, to the huge enjoyment of the family in Thames. On one occasion, the roistering Uncle Tanner did not make it to the farmhouse on his way home, having fallen, or rolled, fortunately front-uppermost, into a horse trough. Finding himself wedged — he was a portly man — and reasonably comfortable (though very wet), he had gone to sleep. His discovery next morning by a farmworker was mortifying in the extreme to saintly Aunt Kate, though regarded as fortuitous by Uncle Tanner himself. Getting him out required the pressing into service of several astonished passers-by. Aunt Kate's humiliation was complete.

Yet another indignity involved Uncle Tanner's arrival home, complete with the usual presents but lacking his gentlemanly trousers, braces and all. (My mother loved this one.) Apparently, when received at the door of his not-very-welcoming home after an episode of high old roistering in the wicked metropolis, Uncle Tanner was seen to be quaintly clothed below the waist. His pin-striped jacket, high collar and waistcoat — even his hat and shoes — were intact (though rather less than immaculate), but his plump nether regions were encased in a terrible old pair of moleskin trousers, with gaping holes at the knee and in the seat, revealing to the world (shocked or amused, according to its wont) the loss, also, of his lordly longjohns. Uncle Tanner had no explanation for this strange deprivation. It was simply anyone's guess . . .

Could all the Uncle Tanner stories have been true? My mother swore that the two I have related were. She added that the beleaguered Aunt Kate was never even able to 'hush things up' between episodes. Uncle Tanner enjoyed his own exploits as much in the retelling as in the happening, and would deliver boisterous accounts without any encouragement at all, in company both suitable and unsuitable.

It has occurred to me only in later life that my parents' celebration of the oddity of these and other relations and friends, and their willingness to accept — welcome, really — a variety of highly divergent people into their, and our lives, was a very sustaining feature of our upbringing. Solemnity is hard to sustain when one has been brought up to laugh.

FIVE

We moved from my grandparents' home in Grey Lynn when I was just over two, and Ross three-and-a-half. I suspect that my father, who had until this time worked in the Norgrove family butchery, wanted to escape his father's domination. Taking a job with a butcher in Onehunga, on the other side of Auckland, accomplished this.

Our first house — really a farm cottage — and the house we subsequently rented in Onehunga, were background to my first conscious (or perhaps *remembered*) awareness that I was *me*. I recall reactions to specific situations: longing to be able to climb the farm gate as Ross could, for example. He would stand on the second-to-top bar, bracing his knees against the top rail and waving his arms at the ragged line of cows that ambled past, twice daily, to the milking shed. I could climb no higher than the second-from-bottom bar, and then must clutch the third for dear life against certain disaster. Once, my father came out and lifted me on to his shoulders, so that I was higher even than Ross. I remember, after the cows had gone, trying to lower my head to the level of my father's. He warned me to be careful, as I might fall; but I was reflecting that, if our heads were level, I would be seeing the world as my father, from his greater height, saw it. I knew that I couldn't explain this to him, but I recall it as a conscious reflection.

I remember, also, being gripped by a sensation that can only have been jealousy. In the Onehunga house, we sometimes played with a girl who was a few years older than us. Ross developed an intense affection for her, and would do anything to persuade her to stay a little longer. Once, when she was about to desert us, he offered to give her one of my two loved if rather battered dolls (called, unaccountably, Mustard and Charlie). I recall, vividly, rushing at the bargaining pair, battering them and shouting with rage. My bemused mother arrived, calmed the other two (but not me; I continued to scream and kick) and finally administered placatory biscuits all round, with the assurance that Mustard and Charlie were safe from abduction.

My mother's assertion that I was a good-natured child falters in the face of another remembered incident. I used to torment a little boy who lived next door, and whose mother would not let him play with us. He would watch us enviously through the fence, and from time to time I would show him something we were playing with and then say triumphantly, 'But you can't have it. So there!' The victimised child (his name was Trevor) would scream (he, also, was about three) and Ross would shout for *our* mother. The commotion would produce *both* mothers, ours full of dismay and apology, Trevor's incensed with rage, which she would vent in a series of hard slaps around her child's legs, meanwhile glaring at me (safe behind the fence) and dragging him inside. These developments, while inexplicable, gave me a feeling of great power. The situation might have been salvaged by the 'nice cup of tea' that my mother was only too ready to offer any neighbour, but Trevor's mother would have no truck with us. Perhaps she saw us as her social inferiors. Interestingly, Ross was just as upset as our mother by my manipulation of the unfortunate Trevor, and did his best to divert me when he saw temptation approaching. But then, he was known to have 'a sweet nature'. I can recall only a sensation of intense satisfaction, with no pity at all for the luckless Trevor.

During these years, and until I was about four, I was known as a very poor speaker. Unlike Ross (who is said to have banged his spoon and shouted, 'More!' at nine months of age, thereafter collecting words at a giddy rate) I said virtually nothing until I was two, and then developed a language style that was comprehensible only to my immediate family. My mother seems to have been untroubled by this apparent retardation, affirming later that she 'had always known that Dorothy was all right'. Her father, my adored Grandpa Brown, had apparently expressed doubt on this point. As words — spoken, heard, read and written — were later to become my stock-in-trade, this early lag was, I suppose, mysterious; and yet I remember loving the sound of words from an early age. I knew that the bush at the bottom of the verandah steps in Grey Lynn was called a fuchsia and I used to savour the word, as well as the bush itself. The flowers were like dancing ladies, I thought. (I knew all about dancing ladies.) I would sit on the steps and watch them moving in the wind. I seem to have gathered words up, long before I could say them. My parents were amused to discover, when we moved into our Onehunga house, that we were flanked on one side by the Hitchcocks, and on the other by the Catchpoles. Ross turned this into a refrain and would stamp about chanting 'Hitchcock and Catchpole!' until dissuaded. I would follow, hysterical with laughter, but never joining in the refrain. Years later, however, I was the one who recalled the engaging fact, astonishing my mother, who had forgotten all about it.

Strangely, I don't recall any frustration at this inability to give tongue to words which I obviously knew existed — or at the amusement that greeted some of my more bizarre attempts to name things or people. Ross, for example, was always Yoey (to rhyme with Joey) to me. When asked years later why I called him Yoey, I said, 'Well, he *is* Yoey.' And he still is, though I have not used it since I was about seven, by which time Val was calling him Yoey too, and my parents thought it was time to be firm, for once.

My adult interest in children's language development relates, I suppose, to this early and continuing love of words. The addiction, as it certainly became, was not, of course, apparent to my family, who were blessedly unconcerned about my intellectual development, in any case. Neither of our parents ever expressed any wish that we should 'work hard' or 'do well at school'. Their sole aspiration seems to have involved our happiness. Suggesting that there might have been something defective about one of us would have been seen as seriously unsupportive.

This cheerful acceptance, delightful in itself, extended to the limit of *not* noticing — or perhaps ignoring — the fact that my right eye was not in perfect alignment with my left. It must have been obvious fairly early that if my infant eyes attempted to swing upwards and to the left, my right eye travelled further than the left. This, of course, compounded the image for me, but as babies and small children have no way of knowing what normally sighted people see (or even that they see at all, in the case of blind infants) I was untroubled. In fact, I used to amuse myself a few years later in school, if the lesson was dull, by contriving to make doors, windows, the blackboard, the teacher, the charts on the wall — any available objects — rearrange themselves interestingly. More usefully, I developed the habit of closing my right eye if I needed a reliably unmoving impression. Long practice of this technique led to mastery; I can still hold my right eye comfortably shut without discomfort, and without squinting the left eye. The surgeon who operated on the eye when I was thirty-five (by which time I could not hold my head far enough back to be able to drive safely) said grimly that it should have been done in babyhood; by now it was possible only to improve the focus slightly. It would never be perfect, and my aging eye muscles would make improvement in any future operation unlikely. I have wondered, in later life, why no one ever told me that there was something wrong with my eyes. I half-believe that this cheerful acceptance — my family's, and by association my own — was the best approach to the disability, given the fact it was not likely to be corrected at an early stage. And how safe and successful were eye operations seventy years ago? Managing with what I had may have been the best deal on offer. And manage I did. My mother was heard to say once that 'Dorothy was born knowing how to read'. This was unlikely, but I certainly read very well, very early, and was later a dab hand at the throwing and catching skills that render one 'good at games', another accomplishment that might have been, but was not, affected by my eye defect.

Life proceeded happily. Auntie and Ockie (now officially Uncle Oscar) continued to indulge us, at the same time compiling a long list of our infant escapades and utterances for future reference. 'Ross is putting shit on me!' I am reputed to have shrieked as we tore through the house, he waving a stick on which he had impaled a large cowpat . . . and Ross, after a mysterious illness, being urged to take his medicine because the doctor had left strict instructions that he must: 'You tell the doctor to give it to his own bloody kids!' My mother was often heard suggesting to my father that he curb his language as she couldn't imagine what might happen to the children when they went to school. He never did, and we never disgraced her in public. I have no idea why, though I suspect that in our family a balance was accidentally established which ensured an early sense of what was fitting in different situations. Our mother was always quiet and 'ladylike' and our father articulate and charming. Only at home did he ever break out, and I think we felt privileged to be included in his audience. ('Christ-all-bloody-mighty!' he would shout, tugging at his curly dark hair when the noise level became unendurable, 'I'll go mad!') He was so unlike the father-figures I later met in books — and recognised among my friends' fathers — that I could only wonder, and be thankful.

We moved to Devonport in late 1928, the precipitating factor being our father's applying for, and getting, a job with the Auckland Meat Company in Stanley Bay. I have often said that I 'grew up in Devonport', and it still feels as if I did. We lived in this lovely old North Shore suburb for only six years, but it seemed like a lifetime. The years between four and ten or eleven witnessed so much change that in retrospect they seem to have taken an infinity of time to live through. This is surely true for all children. You enter this period as little more than a baby, dependent for all your needs on others. You come out the other end a real person; all the more firmly, if people and things don't crowd in on you too obstructively. I was lucky. Wordsworth's 'shades of the prison house' never closed around me. And Devonport was an idyllic place to be let loose in.

The beach, the cliffs, the mudflats and our good fortune in the neighbours we encountered in each of the four houses we lived in combined to make these years a period of vividly remembered happiness. Our little sister Valerie was born while we lived in the first house in Old Lake Road, Narrow Neck. The day of Val's arrival is memorable mainly for the fact that our mother seemed unaccountably to have disappeared and that Mrs Cameron-next-door, who was supposed to be minding us, allowed us to return to our own house where we played motor-racing in the upended bentwood kitchen chairs, ordinarily a frowned-upon occupation. Seated on the chair-back and holding the round seat as if it were a steering wheel, with your feet braced against it, you could propel the whole thing in a series of leaps and jerks along the floor. Particularly wild rolls would spill you out on to the linoleum, in a glorious tumble, the springy wood seeming to give the chair a life of its own. Our mother, being no sort of disciplinarian, allowed us to do this occasionally, but never permitted the excesses we achieved on the twenty-ninth of June 1929.

We were in bed in our own house, quite unsupervised and savouring every minute of it, when our father came to tell us that we had a new little sister. We were not overly impressed; Auntie and Ockie had produced a new cousin for us three months earlier, and babies, while they were cuddly curiosities, did not seem to have much to offer, as far as we could see. But we had had a wonderful day; and hearty Mrs Cameron, whom we loved, and who had five older children of her own, hadn't even *washed* us (I suspect she may have thought we were over-washed anyway).

This was the house in which Ross tried to teach one of the Camerons' fowls to swim in the tub in our washhouse, all but drowning it before its frantic squawking brought our mother, and deliverance; and where one of the bigger Cameron boys taught us to fold newspaper to make aeroplanes that would actually fly. I recall this as a rapturously enjoyable occupation on a summer afternoon. We flew hundreds of the little paper planes from our front porch. I was engulfed in a sort of bliss, which seems in retrospect strange. Was it the sight of the elegant little planes taking off one after the other; the satisfaction of knowing that I had mastered a real skill; the kindly attention of an older child, or something I can't identify? Why should I remember this particular incident, when so much else is lost? Retained, however, is the horror that engulfed me once when playing in the Camerons' house. Ross and I regarded playing with the Camerons as the ultimate ecstasy. There were four boys and a girl, from about thirteen down to seven. I even remember their names: Alfie, Claude, Len, Ray and Mona. Their cheerfully cluttered house, bigger than ours, was full of noise and the smell of cooking. Mrs Cameron's frequently shouted threats or instructions to the unruly mob — which as often as possible included Ross and me — were routinely ignored (my mother reported her as 'having a heart of gold') and no part of the house was out of bounds. Alfie, the eldest, had had 'infantile paralysis' (poliomyelitis) the year before, and wore a leg iron and built-up boot. We were used to this; it was simply part of Alfie. Mrs Cameron used to shout, 'Mind Alfie's leg!' in the face of wild games which were a feature of life at the Camerons. We came to know that this warning was not intended to protect *Alfie,* but any unfortunate child who might suffer an accidental side-swipe from Alfie's iron-girt leg.

On this particular day we were playing hide-and-seek, and I had just hurled myself into a wardrobe. This proved to contain what I realised — but too late — was Alfie's spare leg apparatus: an empty boot, with upright irons and leather straps and buckles. A horror: a detached leg, standing there alone. My stomach turned over. But I did not scream. That would have meant that I couldn't go on playing — an adult would certainly have rescued and removed me — and nothing, absolutely *nothing* could have been worse than that. (An eye to the main chance, I have thought since, characterised my dealings with life from an early age.)

SIX

Ross was now of school age, but his illness at just five, thought originally, but wrongly, to be the 'infantile paralysis' that had assumed epidemic proportions in Auckland at that time, prevented his starting. In fact, he did not go to school until he was well over six. Our parents were by this time looking for a house to rent that would be within walking distance of my father's work in Stanley Bay, and hoped to send us both to Stanley Bay School.

I have long suspected that my mother did not actually want to send us to school at all; I did not begin until I was nearly six, for no reason that was ever explained — and my mother was delighted when the school entry age was temporarily raised to six at exactly the time Val might have been expected to start, during the difficult days of the early thirties. Exactly why my mother was so casual about school attendance has always mystified me. (Other parents wrote angry letters to the papers at their five-year-olds' exclusion.) She believed strongly in reading, but always stressed the enjoyable, rather than the educative quality of books. I have realised in later years that she was an unusual woman. She seemed simply uninterested in the notion of her children getting on in the world, an aspiration embraced by most working-class parents of the day; and yet she had opinions, and talked to us constantly as if we were her equals in understanding. And she enjoyed listening to our tales — the wilder and funnier the better — as we grew older and ventured into the world.

Finally, both Ross and I were at school, and unimaginable vistas opened before us. Not just *at* school but being part of the assorted mob that walked there along the back streets to school, and back in the afternoon; playing in other people's backyards and they in ours, and endless games on the mudflats at the bottom of the road, with sorties to the further-away beach and park. It was all quite heady.

At Stanley Bay School, the four primers all sat in one big room, each class occupying one row. Ross was in Primer Three when I was finally admitted to the glory of Primer One. He and his cohorts seemed like gods, a race apart. They would take turns sitting on a high stool at the front of their own row, *reading aloud* while the others listened. I longed, with a yearning that was a physical ache, to be able to do this. I remember shaking books with exasperation because the meaning that was hidden in the print would not come clear. I could 'do' bits of it, but couldn't keep going. I used to feel that if only I could get a run on . . . and then suddenly I did! I don't recall the book, but I remember, vividly, the passage I was struggling with when it all 'came right' and I was away. It was not a school book; it was one of those bulky volumes with vacuous titles like 'Little Folk's Annual' which had thick leaves like blotting paper. There was a picture of a boy running, and the text said, 'John ran down the road as fast as his legs would carry him.' I was reading it in bed (a lifelong habit established early) and I felt as if I were being physically borne along. It was just like learning to ride a bike: one minute you can't, the next you are wobbling along — and then you are flying!

Every room in our house had at least one text on the wall, and I practised on these. None was religious, but all recommended behaviour that was not just moral, but courageous, and assertive.

> Look up, not down,
> Look forward not back —
> And lend a hand!
> And lend a hand!

we were urged from the kitchen wall. In the sitting room, we were informed that:

> One ship sails East,
> And one sails West,
> By the self-same wind that blows.
> It's not the gales
> But the set of the sails,
> That governs where each ship goes!

and in the front hall we were exhorted towards self-reliance by the last couplet of Henley's 'Invictus':

> I am the master of my fate,
> I am the captain of my soul.

I knew these and other uplifting epithets by heart from an early age but still used to read them, constantly. My father had affixed a copy of Thomas Bracken's 'Not Understood' to the bathroom wall, and chunks of this are still fixed in my mind:

> Not understood. We move along asunder,
> Our paths grow wider as the seasons creep
> Along the years, we marvel and we wonder
> Why life is life? and then we fall asleep
> Not understood.

I sensed, I think, that my father felt 'not understood' by others; and by himself, too.

Some years before my mother's death I was helping her clear out rubbish from an old shed. I caught sight of the back of a tall, narrow framed picture, and said aloud, without conscious thought: 'Where God and man have wrought, and age has beautified.' We turned the battered old picture around, revealing a black-and-white etching of an old, ivy-covered wall, and garden, with these words inscribed beneath. 'But we never hung this again after we left Devonport,' said my mother. 'It was broken, and never fixed.' I wasn't listening. I was back in the front hall of 98 Calliope Road, standing on the hall seat to read the infinitely sad inscription. Why sad? I have no idea. I only know that my heart ached every time I read it. Children's minds and reactions — even one's own, in retrospect — are unfathomable.

Our first teacher, Miss Harty, was elderly, strict and kind. And she

My maternal great-grandparents, Ellen and Edwin Stewart, in their old age.

My maternal grandmother Emily Stewart (Brown) as I remember her best in her seventies. Emily was the fourth of Ellen and Edwin's twelve children.

Left: *George Brown, my maternal grandfather about 1990, in Thames.*

Below: *My father's family, the Norgroves, about 1920. Back row, left to right: sons Harold, Roy, Frederick, Norman, William (my father) and Albert. In front, left to right: Charles, daughter Maud and Alice. Note: The eldest brother Fred had died in the war, and his photo (without legs!) was superimposed.*

Muriel Brown ('Auntie')
aged 1 year, 1899.

Muriel Brown and Emily (my mother), aged 4 and 11, in 1902.

My mother, aged 21, in 1912.

Auntie as the 'Dying Swan', His Majesty's Theatre, Auckland, about 1920.

My father as a young man.

*My mother and father with Ross,
aged 6 months, 1924.*

*Oscar Olliffe (Ockie), my
favourite uncle, '. . . a truly
Dickensian character'.*

Auntie and Ross, aged 4, at the zoo.

*My mother, in her early 30s (Emily
Ellen Brown Norgrove.)*

Ross (above) and Dorothy taken on the same day, Ross's third birthday (Dorothy, 1 year 9 months).

Ross and Dorothy in Grey Lynn, 1927.
Left: *Auntie and Dorothy, aged 2 ¹/₂,*
in Rotorua.

Dorothy, aged 4 years.

read aloud to us, every day, from *The Adventures of Doctor Dolittle*. One might have heard a pin drop. We each had our own half of a wide desk, with our own tin of Plasticine, and another of chalk. We each had our own delineated space on the blackboard, which ran round the walls of the room, and we wrote every day. We also read aloud to the teacher every day, and took our book home at night to read to our parents. I recall 'The Gingerbread Man', 'The Little Red Hen' and 'The Three Billy Goats Gruff' in the first book as discovered gems. Incidents come back. Ross was once hauled before the class in a singing lesson for misbehaviour and required to sing a song alone. I was the only person in the room who was not surprised by his melodious production of 'I'm Forever Blowing Bubbles'; my mother had been playing the piano and Ross singing it the night before. Miss Harty, bless her, led the applause, and often, after this, would request a solo.

I recall, vividly, the sensation of horror that attended news of the terrible Napier earthquake, just after I started school in February 1931. The evening *Star* was full of photographs of the shattered town, two hundred and fifty of its people dead, its streets riven with crater-like cracks, its buildings in ruins. Ten years later, Peter Arnott ('Pinky') who began as Ross's friend and became almost another brother, told us that, with his school falling around him, he had held his arms over his head and run all the way home. As he went, he felt the ground rolling beneath him, and saw people, horses and cars sliding into crevasses. 'It was a miracle I made it,' he said. His mother, who had been widowed several years before, held him so tightly 'I thought my bones would break', he told us. Peter had been almost six. He and I were only a few weeks apart in age. I tried to imagine Miss Harty's well-ordered infant classroom crashing around my six-year-old ears and could not. Would I have been one of the brave ones who ran home? I couldn't know.

On a different note, I remember a small stir when Ross, on my first day at school, took me to the boys' lavatory when I expressed the need to 'go'. We were both mystified by the fuss: I saw nothing amiss and Ross had never noticed that there was a girls' lavatory, decently distant. Wise Miss Harty must have played it all down; it seemed no more reprehensible than hanging one's raincoat in the wrong porch, to either of us.

I had been at school less than a year when I was involved in some sort of horseplay at a friend's party and received an accidental kick in the nose. (My father was heard to remark that any kid might get into a scuffle at a party but that Dorothy could be relied upon to do so.) My nose was rather badly knocked about, and the doctor advised that I be kept at home while it healed. I was actually away from school for five months, and during that time became addicted to books, an addiction that has never left me. This period may also have laid foundations for my adult conviction that schools don't matter nearly as much as homes in children's total development. It certainly made no difference to my later school performance.

I've no idea why my absence from school lasted so long. Much of the time I spent staying with Auntie and Ockie, who by now were running the 'theatre shop', next to the Ambassador Theatre, in Point Chevalier. Equipped with their own small daughter, Pat, they were forever 'borrowing' Ross or me, in a sort of rearrangement of families which suited everyone. Staying at the shop was a great joy; almost like being in fairyland. We were allowed to help unpack things and put them on shelves and in show-cases, and were lavishly provided with chocolate bars (the broken or damaged ones), ice creams and other treats. My memory of these years, both at home, at the shop in Point Chevalier, and at school, is of perpetual sunshine: days that dawned full of promise and more than justified my expectation of laughter and things to do. A recurring memory is of wriggling with pleasurable anticipation in bed at night, planning the next day's activities. These invariably involved some sort of construction: tin canoes, which were held together with tar illicitly removed from between the concrete slabs on Calliope Road, trolleys made from soap-boxes mounted on planks, with iron axles and wheels, and huts in trees, or holes, or stands of bamboo.

Inside we made fleets of paper darts, uncountable kites, peep-shows, 'sand trays' in our mother's cake tins, and innumerable little contraptions from cotton reels (wooden, in those days), matchboxes, candle ends, scraps of material and anything else that came to hand. Our mother was always generous with flour-and-water paste, preserved every scrap of paper and string that came into the house for our use, and never minded mess. There was occasionally a ha'penny — sometimes a penny — for a chew-bar, a 'lamp post', a little bag of aniseed balls or a hokeypokey bar, and the plaited twist on the top of the new loaf from the bakery on Saturday morning was pulled off and halved for us. (I recall our consternation when Val finally arrived at the 'Me too!' stage and things had to be divided into three.)

Mum was not a fussy housekeeper and had no eye for routine. She would suddenly decide on a picnic, if the weather was right, and off we would go. We kept Val's outgrown pushchair for years, and would load it with picnic and swimming gear for these expeditions. When Val was finally too weary to walk we would unload the home-made sacking bags and install her in the pushchair, Ross and I then carrying the supplies. Cheltenham Beach was a favourite spot; an adjacent shop would fill our billy with boiling water for tea, for thruppence, and Mum relished sitting on the beach in her wide-brimmed hat, enamel mug in hand. She always portrayed this as the ultimate bliss. Mum believed in fun. She said to me once, when my own children were young, 'You have no say over what happens to them later, but you can easily make them happy while they are small.' That there is a strong connection between early and late happiness may have evaded her intellectually, but the soundness of the philosophy pervaded her life and enriched ours.

Marbles and tops came in, mysteriously, at the same times every year, and though at school these games were 'boys only', at home and in the street girls played too. Or rather, some girls did, and I was certainly one of them; I could spin a top 'overarm' and shoot alleys, glassies and bottlies with the best of the boys. Then there was cricket and soccer, in season. The necessary gear for these games had been acquired for Ross but I was accorded an equal share. We spent hours bowling to one another and practising what we called 'pots in goal', one of us kicking and the other guarding the goal, usually staked out with peg-box and rubbish tin. This early introduction to the manly sports equipped me well, later, for cricket and hockey, which I played with some success and enormous enthusiasm. I was naturally good at games (though not interested enough in winning to be outstanding), a fact that certainly helped in my Grammar School years. My behaviour was often under disapproving scrutiny, and being good at sport was seen as extenuatingly wholesome (a view that I have never shared).

Other boys would often be present in our games at home, but I don't recall any discrimination. I didn't think about it at the time, but I have no doubt that it was Ross's total, assured acceptance of our equality that underlay my acceptance. I did not know at this stage that boys were supposed to be superior to girls and I suspect that Ross didn't either. He was clearly a natural leader. Everyone wanted to play with him, but this was because he was Ross, I believed, and understandable. We liked to be together and appreciated each other's talents. My mother told me in her eighties that 'Ross always admired you and thought you were clever, from the time you were both babies'. I can recall him telling our boy cousins once that 'Dorothy always has the best ideas'. They believed him; he had natural authority. (I suppose you could say that I believed him too!)

SEVEN

*T*hese were days of poverty for many people, but with the self-centredness of children we lived our own lives and accepted things as they were. We were certainly short of money. My mother made almost all our clothes; expertly, as it happened. She was a superb dressmaker and would comb the shops for cheap materials and also fashion truly stylish dresses for Val and me from used adult garments. Old coats and the legs of men's serge trousers, 'turned', would make tailored trousers for Ross which were indistinguishable — except by their excellence — from other boys' 'pants'. I exasperated her, I know, by my lack of interest in pretty clothes. I was overjoyed when girls started to wear shorts when I was about eight. To my mother's credit, she acceded to my pleas and made me a constant supply thereafter though I could never wear them to school. I don't recall wanting to be a boy; it just seemed unfair that boys' clothes were so much better suited than dresses to the activities I loved most. (My little sister fulfilled my mother's dreams. Val loved frills and flounces and had an eye for fashion from babyhood.)

Others who grew up in those days testify to the forceful administration of foul elixirs like licorice powder to 'open' reluctant bowels, and castor oil for diverse unspecified purposes (often, I suspect, merely to torture the defenceless). Our mother had no heart at all for such persecution of the young. Her own homemade remedy for almost anything consisted of a tablespoon each of glycerine, honey and lemon juice mixed in a cup and fed to us with a teaspoon. I remember coughing in bed at night, and Mum, one arm around me, feeding me the sweet, slightly tart but smooth stuff, and whispering, 'You'll be all right now.' And I was, always. As for the almost universal preoccupation with the bowels of the young, well stewed and sweetened prunes were both acceptable to children, and stimulating to the bowel, she believed, and we agreed, not even appreciating our deliverance. When Ross, at six, was prescribed lovely thick, delicious, positively *chewy* malt to fatten and fortify his thin little legs, I was given it too, though mine were as sturdy as ever, and the expense might well have been spared.

During these years our father mended our shoes on an iron boot-last in the kitchen to extract the final ounce of wear, and polished his own and our shoes nightly. 'Always judge a man by the state of his shoes' must be the sole prejudice he instilled. I'm not sure that I cast it off; when my own children were young, shoes were at least as important as teeth. As winter drew on, old warm coats would be taken out of mothballs and added to our beds for warmth. I recall a magnificent astrakhan-trimmed greatcoat, which I contrived to 'bag' every winter. It was embellished with twirls of silk braid, which you could trace with your finger, always returning to the starting point. I loved that coat, and have often wondered what became of it. Where it came from was a similar mystery. It must have belonged to a highwayman, I used to think.

Everything possible was shared or given away in those (I now realise) bleak days, and we were urged by our parents to be kind to the children at school who had ragged clothes, no shoes, and often no packed lunches. I don't think we paid any heed to this worthy advice; parcelling up your old clothes and toys was one thing, befriending the unfortunate just because they were unfortunate, quite another. It was our good fortune that butchers were in short supply, and that our father was 'in work' for the duration of the worst Depression days. His drinking was still restricted to Saturday afternoons and the occasional (though increasing) after-work drink in the local pub.

Rumblings from the outside world penetrated intermittently. Uncle Bert, our father's youngest brother, was involved in the Queen Street riots of 1932 and Dad supported him in the face of their father's disapproval.

And I recall my mother's scorn at what she called the 'tommy rot' of Anzac Day celebrations. 'Spending money on show, when people are starving!' Although the Great War, as we called it, had been over for seven years when I was born, it was still very much alive in our midst. Almost everyone had lost relations; New Zealand was full of disabled men, war widows, and fatherless children — 'all through sheer foolishness', our mother would tell us. She was a natural pacifist, years before her time — and strong in her belief that women would manage better, given the chance. 'It's men behaving like children that causes all the trouble' was one of her claims. I think my father agreed with her. Made unhappy by his own father as a child, he could not bear to see us upset and would go to any lengths to comfort, explain and make good. 'Never cry over spilt milk' was an oft-repeated piece of advice which has stuck with me ever since.

He was a fallible man, my father, who drank too much, smoked incessantly, spent family money that was needed for necessities, and with it all was totally lovable. He always got up to us at night if we called or were sick. He was intensely proud of each one of us, and never tried to change us in any way. When our mild and accepting mother would finally become exasperated with our behaviour (Ross's inability to remain serious when 'this was no laughing matter', my own habit of 'arguing that black was white' — in the face of all proof to the contrary — and Val's practice of shouting, 'You're all mad anyway!' and rushing out, slamming the door behind her), my father would place a restraining hand on my mother's arm and say merely, 'Leave her (or him) alone . . .' He had a sharp temper of his own ('That's where Val gets it from,' he would say ruefully), and would shout imprecations that were violent and blasphemous — and very funny, so that we would all start to laugh after our first dismay, and in the end he would join us. He was quickly over his 'tempers' — which I think had a cathartic effect — and would apologise to us, even as children, if he felt he had been unreasonable. My father's manners were exemplary, and natural. He made the people he came in contact with, child or adult, feel as if they mattered.

About his drinking, my mother was simultaneously despairing, angry and understanding. She told me when I was no more than ten that he had been a sensitive, rather delicate young man, 'not rough, like most boys', and that he had tried to increase his 'manliness' by drinking. 'He should not have touched alcohol, ever,' she said on many occasions. 'His constitution couldn't stand it, and yet he could never stop.' No one in those days had ever heard of alcoholism. Certainly, no one ever talked about the hopeless plight of intelligent, sensitive people imprisoned in lives that did not suit them, and from which there was no escape. But my mother understood these things, I believe.

We children were largely unaffected by Dad's problems at this stage. Drinking made him happier, and more generous. He was inclined whether sober or not to give away his own and his family's possessions to the less fortunate, anyway. 'We'll be lucky to be left with a pot to boil up our spuds in!' was one of Mum's frequent complaints; and he would bring flowers for our mother and sweets for us when 'under the influence'. I learned later that my astute mother devised ways of making sure that enough of his weekly pay came into her possession to ensure that family needs were met, and always something put aside for the presents she was determined to give us at Christmas and birthdays. My father used to be just as delighted as we were by the appearance of these often lavish gifts. I think that, quite unfairly, he counted on Mum to 'manage'.

I recall long stretches of time spent with books. Reading had by now become an indispensable part of my life. Memories of a wide window seat equipped with heavy dusty curtains in which I used to shroud myself, as in a tent, come back. Ross would urge me to stop reading and come and *play* (a plea never supported by our mother; she had been constantly separated from her book and sent outside to 'play in the fresh air' in her childhood and vowed that this would never happen to any child of hers). I remember telling Ross, and later, Val, long serialised stories, which were mixtures of my own reading and imaginings, in bed at night. According to my mother, I often droned on long after the supposed listener was asleep. Mum never fussed about my reading in bed, though 'turning out lights' was a feature of family economy. Apparently, reading was a justifiable expense. She often told me that I needed less sleep than the others. Almost always, when she came to inspect us before she retired herself, I would still be awake. 'Your eyes would be wide open, and you'd smile at me but not say anything . . .' I remember the shadow from the candle she held, flickering on the wall, and a feeling of delicious comfort. I have always liked being awake, in bed; it seems to me that this is the best time of all for thinking and dreaming and planning. Making stories in my head was a favourite occupation, and bed was the best place to indulge in it.

Mum, of course, was my example in this field. A natural storyteller herself, she regaled us frequently with tales of her own childhood in Thames. These would have been savoured anyway, but her family actually owned, as well as the usual complement of horses, cats and dogs, a *monkey*. Jacko's exploits were prodigious; he was our Pooh, our Paddington. We would often sit on after a meal, pushing back the dishes and resting our heads on our arms, while Mum went through all the 'Jacko' atrocities again. 'Tell us about the time . . .' We all had our own favourites:

Jacko's habit of lying in wait for the little girls coming home from school, snatching their red berets off their heads — the little monkey loved red — and scampering up to the rooftop, where he would abandon the hats and descend looking innocent. Their father, grumbling and protesting, would be obliged to get out the ladder after work.

The family larder was Jacko's favourite room, golden syrup and condensed milk his favourite foods. They were both stored in large crocks and Jacko's delight was to plunge a hairy arm into one of these containers and grab a handful of the sweet, sticky stuff. If apprehended at this point (as he commonly was) he would run through the house leaving a long glutinous trail behind him.

I loved the tale of Grandma, imagining Jacko safe at home, gossiping in the town with a woman-friend who had a baby in a pram, finally bending over to inspect and admire the occupant. There proved to be two occupants, sitting contentedly side by side, tucked snugly under the blanket: a bare-headed, cheerful baby and a monkey wearing a striped woolly hat with a pompon on top. Each was happily eating half a biscuit (Jacko liked to share).

The monkey and the family cat and dog were good friends, though Jacko's idea of fun when the cat was a kitten soon palled; he would grab it, scale the apple tree in the yard, deposit it at the end of a branch, descend, and shake the tree. (He was no match for the cat, later, Mum assured us.) And he used to ride on the dog's back, both animals happy with this arrangement. Once, the dog came home dripping wet, the rain pouring down, but Jacko was snug and dry, hanging upside-down under Rover's belly. 'He was cleverer than any of us,' Mum used to say. We ached to have a monkey, or any pet, but knew that we couldn't. It was hard enough for

Mum to keep *us* healthy and well fed, without the worry of animals.

My reading was, of necessity, a hit-and-miss affair. We did have a few children's books, and these I read and re-read countless times. Notable among them were several books from my mother's childhood: *Carrots: Just a Little Boy* by Mrs Molesworth, and Ethel Turner's *Miss Bobbie*, both of which I have still. Friends' and neighbours' houses were duly cased, and the local Sunday School (the 'Gospel Hall') proved to have a dusty cupboard which yielded an improbable mix. I remember *Nearly Lost but Dearly Won*, a battered Victorian volume surely intended as a cautionary tale for adults. It concerned the Demon Drink, but struck no chord in my bosom. The depicted drunkards were women who swigged gin from bottles, laughed maniacally as they lurched about squalid streets and dwellings, and allowed their babies to die of starvation and disease. I was rendered rigid in the night by this particular saga, but (shades of Alfie's leg) dared not ask for support. It was unlikely that children were *meant* to help themselves to the contents of this particular cupboard, and I did not propose to stop.

EIGHT

Our parents avoided any responsibility for our religious education. Ross and I joined the nearby Gospel Hall Sunday School because we thought it would be fun, and it was. We both performed at 'anniversaries', Ross with talent, I with confidence and a loud voice, and we had frequent tea parties which my father called 'bunfights'. 'A little bit of glory hallelujah will do them no harm,' he would say; he had become disenchanted years before by his own father's pious hypocrisy, and certainly had no intention of dictating to his own children. My mother's father had discharged *his* duty (as a lapsed Catholic) by insisting that his children be baptised in the Catholic church, thereafter taking no further action, a course designed to ensure their subsequent avoidance of churches of any denomination. God was not an issue in our family.

I earned a Bible, 'presented to Dorothy Norgrove for Twelve Large Cards'. I have it still. You were given a card each Sunday, inscribed with a text. You learned the text by heart, and your card was initialled next week by the teacher. Twelve *little* cards earned you a *big* card, and twelve *big* cards . . . Did we really attend for nearly three years? I am assailed by a guilty suspicion that I probably invoked a number of Ross's cards in my race for a Bible. Ross learned texts easily too, was very biddable, and didn't really want a Bible anyway.

I did. It was full of stories that were larger than life, featuring lists of people with extravagant names who begat other people with names of such outrageous improbability that I was moved to laugh aloud and to read them out to anyone who would listen. And anyway, it was a book, with a book's feel and smell, a book to have and to hold, to savour ownership of, when you and it were apart.

Ross was in Standard Two when the door opened one day and the headmaster entered trailing me and a boy called Norman; we were both being 'put up', a procedure that effectively took you out of your year and away from your friends. I recall Ross's broad, welcoming grin as a light in a lonely ocean. These were sink-or-swim days in the educational world; no allowances were made. I remember, too, that after several weeks Norman was 'put back'. He was frailer than I was I think. And, of course, I had Ross. They let me sit across the aisle from him, at first. (We sat two to a desk, but boys and girls never sat together.) And it was here that I surprised even myself by my first profession of outrage at proposed injustice. In those days, a separate copy of the *School Journal*, of blessed memory, was given to each child. Printed in black and white, without a cover, each monthly edition was strung by its spine into a 'journal cover' to be kept for home use thereafter. I suppose that the unsuspecting teacher meant no offence when she suggested that Ross and Dorothy Norgrove needed only one between them; or perhaps the number issued to the class had not yet been increased. Whatever the source, the injustice of the proposal lent me both voice and, apparently, conviction. Two copies it was, for ever after. Our parents were pleased, for both our sakes, that we were now in the same class; no one foresaw any difficulties, and none arose.

But Standard Two was a far cry from Standard One. Ink, mercifully, was still to come, but writing, quite different from printing as practised by the 'babies', demanded intense concentration. It was executed in books designed to rigidly regiment the size and height of one's letters. Each row of writing was produced within four lines, the vowels and other 'low' letters — and the bottom half of the 'd's, 'b's, 'h's and the like and the upper halves of the 'g's, 'j's and *their* like — contained between the two middle lines. Their upper halves (those that *had* upper halves) soared exactly to the topmost (red) line. The exception, for some undivulged reason, was 't', which must reach to a point halfway between the second and top line. (Tricky, this.) The tails of the 'g's, 'y's, 'q's and *their* like descended to the bottom line.

Everything must, of course, strike exactly the slope decreed by authority.

Bearing in mind that the letters bore only a passing resemblance to those learned in the printing regime, plus the need to develop flowing loops to connect them all, the task in retrospect seems daunting. I don't think we were daunted. This was what school was about; and some children will always prefer precision to laxity and vagueness. It was rather gratifying, too, that some of the cleverest children were the poorest writers!

And then, *ink*, in Standard Three, when most of us were nine. The potential for disaster was spectacular. Each desk had a round aperture designed to hold a small china cup with a rolled edge. This would be filled with ink from a large jug with a long thin spout. Ink *stained*: fingers, cuffs, unlikely parts of one's anatomy that came into unfortunate contact with it (dipping the ends of girls' long hair into the inkwell behind them was a hackneyed ploy of poisonous little boys), one's books . . . ink was everywhere. We wrote with pens into which new nibs had constantly to be inserted, and learning to dip up enough ink to write a few words without an excess, which was doomed to slide down and, literally, blot one's copy-book, was a mighty task, accomplished only after much practice and great acceleration of the heartbeat.

Unlucky 'ink monitors' had been known to slip and take the full force of a wave of ink; one's desk could be bumped and an overfull inkwell slop its contents in ruinous directions, or one could be jostled in the aisle and fetch up with ink on the seat of trousers or skirts. Nibs had their problems, too: they broke or splayed if you pressed too hard, and could put your (or someone else's) eye out if brandished recklessly . . . Life, from this point on, was hazardous.

Everyone had their favourite ink story, but nothing compared with Dad's classic tale of Uncle Harold and the inkwells. ('Tell us again, Dad, about the time Uncle Harold threw a whole tray of inkwells at the headmaster!') It was true, too; and it was plump, placid Uncle Harold who had done it, not one of the thin, quick-to-ignite ones like our father or Uncle Roy.

Miss Carnachan, our teacher, expected total attention and instant obedience and, on the whole, got both. I remember her well; she had short black hair, eyes that saw everything, and a brisk, quick manner. She was always fair, good to listen to, and not averse to laughter. Like most teachers in those days, she used the strap for misdemeanours that she considered extreme. In the three years she taught me, she strapped me once: for arguing cheekily on some long-forgotten subject. My two concerns in the face of this ordeal were to withstand the experience without faltering and withdrawing my hand, and *not* to cry. I succeeded in both and actually felt rather proud of myself. I never saw Miss Carnachan deal brutally with any child, but tales abounded of teachers who prided themselves on the strength of their 'strapping' arm. My own punishment served only to assuage Miss Carnachan's exasperation, if it did that. I remained as cheerfully, and no doubt cheekily, argumentative as ever.

I remember Stanley Bay School as consisting outside of large areas of asphalt bounded by low seats. The girls' playground was separated from the boys' by a high wire-netting fence. There was no grass for the girls, but, on a lower level than the main playgrounds, there was a 'big boys' playground', which was grassed, presumably for football. In summer, we used to walk in a long crocodile to Stanley Bay beach for swimming once a week. When only just eight, Ross swam half a mile for his '880 yard' certificate, and was irked because they wouldn't let him continue straight on for the mile certificate. He was totally at home in the water, always. I learned to swim competently, but never excelled. Ross's passion for boats and the water, by contrast, seemed to have been born in him.

We lined up in classes every morning in front of the school, girls on one side, boys on the other, and were brought to military attention with a shouted command: Atten-*shun!* Feet must be together, arms stiffly at one's sides, eyes ahead. After a short address (announcements, instructions and admonitions in the time-honoured tradition of school assemblies) we were marshalled, military style, into school. A teacher shouted 'Left! Right!' and a boy played a drum. Ross and I both aspired to this glory, and practised with two forks on the bottom of empty biscuit tins at home — I without any hope, as girls were not eligible. Why did I not resent this? I am ashamed, in retrospect, but it did not occur to me. Once a week we saluted the flag, 'Salute . . . one *two!*' and sang 'God Save the King'. This was George the Fifth, we all knew. I used to wonder what afflicted him, to warrant this impassioned plea. What did he need saving *from*? But then, I was a child of literal bent, and was often puzzled. (Why should Jesus want the little children to *suffer* to come to him? It simply didn't square with other facets of his character as revealed by the stories in my Bible.)

'Paying attention' was compulsory. When not writing, our hands were to be folded together and placed on our desktops. Occasionally there would be a command, 'Hands on heads!' and our entwined hands would fly to our scalps, elbows braced back. I don't recall resenting these rituals. They certainly produced a background against which teachers could *instruct*, which was, of course, what teachers were employed to do in those days.

In the early thirties, one *learned* at school. Reading was considered a tool, not a subject. One mastered reading in 'the Primers' and thereafter used the skill to acquire essential facts. (This, at least, was the theory.) It was also thought necessary, while children's minds were flexible and sponge-like, to stock them with a multitude of useful, immediately retrievable facts, such as the 'times tables', linear and weight tables, the correct spelling of English words, the geography and history of New Zealand, and the names and locations of the countries of the world (*and* their capitals). 'Times tables' — to twelve times, by Standard Three — were, of course, essential if one was to master computation in pounds, shillings and pence, and one certainly would need these skills to calculate prices and check one's wages when turned loose from school, as most of us expected to be after Standard Six (Year 8, these days). We learned by chanting our tables every day, and rehearsing them at home. No one thought we were clever for knowing them; it was simply necessary. It was also essential to know that there were sixteen ounces in a pound, fourteen pounds in a stone, one hundred and twelve pounds in a hundredweight, twenty hundredweight in a ton, and two thousand, two hundred and forty pounds in a ton. And of course length mattered: twelve inches to a foot, up through yards, chains and furlongs to a mile. We were obliged to *know*, and to these ends constant repetition, reinforced with daily 'mental arithmetic', drove details home. And then there was always spelling . . . We had no 'school trips', and teachers were not expected to be social workers or psychologists. How much easier it must have been to teach in those days!

We did have art (I recall smudgy pastels on black paper) and music. We learned dozens of songs every year, mostly English folk songs, sea shanties and ballads. 'The Ash Grove', 'Strawberry Fair' and 'Old Uncle Tom Cobbly and All' come back unbidden. I suspect that planners of the syllabus took care to avoid any mention of sexual entanglement and were not above altering lines in songs to suit their own pure purposes. The maid who 'dwelt in Amsterdam' was 'a saucy jade' in our version, though I feel sure that knowledge of her status as 'mistress of her trade' would not have sullied our innocent

ears. I, for one, would have assumed that she sewed an especially fine seam
. . . It was all right if the object of desire was dead, and therefore out of
harm's way, of course: 'He sleeps 'neath the turf in the lonely ash grove . . .'
Insobriety didn't seem to matter, either. We used to roar, 'What shall we do
with the drunken sailor?' with enormous satisfaction.

We knew that 1642 was Abel Tasman, 1769 was Captain Cook, 1814
was Samuel Marsden's first sermon, and 1840 the Treaty of Waitangi. We
knew about Hone Heke (we were totally on his side in the spectacular affair
of the cutting-down of the British flagpole *three times*), Hongi Hika, Te
Rauparaha, Te Kooti and the names of the eight canoes. We knew the
words of 'Pokarekareana', and shouted 'Ake! Ake! Ake!' lustily, as a cry of
defiance in our own games. We were presented with the siege of Orakau,
and Rewi's great shout alongside the drama and glory of Trafalgar, and
Nelson's 'England expects . . .' We knew that 'the Maoris' were fierce and
courageous fighters. We were given no 'rights and wrongs' about the 'Maori'
wars, any more than we were directed to take the Royalist, or Cromwell's,
side in the English Civil War. It had all simply happened. In Stanley Bay,
we did not see any 'Maoris' but we knew that Grandma Brown's brother,
Alfred Stewart, had married one. His son, Ernest, had been sent to
Auckland to be educated at St Peters (now Hato Petera) College, and had
often stayed with the family in Grey Lynn. This cousin, my mother told
us, had prospered, a fact verified when, later, we lived in Ponsonby, and
several of his descendants sought us out. Their shiny car, standing outside
our state house, and their expensive and fashionable clothes, were a source
of wonder. I think I was understandably a little confused about Maori, at
this stage.

There was a side to my life at this time that I did not share with
anyone: my devotion to my family of dolls. These I made clothes for, put
tenderly to bed, and taught. I used to make tiny books for them out of
brown paper or anything else I could find, carefully sewing the spines and
inscribing the covers with their separate names. I wrote stories in these little
books and would read them aloud to the listening dolls. I taught them
carefully, sitting them in rows with their books on their knees. I would
never leave the house without making sure they were all comfortable. There
was a big celluloid doll called Doreen and a little china boy doll called
Bruce, with several others between. Each was invested with a total
personality. 'Bruce is shy,' I would say to imaginary company. 'He doesn't

like other people to hold him. Doreen's a real show-off, but she's very kind to others.'

Surprisingly, I never played 'dolls' with other girls my own age. But then, neighbourhood play was almost always conducted outside, and ranged through backyards and streets and over mudflats, beach and cliffs. A boy we knew, Billy Worrall, fell over the cliff on Stanley Point from his own garden, and was killed. He came from one of the 'Point' families, who were known to be both wealthier and higher on the social scale than those of us down on the flat, though he was 'one of the mob' at school. We were all sobered, for a day or two, but it seemed unreal. It could never happen to *us*. Someone suggested, maliciously, that it might not have happened to Billy had his mother not been off playing tennis. 'Rubbish,' said our no-nonsense mother. 'It could have been any child. None of us traipse round behind you.' This was, of course, true.

Val and Pat increasingly aspired to be part of my 'school' games. By the time the two little girls were four and I was eight, I was making little books for them, teaching them to read the simple stories I wrote for the purpose and to write their own names as well as simple numbers. This venture was a great success. No one encouraged either me or the little girls in the exercise. The adults in our lives were always pleased if we were happily engaged and these 'lessons' seemed to occupy all three of us for hours at a time. (I checked with Pat on this point recently. We were talking of a game played by children sixty-five years before, but her face reflected the same remembered pleasure that I experience. And she and Val could certainly read simple text by the time they went to school.)

Among my mother's effects, many years later, I found my own first written verse. I had enclosed it in a somewhat ineptly decorated, home-made card, and given it to my father for Christmas when I was six years old. Punctuation and spelling were arbitrary, though I was obviously determined to get a bit of both in:

> The christmas bells a ringing.
> And all the children singing
> How happy we
> all feel as the
> Bell's play a
> merry pearl.

Underneath the picture of two small, apparently Chinese figures wearing stylised coolie hats and carrying a sedan chair between them, are the words 'We are here to bring you luck'. Two further, rather more carefully illustrated cards, both enclosing an inner leaf that is secured with a piece of fancy cord, were produced for the following Christmas, one for each of my parents. My father's wished him 'Joy and Happyness' on the front and my mother's 'Kind Wishes'. Within, both were inscribed, 'To Daddy' (or Mummy) 'Wishing you peace and comfort from Dorothy'. My mother had often talked about my early, prolific production of cards for family and friends, but I had no idea that she had kept any examples. But she had laughed about my ambitious style. 'The other children would say "Merry Christmas" or "Happy Birthday", but Dorothy always tried something fancier.'

I began a lifelong affair with paper at this time, I believe. Stationery shops seemed to me places of wonder; the very smell of paper, ink, rubbers, pencils and rulers was hypnotic. My mother understood this, and would bring me home a small pad or a new, unsharpened pencil when she brought the others a comic. (Of course, I would read the comics too!)

Meanwhile, I was making repeated sorties into *David Copperfield*, *Westward Ho!* and an unlikely assortment of anything to hand. Our mother had been 'clever' at school, we were told by Auntie. On leaving, at twelve years of age, she had been presented with a complete Shakespeare and a volume of Tennyson's poems — 'For Composition' according to the presentation plate. (It is signed by W. Hammond, a Thames schoolmaster whose name is mentioned with great respect in many histories of 'the Thames'.) The Shakespeare had postage-stamp print and defied my assaults, but the Tennyson had fine bold print, gold edges and romantic illustrations. I treasured it, and read great chunks, hardly understanding but loving it nonetheless. And why, when I was known to be a cheerful, optimistic child, did I so revel in the sombre melancholy of Victorian poetry and song? Tales of lost or unrequited love, of undying devotion, tragic death and lingering sorrow held me captive.

> I stand again in the Northland,
> But in silence and in shame;
> Your grave is my only landmark
> And men have forgotten my name . . .

from 'Thora', a dark heart-rending tale which purports to be '. . . truer and older, than any the sagas tell . . .' used to thrill me so that I visibly trembled when my father sang it. He had a clear baritone voice, and would always perform, my mother accompanying him on the piano, when we had family or friends visiting on a Sunday evening. 'A Perfect Day' and 'In the Gloaming' had a similar effect, and the stirring military ballads fired me with misdirected patriotism:

> And though I've a wooden leg, lass,
> And my eyes are old and dim
> Still I fought for his dear old father
> And I'd fight again, for him!

The old wooden-backed sofa in the kitchen was a treasure trove, for here we kept our comics. Every Christmas brought its crop of comic 'annuals' of English origin: *Comic Cuts, Crackers, Chatterbox, Puck* . . . Magic, unforgettable names! They were stowed under the cushions and brought out for interminable re-readings as the year wore on. Ross and I often read them aloud to each other, laughing uproariously at the absurd bits, improvising wildly on familiar themes, and squabbling endlessly over 'turns'. Each alternate spread was devoted to a written story, with minimal illustration. 'Comics' they certainly were, but there was substance within that is sadly lacking in their modern counterparts. The weekly papers, *Triumph* and *Champion*, were added when we were about nine and ten. Thereafter the intrepid airman Fireworks Flynn, the daring detective Colwyn Dane and their numerous colleagues (British to a man) became part of our lives and games. I am surprised in retrospect that I was not concerned by the total lack of girls or women in these tales. I am surprised also that we never questioned the Englishness of everything we used, and all our customs. (My mother never set foot in England, but like many of her contemporaries would say to the end of her life that someone was having a trip 'home', meaning to England.) We children did not simply believe, we *knew* we were a part of Britain, merely transported bodily to the other side of the world. The change has been breathtakingly fast; my own children feel little if any allegiance, and my grandchildren are quite detached: they are New Zealanders.

NINE

There can be no doubt that the emphasis on 'learning by heart' both at school and informally, at home, through our family emphasis on singing, left me with a vast legacy of words. I must have known, before I ever grew through childhood, the words of hundreds if not thousands of songs — from music hall ditties through romantic love songs to stirring ballads. And from school, poetry. I remember being captivated by Walter de la Mare's 'Silver':

> Slowly, silently, now the moon
> Walks the night in her silver shoon;
> This way and that she peers and sees
> Silver fruit upon silver trees . . .

I used to say 'shoon' to myself, silently. So much richer than the everyday *shoes*! When I was chosen to represent the junior school (the 'Primers' in those days) by reciting at Miss Harty's farewell concert, my mother outdid herself in making me a frilly new dress to befit the occasion. I suspect that I was chosen for my loud voice, and the certainty of those in charge that I would both remember my lines, and not be daunted by the lights and the large audience. I remember standing, grinning widely, as the hall crammed with people applauded enthusiastically. When the elderly and loved Miss

Harty, who was seated on stage, took me to sit on her knee, my glory was complete.

Somehow, my parents had managed to buy a secondhand piano once we were settled in Devonport. The music they must have missed ever since they had left the old family home now returned. When Uncle Bert visited, my mother would happily abandon her piano stool to him and he would throw open the top of the piano and play for my father to sing. Albert Norgrove was a natural pianist. At the age of four he had confounded his older sister's teacher with his untaught, embellished versions of her 'pieces'. Engaged to teach him, this poor woman found the task impossible, as did a succession of male teachers. Little Albert would *not* stick to the music!

As boys, he and my father had played and sung together with enormous enjoyment; it was one occupation that their father would allow. Their pleasure in each other's company was still infectious; this was 'for fun', not to impress an audience. When Uncle Bert came to visit, the windows would be thrown open and the whole family, and like as not the neighbours, would join in the singing. My father told us once that Uncle Bert was not nearly as good an accompanist as my mother — he didn't have the restraint or supportive technique for this role. 'He plays as loud as he can and I shout as loud as I can when we get together,' my father explained. We didn't care. They were both showmen, and we would clamour for more.

If any proof were needed of our parents' determination to have music in their lives, one could point to this early purchase of a piano, and our acquisition of a radio when I was seven, in 1932. We called it a wireless. Thereafter, all the great singers of the day joined in our family lives — it was like magic. Gladys Moncrieff, John McCormack, Richard Tauber, Dame Nellie Melba, Richard Crooks, Peter Dawson and many, many more were all instantly recognised and loved. And all the early radio personalities were suddenly there with us, in a miraculous way. Aunt Daisy sticks in the mind. (The ear doesn't give her up easily, either. 'Good morning, everybody, good morning, good morning, *good morning!*') My mother, and thousands of other women, listened to her every day. Aunt Daisy's brand of fanatical enthusiasm for every aspect of domestic life was irresistible. She was a mine of resource. Household remedies for everything from ink stains to whooping cough and cockroaches, with dazing advice about the care and restoration of vital accessories from false teeth to fur coats, poured from her lips; and of course, *the weather*. Did she *really* once declare rapturously that the sun had been shining right up her back passage that morning? If she didn't, she should have; it is pure Aunt Daisy.

Then there were Uncle Tom and Uncle Scrim from *The Friendly Road*, the one urging us to kindly tolerance:

> You go to your church, and I to mine,
> But let's walk along together!

the other assuring us, in the darkest days that

> All the world's on the way
> To a happier day,
> For the road is open again.

We were supported and uplifted on all sides. A woman with a strong, deep voice used to sing 'The Stranger of Galilee' every Sunday night at eight o'clock. It always made me inexpressibly sad.

> And I knew I could love him forever,
> So tender and gracious was he . . .

Could I be tender and gracious? An inkling that tender and gracious was not my style assailed me. 'Onward Christian Soldiers' was closer: 'Forward into battle, see his banners go!'

On a more vulgar — but delicious — note, Monday night brought us the wrestling from the Town Hall, with Lofty Blomfield and his famous 'octopus clamp' which we all aspired to perfect. It involved a great tangling of legs and was likely to snap bones, if applied correctly. Mercifully, it never was. And there were Dad and Dave, and Mum and Mabel, Australian bumpkins performing their mad and muddy antics in Snake Gully. Our big comfortable kitchen resounded to their harmless inanities, and we all sang along to 'The Road to Gundagai'. All this was truly a miracle.

The family musical streak bypassed me, though I could always sing in tune, and even hold a reliable descant line in the school choir. But the words took root. Several of my cousins did rather better musically. One, Iris Norgrove, played the Civic organ with style and won awards for singing, and my brother, Ross, acquired a reputation as a good man to invite to a party, guitar in hand.

These were the days of 'community singing' in the Auckland Town

Hall, designed to provide free entertainment for the poverty-stricken masses, and to lift everyone's spirits. No lugubrious numbers here!

> Give yourself a pat on the back
> A pat on the back
> A pat on the back
> And say to yourself
> 'Here's jolly good health
> You've had a good day today!'

We used to hear about these concerts from friends at school, but we never went to one. Our realistic mother scoffed at attempts to infuse the populace with artificial good cheer. She simply never told us that we were unfortunate, and contrived somehow to make sure that we never felt so.

But once — only once — she managed to take the three of us to a vaudeville show at His Majesty's Theatre in Auckland. We were well coached beforehand. We would have tickets for 'the gods'. The entrance to these heavenly precincts, way, way up, almost among the stars, opened straight on to a narrow side street. Once the doors were opened, Ross and I were to join the mad rush up the hundreds of stone stairs in an attempt to secure good seats. Mum and Val would come at a more sedate pace behind. Fleet of foot and determined, we arrived panting and triumphant at the head of the horde, and seized front row seats.

The performance transported us to another world. There were magicians, dancers, comedians, jugglers, and clowns — including one who kept appearing from the wings on one side, crazily riding a bike which disappeared with a loud crash into the wings on the other side — and skits, and songs and lights and colour and music . . . We were, indeed, in another world, a magic, unimagined place.

At the end, we descended the stairs in a daze. Mum said she would bring us again one day, if she could manage it. She never could. Heaven knows what economies she had made to manage this once. We knew it was impossible, and didn't ask, but we relived the experience in our minds, and our games, forever.

Ah, but there was always the Winter Show! Was there a child in Auckland, rich or poor, who didn't go to the Winter Show? He or she must have been sorely deprived, if so. It was held in the wharf sheds, and must have been a pale shadow of the glittering, expensive Easter, and Boat and

Home Shows of today; and of course, the war killed it stone dead.

My memories are of 'windmills' and celluloid kewpie dolls on sticks, pink candy floss which enveloped your head and was later scrubbed off face and ears by your determined mother — and usually proved to have also invaded your hair; coconut shies, 'hoopla' stalls (you paid a penny for a few wooden rings and tried — always unsuccessfully — to throw them over one of the trashy trinkets assembled on a table behind a barrier) and a merry-go-round, and music. Goods must have been exhibited, but these were of no concern to us. Tiny samples of boxed breakfast cereals or raisins, though, and tiny, tiny pots of jam or honey were collected eagerly and borne home triumphantly. It was all pure joy.

Our days in Devonport were coming to an end, but we did not suspect this. We were happily settled in our second Calliope Road house, further from the beach, but closer to Dad's shop. This move covered no more than half a mile, but it was still an upheaval, and I loved it. For the last few days in the old house we managed with minimal equipment: one plate and one cup each, the same clothes, roughly flung-together meals . . . and for the first few days in the new house, life was even more Spartan. I was to learn that you cannot find exactly what you want, ever, in this halfway situation. At least one piece of vital equipment — the teapot, perhaps — evades you for weeks, and improvisation is necessary. It is all great fun, however, if you are eight years old. We were to suffer eight more removals (this was our sixth) before I ever left home, but we never seemed to become experts in the business.

At number 98 Calliope Road the night was well advanced before Dad — no handyman at the best of times — had reassembled the beds, Mum had found enough bedding to keep everyone warm, and all five of us had fallen thankfully into deep sleep. Some time later, I awoke in total darkness, not knowing where I was. I seemed to be all wet . . . I was. I had wet the bed! I had often heard Mum tell other mothers about my extraordinarily early 'training' in the toilet field. I controlled my bladder long before I got my speech organs into any sort of order, apparently, and I suppose she had to claim some sort of accomplishment for her seemingly slow daughter. I was simply not used to this sort of thing.

With a loud and uncharacteristic wail (I seldom cried — and never aloud) I stumbled out of bed and attempted the journey to Mum and Dad's bedroom; except that I had no idea where it was, the blackness was total, and the route was an obstacle course. Both my parents, propelled from their bed by the noise, and just as disoriented as I, collided with me in the hall. Dad calmed me while Mum went for the candle, assuring me in her blunt way that this was a perfectly normal mishap, and understandable in the circumstances and that I was 'to stop making that noise at *once*'. Dad meanwhile peeled off my pyjamas and wrapped me in a blanket from the big bed. The impossibility of finding replacement night-clothes resulted in my being encased in Dad's cast-off shirt from the day before. Before long I was snug between Mum and Dad in the big bed, warm and dry — if a little smelly — and luxuriously comfortable. Ross and Val slept through the pandemonium and, I suspect, actually envied me when the story broke in the morning.

It was in this house that our little sister suffered a series of attacks of croup, which terrified our parents and, by association, Ross and me. Mum knew (and of course told Dad, but not us) that her eldest brother, whom she never saw, had died during an attack of croup. He (the 'first George') was a healthy, sturdy little boy, and he was four. He simply lost his breath entirely, and died. Val was four, not sturdy, and often ill.

The attacks would occur at night, and our father would go running, on foot, to fetch Doctor Bennett, in Devonport. He always came, good man that he was, and stayed while Val's attack lasted. They would give her some foul concoction (called, I remember, 'ipecacuanha') to make her vomit, and install her in the sitting room, close to a roaring fire, all windows tightly closed and curtained. Exactly why this treatment failed to carry Val off, as it had poor little George Brown fifty years before, is not clear. The modern home treatment for croup is steam, in copious quantities: damp, not dry air is now known to keep the breathing passages open. So simple — and so lethal in its non-observance. Fortunately, Val 'grew out of' the tendency quite quickly. While it lasted, each attack reduced us all to a state of paralysed dread.

Our former neighbours, the O'Leary's, at the other end of Calliope Road, lamented the loss of our little sister when we moved. While our backs were turned, Val had transformed herself into a character. At the age of three she had insinuated herself into the elderly O'Leary household one evening, wearing Ross's school helmet back to front and carrying a battered old purse given her by Auntie Maggie. She had come to visit, she informed them, and thereafter arrived at the same time each night. 'Is Mick home

yet?' she would enquire. Ross and I called the O'Learys Mr and Mrs, but
then we were never intimate. Val would give them hilarious pieces of half-
truth or misinformation about Norgrove family affairs, accept a cup of tea
and a biscuit graciously, and settle herself to wait for Mick.

Our small sister was the original for *Mary-Mary*, I realised thirty
years later when, with my children, I laughed at Joan Robinson's tales of
this small, bossy female. Val was never a shadow of Ross and me; she
developed an individuality that frequently had us boggling. And she
certainly expected — and got — instant obedience from all of us. (She
would not only scream, but *throw things*, if thwarted.)

This last Stanley Bay house had a big sprawling garden, which sloped
down at the back to a dense hedge of 'cutty-grass' bushes. Beyond this a
derelict old man occupied a broken-down shack on an overgrown piece of
land. He was seen often around the streets, always bare-footed, and always
carrying a sugarbag (or sack) over one shoulder. He was known as 'Old
Mac', and we children always greeted him with a rather mannered 'Hi,
Mac', as we passed him. He would always answer in a low growl, though
he never smiled.

I sometimes played with a small group of girls who lived close, and
one day we decided that we should try to make the old man's life happier
with a gift of some kind. One of our number (who had no mother, but a
father with a good job who indulged her and her younger brother)
produced some money, and we decided that cream doughnuts would bring
a ray of light into Old Mac's dreary day. The delectable buns being
purchased from the home-cookery just along the road (oh, the smells that
wafted from that shop!), we advanced, for the first time ever, into Old
Mac's territory. Or rather, we attempted to; but Old Mac, noting our
approach, came out of his shack shouting and waving a stick. We fled.
Later, on the back steps of an empty house — of which there was no
shortage at that time — we ate the doughnuts: three each. I think we all
felt guilty, and a little foolish, but it was worth it. We licked the sugar from
our fingers in dreamy ecstasy. That night, I told Ross, and he was outraged.
Cream doughnuts . . .? Why wasn't *he* included? And anyway, *he* wouldn't
have retreated in the face of Old Mac's threatened attack! (I didn't believe
this.) In vain did I point out that he had gone off to play with other boys.
Three cream doughnuts each!

Some time later, the tables were turned. I had defected one day after school to play with the McCathie kids, Marie and Jim. I liked them, and their house ran down to the mudflats, which I loved. Ross and several other boys, illicitly cooking stolen potatoes, which we often did, on a fire too close to the cutty-grass bushes, set the whole row alight, and might have incinerated themselves and several houses *and* Old Mac's shack had not the Fire Brigade made a timely appearance, bell clanging, neighbours shouting, dogs barking — and our father, summoned from the shop and still in his butcher's apron, waving his arms and shouting, 'I'll murder the little sod!' I arrived home, my heart thudding in my chest (some kids I met on the way told me gleefully that my house was burning down) in time, at least, to see the fire engine. But soaked, smouldering foliage and a scene of general muddy devastation were no substitutes for the real action. I had missed it entirely. My resentment was intense, and long-lasting.

A great deal of fuss was made about this, but no retribution taken, at least in our family. And potatoes were not really 'stolen'. They were 'pinched' from sacks in the washhouses of the participants' families or occasionally unsuspecting elderly neighbours, who mostly turned a blind eye. 'Boys will be boys' was a generally accepted adage in those days — and included girls, if they happened to include themselves, it seemed.

Gratifyingly, we had a real conflagration shortly afterwards, and I was present. Some English people with a hyphenated name (double-barrelled, my father called it) lived on the other side of Calliope Road further along overlooking the harbour. Everyone knew they were only there temporarily. Their only child was a girl of my age called Celeste — why wasn't I called something romantic like that? — and she and I used to play together occasionally. I was fascinated by her accent which, had I known, was middle-class English, and her airy acceptance of such things as ocean travel, cars, and servants. I was never inside her house, which was large and two-storeyed, with a tower on top, but I imagined velvet cushions, gleaming furniture and beds hung with silken draperies.

On the night before the family left to return to England, the house burned down. The double-barrelled family was quite safe; the whole retinue had already moved into a city hotel. We were hustled from our beds, shrouded in coats and blankets — Dad carried Val — and taken to watch the stunning spectacle. Such splendid free entertainment was not to be missed, and the whole district turned out.

The blaze lit up the whole harbour, and several streets around.

Devonport's valiant fire brigade may have been adequate for the Norgroves' cutty-grass bushes but was no match for *this* fire, and sensibly concentrated on preserving the adjacent church, on one side, and house on the other. There were muttered remarks about the fire being 'an insurance job', but these were hastily stifled. I had no idea what 'insurance job' was, but the suggestion lent an exciting, sinister air to the event, which was a true extravaganza.

When I look back on this time, before I was eleven, I see only sunshine, hear only laughter and cheerful noise. If there were bad times — and there must have been — I have forgotten or suppressed them. But the end of the halcyon days was at hand. In 1935 my father was promoted to be manager of the new Auckland Meat Company's shop in Symonds Street in the city. We were to move 'to town'.

TEN

*I*n 1935 my father was thirty-four years old, and had established his reputation as an outstanding manager with the Auckland Meat Company. A very untypical butcher, he had been pushed into the trade as a young boy by his father, and the Depression was no time to change stream even if he had thought to do so. Instead, he raised his shop to unlikely heights of spotlessness and service. He conceived the idea of using lead-lights to surround the glass in the shop window to enhance its appearance and this innovation was adopted by the company, and used ultimately in most of its shops. He insisted that his staff wear white, starched coats and aprons and that these be fresh every day; the traditional blue-striped apron was banned. The sawdust on the floor of Dad's shop — obligatory, in those days — was changed frequently and raked constantly, and his shop window was always artistically 'dressed' with flowers and bowls of fruit. The refrigerated windows of today were, of course, quite unknown.

We children were never allowed to go to the shop unless expressly sent. Children whose families were known to be 'hard-up' were always, on Dad's instructions, given a thick slice of 'luncheon' sausage if they called in after school, but we never shared in this treat. Having some sausage brought home was not the same; and anyway, our mother gave us meat only once daily. Butchers always received free meat as a condition of employment in those days, and many of their families lived almost entirely on this free food. Not our family; Mum believed in porridge, fruit, vegetables, and Marmite sandwiches. We 'filled up' on as much bread as we wanted and always had home-made jam. There was a family ritual which I have never forgotten: when the big preserving pan of still-hot jam was ready to be bottled, Mum would take it off the stove and put it on the kitchen table, along with a loaf of bread and a plate of butter. Then, whatever the time of day, we would all eat slabs of bread running with the hot, delicious stuff straight from the pan, no one caring if it slopped off the slice and on to child, table or floor. The joy of this voluptuous exercise is still with me.

We had golden syrup, too, on porridge and bread, but, for some un-revealed reason, never that favourite Depression delicacy, bread and dripping. Perhaps it was part of Mum's 'not too much meat' policy. No one drank milk beyond babyhood. It was expensive, and one 'billy' per day was bought at the door from the milkman, who came in a horse-pulled cart. The horse, on shouted instruction, would move a few yards along the road and wait patiently for its master to serve each house in turn. We were given weak tea or cocoa made with hot water, with a dash of milk and a spoonful of sugar. Mum always suggested a hot drink whenever anyone looked tired or out of sorts, and this habit took root in my being. A 'nice cup of . . . something' still seems to help, and is always suggested in our family. (I suspect that this was a colonial tradition in New Zealand, and still survives.) Weet-Bix, then as now, was an alternative to oatmeal porridge and, in our case, often given as a snack before bed if 'tea' (New Zealand for dinner or supper) had been early and we had been playing outside. I remember Mum talking about children who had to go to bed with their stomachs empty. Not her children. Boiling water would be poured over the Weet-Bix, a dash of milk added and sugar or golden syrup slopped generously over all. We loved it.

It seems to me in retrospect that, if you are to be poor, you do well to have a mother who is not intent upon keeping up appearances. No starched table napkins or polished silver, with tiny helpings and tight-lipped resentment in the face of reduced circumstances for us! Mum would have filled our bellies with bread and jam, spreading newspaper as a tablecloth, and never divulging our poverty to us even if things had got worse. She'd have kept us laughing too, lost in the true or fabricated tales she would tell us, abandoning duty and taking us on picnics at the drop of a hat.

The news that Dad was to be promoted was greeted with some ambivalence by his children. Ross and I didn't want to leave Stanley Bay School and our friends but the thought of moving to town was exciting — and Dad seemed to be delighted, and kept assuring us that the change would be good for us all. I learned years later that Mum had been filled with apprehension. Stanley Bay was like a village; it was unusual to meet anyone in the street whom you did not know, and this necessarily had a constraining effect on everyone's behaviour. Mum wasn't worried about her own or her children's capacity to withstand change. It was her husband she feared for. But glory surrounded the coming move from Dad's point of view, and rubbed off on to us. He had been informed by the 'big bosses' that he had a great future in the company. He could not be expected to moulder away in the little Calliope Road shop, however much his family enjoyed 'shore' life. Our fate was inevitable.

Dad was duly installed as manager of the large, new A.M.C. shop in upper Symonds Street, we moved to a house in Mount Albert, and Ross and I were enrolled at what was then known as Gladstone Road School (now simply 'Gladstone'). I had turned ten in April of that year, and Ross eleven on the last day of the year before. (It has always seemed appropriate that party-loving Ross should have been born on New Year's Eve.) Our house, although an impressively new bungalow, as against the draughty old villa we had quitted, was low-lying, and Mum was prone to bronchitis, so we shifted again. The second house was a step up in more ways than one. Modern and spacious, with expansive views, it was literally on the side of Mount Albert. We knew that this house was on the market, and hoped, with Dad's improved and improving prospects, to save enough money to put down as a deposit on it. Imagine: we would own a house — a beautiful house! (I recall that it was offered to us at eleven hundred pounds.)

I have never known at what point my father's serious descent into drinking and disaster began. He had always spent Saturday afternoon at the pub, arriving home fit only for whatever food Mum could get into him, and bed. But the pub had been just down the road in Devonport, and his drinking mates were men we knew. Now, there was no local pub, and the shop in Symonds Street was surrounded by city hotels: two within a few hundred yards. Mum's fears proved to be justified; but to begin with, all

seemed to go well. Dad's enthusiasm and energy were boundless, and he
soon had this shop, too, running the way he wanted it. Butchers always
started work at five o'clock in the morning and sometimes earlier in those
days; everything sold was cut up and prepared for sale on the premises. Dad
would walk the half-mile or so to the main road and catch the first tram
to the city, returning by the same route at the end of the day. At least, this
was his intention, and Mum's hope. Gradually, his arrival home became
later and later.

We children had no suspicion that, behind the scenes, the drama of
Dad's downfall was starting to be enacted. Mum still devoted herself to us.
Concealing her growing unease was, I suppose, merely part of her 'keeping
the children happy' policy. We were now within walking distance, in those
car-less days, of Auntie, Ockie and Pat in their shop in Point Chevalier,
and this fact was obviously a comfort to Mum, as well as a joy to us. The
move to town was not without its advantages, we started to think.

I remember our first day at Gladstone School. Ross and I knew no
one — we might have been in another country — and were directed to
opposite sides of the room, to sit in desks that each happened to be
occupied by only one person. I remember that my desk-partner was a large,
gypsy-like girl who looked dull, and wore ragged clothes and actually
smelled. I had never met anyone like her, poor girl. I smiled at her (I always
tried to be as much like Dad as possible, and *he* always smiled at people)
but she didn't smile back. The teacher, meanwhile, was writing sums on
the blackboard, the class starting to copy them into their books. I
recognised the type: long division in pounds, shillings and pence. We had
been about to start these at Stanley Bay. Neither Ross nor I could do them!
We were both stunned, but the teacher noticed our shock, and called us
up to her desk. She told us to eat our lunch quickly at lunchtime, and come
back into the classroom, where she would teach us. We did this — and so,
obviously, did she — and we worked on 'long division in money' for the
rest of the hour. We both learned. (At least we knew our tables.)

The playground at Gladstone School seemed like a desert of asphalt,
but at playtime teachers appeared bearing huge enamel jugs of hot cocoa,
and a girl called June Lawson lent me her mug, and the rich sweet drink
warmed the cockles of my heart, as Mum would have said. Ross reported
receiving similarly kind treatment in the far-off boys' playground, and we
brought our own mugs the next day — and our thruppences for a week's

supply. (Children from poor families did not have to pay, but that did not include us, Mum insisted.) We both made friends easily, but it was never the same; some of the light had gone out of our lives with the shift to town. And life *was* different. Comfortable evenings in the old sitting room in our Devonport house, when Mum played the piano and Dad sang, had gone forever.

But living on the mountain had its points. We used to play in the old Maori fortifications and scramble round the steep sides of the crater, and — blissful chance — found, under our house, abandoned by its former owners, a stoutly built wooden sledge. Its purpose was immediately clear; other children were to be seen speeding down the grassy slopes of the mountain on similar sledges, and we happily joined in. Everyone used to grease their runners with meat fat, and our father, being pressed into providing tins of the stuff, certainly increased the Norgrove kids' popularity. We roamed all over the mountain, and on the Owairaka side, where much of the land was still rural, we found a house with a notice on its gate: BANTAMS FOR SALE. We were giddy with joy when Mum said yes, her family had had bantams . . . we could have two, a cock and a hen. Obviously we were now rich. Bennie and Bessie, they were: *our pets!* Bennie was a royal little bird in his rich red and purple plumage, Bessie modestly, beautifully speckled, a serene little body. Perhaps she would lay eggs, and we might have bantam chicks . . . We made them a house out of a packing case, but gave them free run of the garden. They stayed close, and even sometimes came into the kitchen. We loved them passionately.

Then, one day, Bessie flew into the kitchen in a state of outraged alarm, flapping and squawking. Imagining a marauding animal at least, Mum (we were at school) rushed out, to witness, over the fence in our neighbours' fowl run, Bennie strutting, emperor-fashion, back and forth while a cluster of white hens, at least twice his size, looked on admiringly from the sidelines and clucked appreciatively. This was funny enough, but Bessie's fury was even funnier, our mother told us. We were home the next time it happened, as it did at intervals. The temptation to strut his stuff in front of a potential harem, however unsuitable, would overcome Bennie and away he would go. Bessie would advise us immediately. Fortunately, the neighbours were amused, too.

Bessie *did* lay eggs, but never sat on them (Mum assured us that Bessie would know when there were chicks to be hatched). The tiny little eggs, hardly bigger than marbles, made a delicious mouthful, lightly boiled. We children took turns eating them for breakfast.

Auntie had meanwhile opened a children's dancing class behind their shop in Point Chevalier. This was a cheerful, music-hall style venture, and Ross and I both joined. We used to walk down after school two days a week, and then home to the mountain after our lesson — a considerable distance, but we didn't mind; we loved these days. Kind Auntie always regaled all her pupils with biscuits and a drink before the lesson began, and Ockie would pop in and out between customers to see how we were all getting on and, like as not, issue sweets. We liked the other children we met at the class and enjoyed the dancing: the Sailor's Hornpipe, the Irish Jig and the Highland Fling, as well as items for a concert we were to give in the convent school hall when we were all adjudged professional enough.

In the event, this proved an uproarious affair. Our father was dragged into service and forced to revive his long-dormant stage skills. Cast as the 'dame' in a pantomime skit, he charged about the stage in a long skirt and an old black bonnet of Grandma's wielding an umbrella, and was the star of the night. Then dressed as a Victorian schoolmarm, he officiated in the 'school scene' in which we all behaved very badly (by design) but sang and danced with enormous enthusiasm. My mother played the piano, Ockie took the money at the door with gracious aplomb, and there was standing room only in the hall. The proceeds were to be donated to the St Francis convent school, which Pat was to begin attending shortly. (She later transferred to the local state school, to be with us.) I recall my mother's outrage that the kindly and hardworking nuns were permitted to help the children with costume changing behind the scenes but on *no account* to actually witness the show. Music hall as a 'no-no' applied even to the cavorting of the young it seemed. By contrast, the parish priest and several other clergy enjoyed the show from the front row!

Not long after this, Ross and I performed at an Auckland Meat Company function: a dinner for managers and executives at which entertainment was provided on a stage in a very ornate, large room in a city hotel. At that time there were two very well-known radio personalities called 'Dorothy and Neddo', and this pair had been engaged to conduct the evening's entertainment. Ross, dressed as a tramp, with his swag on a stick over his shoulder, sang a song called 'The Old Sundowner' and did a tap dance; he and I performed a gypsy song and dance together, wielding tambourines, and then, devised especially for the occasion, a minuet. Ross stood by in his beautifully made (by our mother) evening suit with frilled shirt and white bow tie, holding his top hat while I recited, in a good clear voice (with *expression*) a poem taught me by Ockie (who had a fine voice himself, and had performed in *Shakespeare!*).

> Grandma told me all about it,
> Told me, so I couldn't doubt it,
> How she danced, my grandma,
> Long ago.
> How she held her pretty head,
> How her dainty skirt she spread . . .

Then, to our mother's accompaniment (she was wearing an *evening dress!*) we danced a real minuet — and the applause was thunderous. Dorothy and Neddo insisted then that we sit at their table, and we knew that our parents were proud of us, and we beamed accordingly. Ross was, as usual, full of shy charm; he had a sweet, clear singing voice, and received much praise (and I could be relied upon to answer all the questions). I was resplendent in a pale green satin gown, with rows of flounces to the floor, and a poke bonnet in the same material, lined with pale pink and trimmed with tiny flowers. We both recall feeling that this was probably a dream and we would wake up. We could simply *not* believe it when later we received five pounds each! (Mum sensibly took this wealth in hand, but we knew it would be spent on us.)

ELEVEN

*D*uring our second summer on the mountain I made friends with a girl of my own age, who lived in a big house below ours and went to a different school. Her name was Josephine Caughey — of 'Smith and Caughey' connection according to Mum — but to me Josie was simply a good new friend. She and her cousin Jeanette Caughey, who lived opposite, went to school and returned daily *in a car*, which I felt must be very dull. Half the exciting things in life happened on the way to and from school. Their school was the original Hilltop, then in Khyber Pass Road in the city, and now, greatly expanded, in Blockhouse Bay. I *was* impressed by their brown uniforms, though; just like those worn by the girls of St Whatever's in the English school stories I read.

Josie and I spent a wonderful summer making and equipping a hut in a large rectangular hole that had been dug in an empty section of land between our drive and the Caugheys' house. In all likelihood, the land belonged to the Caugheys; the hole itself was probably the proposed site of a tank of some sort. In this long, dry summer our hole had a firm floor and sides and was ideal for our purposes. Josie's mother provided an old bed cover for our roof and this, mounted on supporting props at the corners, let in light and air all around. I have never forgotten the bliss of this little hut nor the companionship we experienced in its making. We built a ladder-like staircase for access and improvised shelves and seats from planks discovered in our garage. We found an old piece of matting for the floor, and assembled a collection of cracked and discarded cups, plates and ornaments to sit on the shelves. We hung improvised pictures from pegs driven into the walls, and fashioned a little couch from boxes and old cushions. We both liked reading, and often immured ourselves in our hideout for hours at a time, away from the world and the demands of brothers and sisters. Josie's little brother Richard and my little sister Valerie did their best to infiltrate, but both our mothers — who never met — contrived to preserve us from invasion, and the long summer days seemed to go on and on. I had been involved in hut building before, in Stanley Bay, but those had always been boy-style huts — forts, really — which we would then be obliged to defend against marauding, if friendly, neighbourhood kids. That had been fun; but this was different.

I am reminded on looking back of Padraic Colum's poem:

> O to have a little house!
> To own the hearth, and stool and all!

I think that my home-making instincts were being prodded into life; like Mole, in *The Wind in the Willows*, I have always loved the sights and smells of home. Josie's very well-kept garden sported a professionally built playhouse, but after a short admiring inspection, I spurned it, as did she. Our *own* little house was quite different, and altogether superior. Josie's father came to visit us one day and was suitably impressed, we thought.

The summer ended sadly. A boy called Ken Stacey from our class at school used to play with Ross, and both of us liked him. At Christmas he had received a new bike, and we were filled with envy and admiration; it shone with newness, had a bell that rang, and a *light*! One morning Ken brought his younger sister and little brother to see us. I remember my mother saying what a likeable boy he was. And he was. Quiet, but not shy, with his smooth olive skin and friendly smile, Ken was every mother's idea of 'a nice boy'. That same afternoon, he was riding his new bike from Mount Albert to Avondale on an errand for his mother. We all wore wide-brimmed straw hats that summer, supposedly to protect us from the threat of polio, and Ken was wearing his. Keeping it on while riding his bike proved difficult, and he kept lowering his head. Ken never saw the stationary truck that he rode into. He was dead when they picked him up from the road.

This death, more than Billy's two years earlier in Stanley Bay, had a lasting effect on me. I can still see Ken now, proudly showing his very little brother to my admiring mother, only a few hours before his death. Many years later when our own twelve-year-old son swung out on his bike from behind a bus, tipped the back of it and was catapulted across the road, miraculously missing oncoming traffic, I suggested banning any further bike-riding on public roads in our family, and Roy agreed. Neither of us believed then, or think now, that children, with their in-built faith in their own immortality, are safe on frail, exposed machines in the mad whirl of modern traffic.

This same summer a boy called Albert made what I suppose would have been called 'an improper suggestion' to me, but I said, 'Don't be mad!' and pushed him backwards into a bush. Poor Albert. He had weak pale eyes and a stammer, and spent the year at boarding school. He lived in a large house nearby and was looked after in the holidays by a housekeeper. My mother (whom I did not tell about this incident) said that we should be sorry for him, as he was neglected. Small wonder that none of us ever equated wealth with privilege! Ross had a fight with Albert (whom we called Allie) once, and his absentee mother actually appeared and complained to ours. Neither boy was visibly battered, and Mum suggested 'leaving it to the children'. (She probably offered a nice cup of tea as well, but I doubt it was accepted.)

And this was the summer of the beehive. It does not seem likely that someone would give an eleven-year-old boy a beehive, but this happened to Ross (and of course, interesting things have always happened to Ross). Because I was not sure of the details, I faxed him at his home in the West Indies. (We keep in touch by fax and phone these days.) Ross's answer arrived promptly. Here is his account of his triumphant trip home with his trophy:

> . . . so I loaded the beehive on to my trolley, and surrounded by a cluster of its dislodged occupants, all buzzing in an unfriendly way, started off home. The course led right through the Mount Albert shopping centre (in those days called the terminus). I can still remember the pavement clearing magically before me as I passed through — people scuttling into shops or shooting to the other side of the street. All of which makes me think that the way to

clear an immediate path through any crowd (a path wide enough for a ten-ton truck) is to introduce a small boy with a trolley and a beehive . . . My arrival home received Mum's full, wide-eyed, undivided attention . . .

I laughed aloud at this, for it describes Mum's invariable response to our excesses, exactly. Ross went on: 'I put the hive way down the garden and would lie underneath it for hours, watching the bees at work. And I never got stung.'

What was I doing while Ross lay under his beehive? Luxuriating in the underground hut with Josie, I suspect. I certainly recall my brother's devotion to his bees — and everyone else's apprehension. The potential for disruption, if not disaster, was considerable, but Mum, typically, took no action. She may have regretted this in the end.

One day, without warning, there was seen to be a general exodus of bees from the hive. This had a furious quality about it that prompted even Ross to take hasty shelter behind a closed window in the house. We watched, fascinated, as the bees selected an article of someone's underwear on the clothesline and, in their thousands, settled on it. The resultant structure dangled like an immense, elongated football. Those bees that hadn't seized a place at first landing made frenzied, repeated attempts to infiltrate, and the whole seething bundle swayed frighteningly.

It was soon apparent that the neighbours were just as perturbed as we were. Fortunately, someone knew a man who kept bees — officially — and he, being summoned (some people in Mount Albert had *phones*), appeared with alacrity, donned enveloping, flimsy robes, which made him look like a medieval magician, and before our enchanted eyes took appropriate action. He also took the beehive when he left, at Mum's suggestion. Ross's distraught objections went for nothing, this time.

❧

The summer of the hut-in-the-hole, the bees, the sadness of Ken, and the puzzle of Allie (why was he so unlikeable, and why did he hate Ross so much — Ross who always grinned and forgave anyone?) slid past. Another shock was in store for us.

But Ross and I had had a wonderful year. If we had been less absorbed in our own affairs, less insulated by Mum's determination to keep us happy, we might have paid more attention to Dad's lessening influence in our lives. The fact was that we seldom saw him. He left for work so early and came home so late that he was in evidence only on a Sunday, when he seemed to be in bed for most of the day. Of course, he might have come home as soon as he finished work at noon on Saturdays, but by now the Symonds Street pubs had claimed him. Increasingly, Mum contrived to take the three of us out on Saturday evenings — usually to Auntie and Ockie's, but occasionally to the 'pictures', which Ross and I loved (Val would simply go to sleep) — in the hope, I imagine, that Dad would have returned while we were out, and gone to bed. This must have been for Mum a sad and sterile state to be reduced to from what was once a happy marriage. It is hard, in retrospect, however, to see that she could have done any better, given her resolution to keep the family intact. On one of these Saturday nights we came home to find charred steak in a smoking pan on a red-hot element, and Dad asleep fully clothed on the bed. Another half-hour, or less, and the house might have gone up in flames.

But our Standard Five (Form One) year at Gladstone Road School was superb. By this time, we knew everyone in the class and were sure of acceptance. Mr Watson, our teacher, had a reputation that everybody in Standard Four knew about in advance. In Mr Watson's class, you *worked*. From the first day, there was no doubt in anyone's mind. You were meant to achieve, and Mr Watson proposed to make sure that you did.

There were more than fifty children in the class. I did not realise until I resurrected the photo and counted them: fifty-three with twice as many boys as girls (I had not been conscious of that, either). There may even have been more. One or two children may have been absent on the day the photo was taken, though 'staying away' was a risk one took advisedly. Neither Ross nor I missed a day all year.

Disciplined attention was compulsory, and always observed. The magnetism of the man in front of us ensured this. I suppose there was an element of fear in our response, but I don't recall this — rather a heightened awareness of the need to exert oneself in the face of new demands. In Mr Watson's class, you *listened* and *looked*. Success in the essentials — spelling, computational arithmetic, handwriting and composition — was achieved through extra instruction at lunchtime and after school for those who needed it. Neither Ross nor I fell into this category (thanks no doubt to two-and-a-half years of Miss Carnachan at

Stanley Bay) but no one was spared if Mr Watson felt they were giving less than their best, and we both fell foul of this judgement at one time or another.

I first became conscious during this year that I could write rather more easily and clearly than most. Mr Watson told me this, and encouraged me, and I enjoyed the attention. I had never thought of this before; surely, everyone could write? But I was pleased at the marks I received for my weekly 'composition' — they compensated in part for the trouble I was having with 'problems' in arithmetic. I had always been good at mechanical arithmetic but, until I encountered Mr Watson, I was shaky on problems. No longer! In Standard Five at Gladstone Road School we were taught to approach any task methodically. Each 'sum' must be headed 'Answer Required', underlined. (Heaven help any child who proffered, as answer, the number of hours it took to dig a trench of specified width, length and depth when what was required was the number of necessary men!) We were ranked by weekly tests in the main subjects — *always* ten problems in arithmetic — and Ross and I were consistently in the top ten. I don't recall any glorification of the people at the top, or derision directed at those at the bottom. A boy called John Burns was always top, and a year later won a Rawleigh's Scholarship to secondary school, as one of the top boys in Auckland. (Girls were not eligible!)

I became conscious, for the first time, in this class, of the agility of some other children's minds. I am quite sure, in retrospect, that Warnock Watson's vigour and personal style — virtuosity, really — kindled intellectual activity in an extraordinary way. It seemed natural to follow the patterns he set. Ross and I had never been required to do homework before — except, of course, learning spelling and times tables — but we now worked every night, usually finishing work started at school, or repeating problems we had done wrongly. Everything was always corrected, everything wrong put right. One can only wonder at the hours such a teacher devoted to his job.

One aspect of life this year was a great joy to both of us. Mr Watson loved music, and taught his class to sing in harmony. (He was a young man, at this time. I learned later that he had achieved prominence as organiser and conductor of primary school festival choirs in Auckland, when these were instituted.) He also believed in choral speaking, and taught us to breathe properly and use our voices to best effect. We all stood, for this exercise, and he conducted us like a choir. No one was allowed to coast; Mr Watson claimed that anyone *could* use their voice and lungs if they only *would*. As he made it plain that we *must*, the evidence was likely to support this view.

I have made Warnock Watson sound like a tyrant, but he was far from that. He would tell us amusing stories, often involving his own baby daughter; and he encouraged us to read by reading parts of books aloud to us. He had little need to punish, for no one disobeyed him. I was once ejected from the classroom for arguing (cheekily, I have no doubt. Questions were encouraged but contradicting the teacher was another matter). After an interval, Ross was sent out to suggest that I come in and apologise, but I refused. It was late in the day, and at three o'clock everyone else went home, leaving me still in the school porch. Ultimately, Mr Watson came out and told me that I could go, too. But he smiled at me. I liked him, and I knew he liked me.

'I thought you were for it!' said Ross later. (He had been skulking around to see what would happen.) Neither of us knew what 'it' was, but we were both a bit scared. It was not usual for anyone to 'stand up to' Mr Watson.

TWELVE

he blow fell suddenly. My father's dereliction of duty in his new job resulted in dismissal: 'the sack', it was called. His alcoholism was now well advanced. There had been a frightening spell of what Mum told us was 'the DTs', during which he shouted hysterically and groaned in his sleep. I realise now that he needed treatment, desperately. He was thin and haggard, and although always loving towards us, had little of his earlier sparkle. The state of his mind does not bear contemplation. He had failed utterly when the future had seemed bright. He must have believed that he had betrayed his family, and could probably see no hope of regeneration.

We children were not given details of Dad's disgrace; we were simply told that he was not now working for the AMC, and that, once again, we were going to move. I think that Mum wanted to get away from our new neighbours in Mount Albert anyway, before the situation deteriorated further, as surely it must. There was little likelihood that Dad would get another job; in 1936, times were still hard, and in his present state he was scarcely capable of working anyway. One could hardly imagine him chipping weeds on the roadside, with other unemployed men. Far from buying our lovely house on the mountain, we could not now afford to pay the rent.

I can only speculate as to why Ross and I were not devastated by these events. I suspect that we both have always had, in common, an intense interest in whatever we are doing or thinking ourselves, and that as children this inoculated us against too much consideration of our actual situation. And of course, all children rely on their parents for security, and our parents were devoted to us. There was never the slightest chance that we would not all be together, wherever we went. But we didn't want to leave Mount Albert.

Looking back, I think that Val suffered more than any of us. From birth she had been less robust and confident; and she had been too young to experience Stanley Bay in the way Ross and I had. By the time Val entered the six-to-ten stage, which we had lived so fully at school and on beach, mudflat and street in Devonport, the family had embarked on the uncertain ocean of 'town'.

Just before school started in 1937, we moved to a little, very old cottage in Johnstone Street, Point Chevalier. Grandma Brown came to live with us, I suspect to help financially. Although she had only her modest widow's pension, her board would certainly have helped. The need to give Grandma a bedroom meant that the small, narrow kitchen, mercifully complete with coal range, became the sole living room for the family of three adults and three children. Val and I slept in a tiny room off the kitchen, and Ross in a 'room' that had been made at some time by partitioning the back verandah. The cottage was shabby, both outside and in, but was on a large piece of unkempt ground with a neglected apple orchard behind the house. A huge, sagging old shed — big enough to build a boat in, Ross said — completed the picture, and we children usurped it immediately. This shed must have been a blessing to my mother. The three of us, and the friends we soon made, spent almost all our waking non-school hours in it during the winter. I suppose it was cold — the wind blew through cracks and the big double doors never met, and had to be dragged shut — but the last tenants had left a dazzling quantity of rough timber and miscellaneous junk. We built structures of every imaginable sort, and a rickety stage, on which we held concerts.

Val at last started school, and our cousin Pat joined her from the convent school. Point Chevalier School was only a few streets away, and we were all enrolled. The news was broken to me that, as my parents knew they would have little spare money available at the end of the coming year to outfit both Ross and me for secondary school, I as the youngest, was to have another year in Standard Five. In this case, too, I don't know why I was unconcerned. I have thought about it since, and wondered if perhaps I *did* mind, but concealed or repressed the feeling. But I don't think so. I seem to have accepted the fact that this was how it had to be, and simply got on with life. Making the most of the here-and-now seems to have been an inbuilt characteristic. (I feel faintly puzzled about this. Surely any normal, supposedly intelligent child would have seen this as an act of unfairness? It simply didn't occur to me.)

The school year had already begun when I came round the corner of the house one evening (full-tilt; we were embarked upon a wild game) to find Mum at the front door, talking to Mr Watson! I was agape, and so was Ross when he arrived, almost bowling me over. Teachers simply did not visit homes — and Mr Watson was not our teacher anyway, now. He had come on his bike, and was suggesting to Mum that Ross and I might be re-enrolled at Gladstone School if *we* had bikes, which he was sure he — or the school, I'm not sure which — could provide. The distance was, after all, only about two miles . . . Mum, who did not invite him in, was polite, but also firm. All three of us and our cousin were at Point Chevalier School now, and there we would stay. She did not tell Mr Watson that I was repeating my Standard Five year, and Ross and I did not let her down when he spoke briefly to us. We were bereft of speech anyway; social contact with teachers defied imagination and paralysed the larynx. Mr Watson rode away sadly, giving us his sweet smile as he mounted his bike, and wishing us well. (He had told Mum that we were both very able children, and that he had taken his class on to Standard Six, and had had high hopes for her son and daughter.)

Poor Mum. Our shabby little house with its neglected, overgrown front garden was a far cry from Mount Albert. She would not have felt able to invite Mr Watson in, and this would have offended her own hospitable nature. Ross and I simply did not mention the incident again, either to one another or anyone else. I don't know whether or not Mum told Dad; he was by now out every day looking, hopelessly it seemed, for work. She probably spared him.

The Standard Five I arrived into was a delightful place, but so different from Mr Watson's class that it seemed like another world. It was a composite of 'leftover' Standard Three, Four, and Five children. In each case, there was another, full class at that level. How the children were chosen I have no idea; but the Standard Five section of which I was part included Jack Sinclair (who later became Professor of Physiology at Auckland University) and several other children who, like Jack, were very young, and very bright. We were an odd assortment: there were even several very slow children who needed extra care, which Miss Foster gave them, lovingly. Perhaps we were all chosen for our 'special' nature, however diverse. It is likely that I was included as a second-time-rounder whose progress card, which followed you everywhere in those days, revealed that I should have been in Standard Six. (A sort of 'specialness', I suppose.) In better days, the school might have protested; but these were Depression days, and the reason given by my family for holding me back was likely to be accepted.

Those of us in the upper section of the class were expected to work independently a great deal of the time. Miss Foster had very liberal ideas, I have realised since. Of course, it is likely that the poor, overworked woman, who was kindly by nature, simply felt that her senior pupils, being all reasonably bright, would come to no harm 'doing their own thing' for a year. Stern things were certainly ahead: from Ross's class next door, not a sound could be heard except the teacher's voice. Very bossy it sounded, too, I thought.

I spent most of the year writing, and ultimately producing, a play which I recall as a weird amalgam of *Treasure Island*, *The Scarlet Pimpernel*, *Peter Pan*, and *Tarzan of the Apes*. We would often be banished to the play-ground for rehearsals. I recall a grassed area with a hedge from which we leapt, brandishing wands or cutlasses as appropriate, everyone embroidering the original script enthusiastically. When it rained, we retreated to the shelter shed, which smelt of fish-paste sandwiches but had a seat all around from which we could leap. We performed the play only for Miss Foster and the rest of the class, in the end — and then in a highly disorganised way — but we all thought it a great success. In fact, nothing has remained in my mind about that school year, except that particular enterprise. Ross was filled with envy. Stuck in a desk inside, with a teacher who had Mr Watson's standards but not his flair, life for him was dull.

But out of school, we had beach, cliffs and mudflats again. For a few months, before winter set in, there was swimming every day, new friends to be made and games in the park behind the beach — the reserve, it was called. I remember hockey, played with sticks improvised from branches of the pohutukawa trees that ringed the park. My cricket experiences helped here; I was often the only girl playing but could hold my own easily.

Opposite us in Johnstone Street, and slightly further down, lived the Sinclairs. Keith Sinclair was a year older than Ross, and already at Mount Albert Grammar School. I recall seeing him coming home some afternoons, a slight, lordly figure with a huge bag of books, but have no clear memory of him otherwise. (Many years later, after he had become Professor of History at Auckland University and I was involved in writing and editing, I included his first children's story in my anthology *The Magpies Said*.) I knew his sisters, Jean, Shirley, Marge and Gwen, and his brother Jack — Shirley and Jack were both in my class at school — and soon got to know the rest of the family. The Sinclairs fascinated me. There were eight children — ultimately ten — and I loved being part of the cheerful confusion that seemed to reign in their backyard. (Rather like the Camerons, all those years ago, or the Pritchards in Stanley Bay, a huge extended and ever-expanding family who had Percy, Ivy, Jack, young George, Uncle George, Bob, a grown-up sister called Flo who had a little boy called Billy and was married to an absent sailor — and a huge hearty mother who cooked all day, and a thin, wispy father called 'Pop' who chopped wood incessantly. They were from the 'East End' of London — magical location! — and had voices that vied with the sound of Pop's saw and could be heard all over the neighbourhood. I loved them all.)

'Why don't we have more children?' I asked Mum, but I didn't get a straight answer. The mere thought must surely have appalled her at this point in our lives. I later re-met all the Sinclair girls except the youngest at Grammar, and had a nostalgic chat with Jack years later in my bookshop. With the rest of Auckland I can claim acquaintance at one remove with Geoff, longstanding talk-back host at Radio Pacific, an ex-teacher with a fine line in common sense and kindly humour. My mother and Mrs Sinclair used to chat together when they met in the street. In those days, housewives made interminable trips to and from shops, often carrying heavy bags for miles. It seems strange that no one had invented the shopping trundler, at a time when so many people would have benefited from owning one. It was a common sight to see babies in prams and pushchairs almost buried in bags of potatoes, loaves of bread and the familiar brown paper parcels that contained meat. It is likely, of course, that few working-class housewives could have afforded a trundler had they been available.

Reading Keith Sinclair's autobiography *Halfway Round the Harbour* gave me the feeling that Mum and Mrs Sinclair were much the same sort of woman: quiet, but strong, though I suspect that Mum had a free-and-easy approach to life that was not shared by many of her female peers, including Mrs Sinclair. (Auntie had it too.) But my mother and the Sinclairs' mother may have had more in common than either had time to find out.

Ross and I felt at home at 'the Point'. We had earlier trudged the length of the main road for innumerable trips to the beach and reserve with Auntie and Ockie from their shop at 'the Hall'. When we lived in Mount Albert, the Point was our nearest beach for picnics; moving to Johnstone Street, only a stone's throw from a spot we already loved, had its attractions.

In his autobiography Keith Sinclair wrote a wonderful account of childhood, in a chapter called 'At the Point'. 'The Point was magic,' he said, '. . . it could have been hundreds of miles from a town. We lived, not close to nature, but part of it . . . We were people of the land. We owned it. Our life was timeless.' And further on: 'Our community was the street, which had a life of its own.' For a while the three Norgrove children were part of this same street, though, as newcomers, we could never truly belong. But we felt welcome, and in the way of children, explored our new world and found it good.

Meanwhile, we were having more contact with Dad, who was simply not able to drink, as there was hardly enough money for us even to eat. He was loving, and funny, and life for us improved. Dad searched for work constantly. Mum was desperately disappointed when he just missed out on a job running a country store somewhere near Putaruru, with living accommodation. I think she believed that Dad's only hope was to become part of a small community again.

Our apple trees were squat and gnarled, but their branches sagged with large green apples: thousands of them. They were very hard, and not very sweet, but we children munched our way through them anyway. Stewed with sugar, they were transformed into a glorious, smooth fluff. Mum peeled an enormous pile every night, pressing us all into service, and cooking them in our old preserving pan on the coal range. (She was always an unconventional housewife, and liked working at night.) We ate bowls of stewed apple at every meal, and whenever we were hungry in between. I remember getting up early on a hot summer morning and helping myself to plate after plate of the luscious, cold stuff. From February until about May, when we moved to a slightly better (according to adult taste) house a few streets away, we were kept alive and well on apples, and Grandma's famous girdle scones. Mum made plum jam, swapping apples for plums in the way of all New Zealand housewives in those days, and we were never hungry. And Auntie and Ockie, as usual, helped.

Leaving Johnstone Street was a tragedy, Ross and I felt, but Dad had managed, through a friend in the butchery trade, to get a temporary job, and we had a regular, if modest, income again. Even better, if Dad managed to stay sober he would have a reference with which to apply for another job when this one ended. No one doubted his capacity to impress an employer given the chance.

THIRTEEN

his was Coronation year, and we were bombarded with details of the coming pageantry. Daily eulogies of the future George VI, his queen, and their two daughters, Elizabeth and Margaret Rose, poured from newspaper and radio. In strict contrast to their modern counterparts, the media were totally, and fulsomely sycophantic: the royal parents were nobly virtuous, the children angelic. The radio announcers we heard daily adopted voices of simpering servility to tell us that 'the two little princesses play happily in the gardens of Buckingham Palace, unaware that the world is waiting with bated breath, for the day when their father . . .' Baloney, said Ross to all of this, but I was captivated, an ensnarement of which I am now somewhat ashamed. We had stopped taking the *Auckland Star* as one of our economies, but Ockie faithfully bought a *Star* for me every day while the excitement lasted. When photographs of the magnificent event finally appeared, in thick supplements in both daily papers, he got up especially early to secure a *Herald* for me, later in the day queuing at a local shop for a *Star*. I was waiting at the gate, that morning. I remember seeing Ockie's tall figure coming sedately down Johnstone Street, brandishing my *Herald* in a dignified wave — a truly Dickensian character, with his bald head, portly build and serene smile. Eighteen years older than Auntie, he had now

retired, and they rented a house nearby. Their income was small. Ockie had
been married before, and divorced (unusual, for those days) and although
he had no children from his first marriage, alimony payments made harsh
inroads on his income.

I have realised only in later years how much Auntie and Ockie's
support — and good cheer, in the face of all eventualities — must have
comforted my mother. And my father, too, for they never judged him. He
was, after all, Bill, and that was how he 'was'. When Ockie appeared with
a thick scrapbook for me to preserve all my precious pictures and articles
in I was dizzy with joy. I kept that book for years. What happened to it in
the end I have no idea. Nor have I any idea what sparked my obsession. I
knew the name of every single member of the extended royal family, their
spouses and children, and longed for more information about what was
going on in London. This may have related to a serious shortage of books
in my life at that time. I don't recall ever being bored, but I think I was
compelled to fill my life with whatever came to hand — and the
Coronation came to hand. (The Abdication the year before — 1936 — had
hardly interested me at all, although I was wide-eyed at Grandma's
reference to 'that woman'. The sight of Grandma's kindly face, so often
creased into lines of quiet laughter, now set with rigid mouth and steely
eyes, was curious indeed.)

I discovered that some people belonged to the Point Chevalier library,
within walking distance, at 'the Hall'. I discovered also that you could join
the library only if your father was a ratepayer. Mine wasn't. I have learnt
since that some kindly ratepayers in those days would sign forms for
ineligible people, even children, and take responsibility for their returning
books, but no such kindly ratepayer swam into my ken — and anyway,
before the year ended, we had moved to Grafton. (Here, also, there was a
library — a great, grey, austere edifice, which I nonetheless would have
stormed had a kindly ratepayer surfaced.) My only recourse was to keep
reading the books I *did* have.

Several years before, my repeated assaults on *David Copperfield* had
brought me, finally, to the end — at which point I simply began again. If I
had been asked, I'd have said that I liked reading because I liked stories,
but I now realise it was more than that. I would re-read paragraphs that I
particularly enjoyed in *David Copperfield*, over and over again at speaking
speed, relishing the words. I had favourite passages, and would turn these

up constantly: Betsey Trotwood and the donkeys and her rescue of David from the clutches of the fearsome Mr Murdstone; the antics of the amiably mad Mr Dick; the deaths of both homely, faithful Ham and sophisticated, faithless Steerforth in the same terrible tempest, and the pompous posturing of Mr Micawber. My mother had read this same old copy, bound in leather by her father, when she was a girl, and had included incidents ('Barkis is willin'' and Uriah Heep and his 'umbleness) in the stories she told us. David Copperfield and his vast community seemed like part of our family. I think I lived, for some years, more intensely between the covers of this, and other books, than in the real world: in escape, some would say, from the less attractive aspects of my own life. Perhaps so. I did not speculate then, and now I regard escape from the 'real' world as a major function of literature. Who, in any age, and of any age, can find in their everyday lives the fascination, mystery, humour and sheer, dazing interest that is there, between the covers of books? And this capacity of the book, which is really a power to stimulate the spirit, does not cut off as one returns to real life. A proportion of it sticks, each time, so that one finds oneself smiling fondly or foolishly, reflecting sadly, or screwing one's courage to the sticking post in the face of adversity. You may have escaped for a time, but the break was beneficial; you return strengthened, better able to cope, more aware of the complexities of other people's natures and reactions.

A girl at school lent me a copy of *Tarzan of the Apes* — the book a far cry from the Hollywood 'Me-Tarzan-you-Jane' version. The same girl brought me a copy of Baroness Orczy's *The Scarlet Pimpernel* ('Is he in heaven, or is he in hell, that *demmed* elusive Pimpernel?') and I was immediately transported to Paris of the Revolution, firmly on the side of the aristocrats. (I was won over to the peasantry some years later.)

Things were about to change again. I recall very little about our life in the house in Wainui Avenue, to which we moved from Johnstone Street, though I got to know it quite well in later years, as Auntie, Ockie and Pat shifted into it on our departure. We were able to leave Bennie and Bessie with them; a source of grief, but much better than losing them entirely. I remember very well, though, coming home from school one day before we left the Point, to find Mum and Grandma both red-eyed and distressed.

Auntie Lillian, wife of my mother's oldest brother Ray, had dropped dead
of a heart attack. Our three cousins, Irma, Shirley and Maurine, were
consequently motherless. Grandma had already made her intention clear:
she would move in at once with her son, and care for his children. Ross
and I were guiltily ambivalent about this. We were wide-eyed and solemn
about Auntie Lil's death. (What if *our* mother were to die? It was not
possible, of course, but . . .) On the other hand — *our* grandmother, happily
settled with us, was deserting us for our cousins!

Uncle Ray was besought by Auntie Lil's three married sisters to let
them have a girl apiece to care for, but he declined politely. His motherless
daughters (thirteen, eleven and nine at the time) must be kept together.
He and Grandma would cope: and they did. Grandma was seventy-seven,
but she did not die until she was ninety-three, by which time the three girls
were launched successfully into the world.

Emily Stewart Brown was not one to shirk duty, but she had an eye
for fun, too. None of her children inherited her passion for playing cards,
and 'going to the races', but none ever disapproved, either. She was a
character; almost eccentric in some ways, but in the course of a long life,
which knew tragedy as well as contentment, she never lost her resolute
ways, or her sense of humour.

In our last Point Chevalier house, Ockie paid me sixpence a week to
water his garden every night. They lived in a tiny house in Meola Road,
which adjoined an empty section behind our house, and we all enjoyed this
arrangement. Watering Ockie's large garden involved filling buckets at the
house, carting them some distance, and dribbling water plant by plant,
through the holes drilled in the bottom of a jam tin. Ross, as the eldest,
had been offered this job, but had turned it down after a short trial, in my
favour. It was too slow for him. I was delighted. The money was dazzling
wealth, the job itself a total satisfaction. This was my first real contact with
things that grew if tended and encouraged, and answered an unspoken
need in my soul, it seemed. *And* no one could require anything else of you
while you did it. You were free to think, and dream . . . another of my soul's
requirements, apparently.

And, at last, we had baby chicks! Despairing of Bennie and Bessie as
a fertile couple, Mum cleverly obtained four inseminated eggs from a
neighbour. Bessie adopted them with fervour, and Bennie (who we came
to believe was not very intelligent) guarded his broody wife, and family of

huge eggs, with paternal pride. All four hatched successfully, producing utterly enchanting, tiny Black Orpington chicks. Both surrogate parents were ecstatic — though Bessie's attempts to keep her brood snug under her wings became less and less successful; they were soon as big as their mother. Neither they nor Bessie — and certainly not Bennie, who was doing the proud Victorian papa thing, strutting about issuing orders — appeared to notice the disparity in size. Once the 'chicks', now huge, were totally independent, they were returned, despite Ross's, Val's and my protests, to their true home, where they 'settled in' immediately, we were told.

From the Wainui Avenue house, Dad and I several times walked across the mudflats, where now the Meola Road extension spans the distance between Point Chevalier and Westmere, to visit his parents in Cumberland Avenue. (I was always the one who answered Dad's requests for company immediately.) We went in bare feet, carrying our shoes and socks in one hand, and taking turns with the basket of scones or fruit without which no visit was ever made. I still have this basket. Over the years I have despatched innumerable children and grandchildren with just such offerings, in its well-designed depths. Mum had painted it red some years earlier, and it is still proudly, if a bit shabbily, red. It had belonged to Grandma Brown, originally, my mother told me: my grandchildren's great-great-grandmother. Dad and I would choose a grassy spot on the Westmere side of the mudflats to sit down and pull on socks and shoes over our wet, muddy feet, before facing civilisation. How much closer could one be to one's father than this?

The job that Dad managed to get must have struck dread to Mum's heart. It was in Symonds Street, scene of her husband's fall from grace less than two years before and almost opposite the AMC shop, of uncomfortable memory. Dad was to open and manage a delicatessen for a private Auckland company, and we were to live in the rooms above. We children were simply told that we were to move, and that we would return by tram each day to Point Chevalier School until the end of the year. Ross would then go to the Seddon Memorial Technical College ('Tech') and Val and I to Grafton Primary School. I would follow Ross to Tech, in due course. If we had opinions at all, they were spiced with excitement at the idea of living *over a shop, in the city*.

We moved. Our new quarters were old, dilapidated and dirty. The lavatory we used was downstairs, at the back of the shop, and was shared with the shop staff. (Old, outside dunnies screened by vine-festooned trellises at the bottom of gardens must after all have seemed attractive to poor Mum, but we kids didn't mind — though her insistence on accompanying us into the Stygian depths at night was mortifying.) These dank regions were cleaned nightly by a charwoman — the term was still in use in 1938 — a bent, scurrying little woman who made a mighty clanging and banging as she went about her unenviable chores. The first time I ever presented the cup of tea that my mother insisted the 'poor old thing' must have, she took it in her reddened hands, muttering what could only be 'Thank 'ee my dear.' I was startled; she looked like Mrs Gamp, straight from *Martin Chuzzlewit*, though I recognised her again, years later, in Mrs Tiggy-winkle, and I wondered with anguish where she came from. What unfeeling mob let their old granny out in any weather, in pitifully inadequate clothes, at *night*, to slosh soap and water around in the cold 'backs' of ancient shops? My mother used to try to chat to her. (We never elicited a name.) Once, receiving Mum's sympathy for the hard work she had to do, she replied, 'Well, if y' 'ave t', y' 'ave t',' which remark has stayed with us down the generations.

Val's and my bedroom window opened, as did the antediluvian bathroom, on to an interior well, which admitted little light and barely any air. Mum and Dad's room, tiny like ours, had only an opening roof light, which leaked. Ross slept in the bigger, front room, which looked out over the shop verandah on to Symonds Street itself. This was intended to be a living room in which a boy slept. Ross was doubtful at first, but quickly got used to the idea. The room was jam-packed with furniture: a 'chesterfield' suite (old and dusty, but comfortable), the piano, and assorted paraphernalia for which no other storage place was available. We often played wild games there, leaping from one piece of furniture to another, a diversion usually instigated by our little sister. Val used to plead with us to play with her. Symonds Street was not a fertile field for small playmates. I spent long hours in this cheerfully cluttered room, curled up in one of the sagging chairs, reading, while trams and other traffic clattered by a few yards from my head.

We shared our back door with the shop. It opened on to a narrow alley, which ran parallel to Symonds Street, and opened at one end on to Newton Road. Dotted with malodorous rubbish tins, it was best navigated quickly. The shops are still there, as is the alley. I note with some amusement as I drive past that it is now dignified as 'Stable Lane'. (No name in our day, and no stables either, though these may have existed at an earlier date.) We made do with honest squalor sixty years ago; quaint antiquity is the keynote now.

One night we all awoke to the sound of heavy feet on the stairs and a voice calling 'Police!' Val and I lay petrified in our beds. But it seemed we were not all to be bundled into the Black Maria and whisked off to prison after all; the two genial policemen were merely checking that all was well. Patrolling our back alley, they had found our door open. Dad, hastily pulling on trousers over his pyjamas, was obliged to accompany them downstairs to check the shop for possible burglary. We children, by this time thrilled by such unexpected midnight entertainment, were wide awake and anxious to be part of the action. Ross managed to infiltrate the search party downstairs, but Mum was firm, for once, about the unsuitable nature of this venture for me. She did, however, make cocoa to calm us all — and the inevitable cup of tea for the friendly cops. Dad's mortification when he was obliged to admit that he couldn't recall securing the door was touching, but the flavour of the incident, from his children's point of view, was one of sublime satisfaction. We couldn't wait to dine out on the delicious details next day at school.

Once again, Ross and I looked around us, identified, with eyes that were by now well seasoned, the opportunities of our new environment, and set about exploring them. While Dad quickly turned the shop below into a showpiece, Mum vied with dirt and antiquated facilities above; and Val, only seven years old and newly wrenched from our cousin Pat's daily company, simply clung closer to Mum and looked out at the world with wondering, if not apprehensive, eyes.

FOURTEEN

Another home, another school, another place to explore. But first, we children must finish out the school year at Point Chevalier. This involved a walk through narrow city streets to Karangahape Road, from which a tram to the Point left. No one had heard of 'K Road', as it is now so sloppily — or cleverly — called. (Was this change a marketing ploy?) There was an old joke that documented the arrest of a disorderly drunk in Pitt Street. It was revealed in court that the undesirable behaviour had actually occurred in Karangahape Road, but that, as the constable had trouble with his spelling, he had hauled the inebriated offender round the corner into Pitt Street before taking out notebook and pencil. One suspects that the change to 'K Road' may relate to just such difficulties.

Ross and I could certainly spell 'Karangahape', although, with the rest of Auckland's Pakeha population at that uninformed and insensitive time, we pronounced it 'Kranga-happy'. We used to challenge one another to spell hard words, a game introduced by Mum when we were quite small. And Grandma Brown taught us to spell 'Ightham' — pronounced 'item' — the name of her family's village in Kent, before we went to school. Grandma, looking wicked, instructed each of us in turn to ask our teachers to spell 'Ightham', and correct them when they responded with 'item'. And we both did, triumphantly.

We quite enjoyed the journey to school by tram. At least it was summer, with the close of the school year in sight; and, at 'the Point' end of the trip the tram dropped us a few short yards from the school. Here, all was levity in Miss Foster's class as the year drew to a close. We spent the day making Christmas decorations, cards, calendars and unidentifiable presents for unlucky relatives, and singing lusty renditions of 'Good King Wenceslas' and 'God Rest Ye, Merry Gentlemen', to Miss Foster's thunderous piano accompaniment. 'You make a terrible din, next door,' said Ross with ill-concealed envy. He had just finished a year of solid academic grind. 'He's harder even than Mr Watson, and much crabbier,' he reported of his teacher. I recall a sensation of guilt, as well as sympathy, that while I led a blissful life in one room, Ross was kept head-down and joyless in the next.

This enforced effort had, however, raised Ross to spectacular heights. His Standard Six report, discovered, surprisingly, among my mother's effects on her death in 1982, revealed that he had been Dux of Point Chevalier School in 1937. Characteristically, no one in our family gave any attention to this distinction. If I knew at all, I had long forgotten by the time I found the report, and Ross had certainly never mentioned it in all the time between.

I have thought, in later years, that this family habit of treating us as infinitely valuable members of the human race, while never requiring us to provide any evidence to justify the assessment — or even taking particular note if we did — rubbed off on us, and explained in good part our total acceptance of our father's less-than-worthy performance. It simply wasn't part of family policy to judge or compare. And of course, Dad's endless generosity, good humour and charm, and his habit of treating his children as friends, rather than vassals, made it easy for us to overlook his short-comings as family breadwinner. Mum must have found this infinitely harder, but the evidence never wavered that she was prepared to go on supporting him, whatever the cost. Nor could one doubt his devotion to her. Our family life may have had its irregular features, but it never included dissension or ugly scenes. Dad was a cheerful and biddable drunk; getting him to bed as fast as possible was Mum's policy, always. His compliance was everyone's good fortune.

If I received a report at all that year, no one thought to keep it. It is quite likely that dear Miss Foster did not believe in ranking children academically or indeed inspecting them critically in any way. I know that I wrote good stories, because Miss Foster often read them aloud to the class. I suspect that I spent hours scribbling away happily — hours that were probably designated on some remote 'scheme' for earnest acquisition of facts mathematical and scientific (which I did not find attractive). Where did she come from, and go to, delightful, woolly Miss Foster? There are people like her in every generation of teachers, I suspect, but they are seldom admired by their colleagues or rewarded by bureaucracy. Children remember them though. They seem to think that you are all right the way you are, which means, invariably, that you flourish, and even improve in their care.

❧

We fronted up, Val and I, to Grafton School and whatever it had to offer, in February 1938. Ross was despatched on foot to Seddon 'Tech', on the site of today's Institute of Technology in Wellesley Street. His curly hair was crammed into a cap, which was striped like a beehive in green and yellow, and his socks, with similar green and yellow tops were, like his shorts and shirt, made of warmest wool. Almost one hundred years after 'the first ships to Auckland', no one had acknowledged the fact that the climate bore little resemblance to that of England. I suspect that it went further than that: no one *wanted* to admit that the Old Country could not be replicated exactly in the farthest reaches of the southern ocean.

Equally close to our new home, down Khyber Pass (without the appendage of 'Road' in those days) and up leafy Mountain Road was the Auckland Grammar School. Sixty years ago, this now famous school had already gained a reputation for scholarship, and stood in attractive grounds, with extensive playing fields. Both Grammar and Tech were state schools. Why my parents chose 'Tech' for Ross, when he was clearly capable of academic achievement, I have no idea. One might have thought that his Standard Six teacher or the headmaster of Point Chevalier School might have made a recommendation for the future education of their top student, but this did not happen. Ross was to do 'Accounting', whatever that entailed. His notable grin and air of cheerful confidence were shaky on the morning he first set off on foot, shoes polished and new schoolbag on back, but that was to be expected. The Seddon Memorial Technical College looked like a vast, grey jail. It rose unrelentingly from its street frontage and had no gardens or playing fields at all. For a boy who loved sea and air and sky, entering its grim portals must have seemed like beginning a prison sentence.

❧

A. E. Manning taught Standard Six at Grafton School. Later, he achieved modest fame as author of a book called *The Bodgie*, which described, and sought to explain, the emergence of New Zealand's first teenage cult. He was an interesting man, short and stocky, with sharp eyes that gleamed behind thick glasses, but shot fire if he was provoked. I liked him, as he clearly liked me, and encouraged me to write — but I squirmed, sometimes, at his derisive treatment of less able children, particularly boys. But he was innovative, too. Once, he asked us for ideas as to how we could make the school day more interesting. I suggested setting up an imitation radio station in the corner of the room to provide news and items every morning. Everyone agreed, and we constructed a 'studio' using an easel and blackboard augmented with junk of a diverse and interesting nature which we found in the bowels of the ancient school. I seem to have appointed myself architect, programmer and announcer of this project — and proved a powerful force in extracting items from reluctant performers. If the worst came to the worst I would simply recite myself. I acquired a vast repertoire of poems by heart, this year. There was always Tennyson:

> Break, break, break,
> On thy cold gray stones, O Sea!
> And I would that my tongue could utter,
> The thoughts that arise in me . . .

and Thomas Hood:

> I remember, I remember,
> The house where I was born
> The little window where the sun,
> Came peeping in at morn . . .

The melodramatic and the nostalgic was my style. Standard Six at Grafton School approved, and I indulged myself mightily.

Later in the year I founded a handwritten (by me) broadsheet which

I called, grandly, 'The Grafton Clarion'. The notion was that people would contribute to this weekly paper and that I, as editor, would choose, collate and 'publish' it. Extracting *written* copy proved much harder than persuading or bullying people into offering vocal contributions from the anonymous depths of the radio station, I found; and my natural arrogance led to shameful and arbitrary editing of any offerings that offended me or were, in my opinion, poorly written. But no one seemed to mind. I was conceited enough to believe that any change I rang in other people's texts was certainly for the better, and everyone was always delighted by the paper, which was handed from desk to desk on Monday mornings. Only one copy, of course — the days of easy duplication were still far ahead. I used to spend long hours in the weekend printing the paper out by hand, writing fill-in bits, jokes, a weekly serial, which I produced myself, and garnishing the whole with illustrations. I have always had a minimal but useful talent at drawing cartoon-style figures, and this stood me in good stead in 'Clarion' days.

Late in the year, by which time I had produced a Christmas edition — lavishly festooned with holly, candles, robin redbreasts and tiny snow-girt churches in the best English tradition — an inspector visited the school. All copies of the 'Clarion' to date were kept on Mr Manning's desk. They were proudly exhibited to the inspector, and subsequently borne off by him, to be shown, he said, to colleagues. Naturally, he would return them. Predictably, he didn't. I don't remember giving this omission much thought. It had been the process, not the product, that had engaged my passionate attention. But I have wished since that at least one edition of 'The Grafton Clarion', 1938 model, had survived for its owner, editor, chief reporter, writer and illustrator to chuckle over later.

In characteristic style, my mother sighed over my weekend dedication to its production. Often she and Val would decamp to 'the pictures' on Saturday afternoon, leaving me poring over my task, 'putting my paper to bed'. I never minded. This was the start of a period spent pursuing my own (usually solitary) interests in the face of family perplexity, which fortunately remained just that. 'You know Dorothy . . .' my mother would say tolerantly, if faintly regretfully. Disapproval never invaded the scene.

With a steady income we were able to subscribe once more to the *Auckland Star*. There was a complete section, at the weekend, devoted to children's cartoons (the Katzenjammer Kids were everyone's favourites), and a page run by an imaginary 'aunt' or 'uncle' which printed children's stories and poems, awarding points which ultimately translated into real money. For a few months I contributed to this, with considerable success; I even won a competition for which I received the heady sum of *one pound*! I handed my earnings over to Mum; we were saving up for a trip to Rotorua, where we had distant relatives who had invited us to stay. This trip did not actually take place for several years, but Mum kept my money, faithfully.

I wonder, now, why I was not more enthusiastic about seeing my work in print. I soon tired of making submissions to the *Star*. It seems likely that this was a manifestation of a trait that has characterised my life: a preference for individual rather than group activity. 'The Grafton Clarion' — my paper — seemed infinitely more important than the *Auckland Star*. And I seemed not to derive as much pleasure from seeing my work in print, as other writers have reported. I wanted to 'run my own show', and I did. The satisfaction of printing it all out, arranging articles, filling in corners with jokes, puzzles or illustrations and finally knowing that I had produced something, was enough.

Ever since my days in Mr Watson's class at Gladstone School, I had been writing poetry. My models were all English, and the resultant poems were mannered, sentimental, often pretentious, usually adopting a high moral tone and, in retrospect, mortifying to recall. But they showed, I suspect, that I could handle language, manoeuvring it into a rhythm-and-rhyme form which revealed a degree of skill, if an under-use of imagination. Teachers in those days did not encourage children to *write* poetry, or explain to them that poems should express personal feeling and experience. But they did teach us to say by heart a great deal of poetry, by the English authors who were writing for children at that time: Walter de la Mare, A. A. Milne, John Masefield, Robert Louis Stevenson, Eleanor Farjeon and others.

We had poetry galore in Standard Six at Grafton School, and I think I started to see what poetry *was*. I certainly loved it. Belloc's 'Tarantella', for example:

> Do you remember an Inn?
> Miranda?
> Do you remember an Inn?
> And the tedding and the spreading
> Of the straw for a bedding

> And the fleas that tease in the High Pyrenees
> And the wine that tasted of the tar?
> And the cheers and the jeers of the young mulateers . . .

We all had fun getting our tongues around Hilaire Belloc's tricky lines, and then were suitably sobered by the chill, echoing ending:

> Never more
> Miranda,
> Never more.
> Only the high peaks hoar:
> And Aragon a torrent at the door.
> No sound
> In the walls of the Halls where falls
> The tread
> Of the feet of the dead to the ground.
> No sound:
> Only the boom
> Of the far Waterfall like Doom.

I've always loved the story of the boy who said he didn't care for poetry; it was 'all hey-nony-nonny and bloody daffodils'. I wonder if anyone had ever introduced this discerning child to 'Tarantella', or 'The Highwayman', or any of John Masefield's stirring sea poems or the wealth of funny, romantic or dramatic poetry that is available? I, in company with other children of my generation, piled up a rich store of such poems during our school life, poems that still today, in sudden snatches, spring into consciousness. (One night last winter I and my friend Nancy Fox sat in front of my fire, and for some reason started to review our separate, but overlapping hoards. We proved to have remarkably similar repertoires. New Zealand educators of the twenties and thirties were obviously intent upon sending their charges out into the world equipped with deep reserves of the English tongue as used by masterly practitioners. Patterns were laid down, and took root, even in unlikely soil. Priceless booty, indeed.)

Symonds Street, as a place to live, revealed features that had been undreamt of in my life before. We quickly got used to the noise and clang of the traffic (trams have their own unique sound: 'clang' is the only word for it), the ceaseless clamour from adjacent factories, and the seemingly endless stream of anonymous people we passed in the street. I soon discovered a new delight: a poky, dark little shop down Eden Terrace whose owner styled himself a 'newsagent' and, as a sideline, operated a system whereby books and magazines might be exchanged for a few pence. I liked the old man who ran the shop. He never objected to my endless perusal of his stock, and even gave me a stool to sit on. Along with my own books, notably the Tennyson, the old man's rather doubtful wares constituted my main reading diet this year. 'Westerns' were a revelation. I must have read his whole stock; and *True Romances* — eclipsed, once I discovered it, by *True Confessions* — had me wide-eyed and longing for more. Far from disapproving of this descent into the murky and sensational depths of popular literature, Mum used to share my booty (and must have financed the deal, as I had no income). I cannot, now, recall one story or article in detail from the hundreds I must have gulped down during this period. If any of them featured real nastiness or depravity, it went unnoticed by my innocent eyes; and of course there was no overt sex in any magazine generally available in New Zealand sixty years ago. The violence I recall was mainly of the gangster-speakeasy type, which we had always included in our games, along with the cowboys-and-Indians bang-bang-you're-dead variety. All very bloodless, really.

I realise now that as I trudged home almost daily with my delightful loot I would pass within a few hundred yards of the great gaunt Grafton Public Library, from which I was debarred by City Council edict. Resentment never entered my mind. It was unlikely, anyway, that I should have struck up a valued friendship with the librarian in that forbidding place. I went in one day to look, and there was a notice on the wall saying SILENCE. Chatting about this and that to my old man in the bookshop was a better deal altogether.

I was seeing less of Ross since we came to the city. He arrived home from school an hour later than Val and I, and was then engulfed, it always seemed, in homework. But we went to an occasional film together, especially in the holidays. From choice, this would be a funny one: Laurel and Hardy, or a new team, the Marx Brothers, whom we both loved at first encounter. We would give Mum and Val a blow-by-blow description on arrival home, and re-live the best bits for months afterwards, hooting with laughter all over again. 'Remember when . . .?' and we would be away.

We had been in Symonds Street for a year when our tenure assumed a slightly doubtful status. This did not relate to any fault of Dad's.

Seemingly, the owner of the business, having engaged Dad to open and establish the enterprise — which he had done superbly, with the help of only one assistant — now proposed to move in and manage it himself. There was no question of Dad's becoming the assistant; this was a competent but doubtless underpaid woman, who made sandwiches, loaded and guarded the pie oven, and did the cleaning. We might stay on upstairs until we found other accommodation . . . and Dad, of course, must find another job.

With Mum on the spot, Dad's drinking, though it certainly hadn't stopped, had decreased, and was manageable. It was ironic that fate should deal him such a blow when he had achieved so much, and was at least in part-control of his drinking. Dad must have seen the blow coming. He must also have been conscious of Mum's strong, though unspoken (in her children's hearing, at least) objection to remaining indefinitely in sub-standard living conditions with nowhere for Val, in particular, to play. It was revealed, in time, that several months before Dad became jobless, our parents had applied for a state house. During the year before (1937), the Labour Government had launched its housing scheme aimed at providing at least some families who were living in unsatisfactory conditions, with well-equipped houses at low rentals. We had been inspected, and apparently found needy; but houses were limited, and only a few of the throng of applicants could be successful. Our parents were dazed when advised of their selection as state house tenants, I recall. It must surely have lessened the blow of the recent disaster.

We were all stunned, I think, as we packed up to leave Symonds Street. *A brand new house!* And a garden! The people who ran the dairy down the road sent us two big boxes filled with chocolate eggs left over from Easter, and we children made ourselves sick eating them. All the adjacent shopkeepers were angry on Dad's account, Mum told us later. They thought he had been treated shabbily — and of course, they had all been charmed by him. People always were.

FIFTEEN

*R*oss and I talked on the phone yesterday. Faxes are convenient and cheap, but there's nothing like the sound of a voice from time to time. The thousands of miles that separate Kare Kare in Auckland, New Zealand from Tortola, one of the British Virgin Islands in the West Indies, disappear as we speak.

I know Ross and Minine's home well. I have been there five times in the last twenty years. I can see the huge living room bounded by terrace and blue sea on one side, with palms and tropical flowers moving in the faint breeze at either end. I can feel the cool parquet floor under my bare feet, see the comfortable cane furniture on the seaward side and the heavy, polished table and chairs and huge old sideboard on the landward side of the room. Ross will be sitting in his wheelchair in light cotton shorts and shirt, with bare feet.

'That was the best thing that ever happened to us,' he says. He is talking, of course, of our move to the Casey Estate. I think he is right.

❦

We moved into our new government house in mid-winter, 1938. The Casey Estate, as it was known then, and indeed for many years after, occupied a hollow between the Auckland suburbs of Grey Lynn, Ponsonby,

114

Herne Bay and Westmere. It was the second state house project in the city
— Orakei was the first — and was widely vaunted as a sign that better
accommodation for working-class families was on the way.

My mother remembered galloping her brother's horse over the
Caseys' fields from her home in Grey Lynn years before, with friends, to
picnic at the Herne Bay beaches. 'Tell us about it, Mum,' one of us would
say. Quite ordinary events were transformed by Mum's aptitude for
reporting. She never exaggerated for effect; merely found words that
brought situations to life, often curious or hilarious life. It was a natural
talent, fed perhaps by her tendency to re-live the past, dreamily, when the
present seemed less than tolerable. It was her way of escape, and our good
fortune.

'In those days,' she told us, 'the countryside was beautiful, with green
fields, and hills and valleys, and trees.'

The hills and valleys were still there, but they were stark and
mutilated; neither tree nor blade of grass had been left. But, of course,
people needed houses. *We* needed a house.

After the shabby squalor of the quarters above the shop in Symonds
Street, the glistening newness of Number 9 Tawariki Road had us speaking
in uneasy whispers at first visit. We tiptoed from room to room, enveloped
in the smell of new paint. The electric stove still had its sales ticket
attached. For the first few weeks our mother urged us to avoid marking
the wallpaper or scratching the new paint and varnish, but she had as little
heart for policing these instructions as we had inclination to listen. In no
time at all, we resumed our cheerful, cluttered way of life. Moving was, of
course, no novelty. This was our twelfth 'shift' in as many years: almost my
whole lifetime. But my attitude to this new house was ambivalent. I had
always savoured the evidence of other people's lives in former 'new' houses.
One could speculate about the pictures that had left faded rectangles on
drab wallpapers and departed with their owners to new settings. Like as
not, dim corners of dusty cupboards would yield up unsuspected treasures:
in our fine Mt Albert house, an ancient copy of *The Prince and the Pauper*,
which I embarked upon immediately behind the packing cases, feigning
deafness when hailed to help unpack — and a *harmonica* — not a cheap
mouth-organ, but a real musical instrument. Ross seized it immediately,
and gave us such a tuneful rendering of 'Swannee River' that we were all
enchanted, my mother protesting too late that the instrument might have

harboured 'someone else's germs'. Obviously it hadn't, and obviously it was Ross's for the rest of its long life (I could play it rather falteringly, but never with Ross's style and expertise). Even the odd old chest or table might be found abandoned in newly rented houses, and the gardens were sublime.

Oh those overgrown, jungle-like thickets, enshrouding, if you were lucky, long-abandoned fowlhouses or sagging old sheds! The latter would invariably contain ancient and broken garden tools, buckets, wheels and unidentifiable, mysteriously fashioned pieces of leather and iron — that indescribable detritus of human occupation which children so readily and happily convert to their own use if no one insists on 'cleaning it up'. In our shining new government house we had none of these treasures, and were surrounded by a sea of mud. Sadly, we recalled the fruit trees we had found in former gardens, promising as they had — and usually delivering — lavish crops of plums, peaches, pears or apples . . . even, sometimes, figs. My mother and figs are inextricably entwined in my memory. Mum was renowned for her fig jam and somehow always contrived to arrange a yearly supply. Someone's aunt or grandmother would have a fig tree (or know someone who had) and the baskets of precious fruit would be conveyed to our kitchen. Those involved in the supply chain would expect to receive a pot of jam in due course, and were never disappointed. (The rules were unspoken, but unbroken.) And how could I ever cease to cherish in memory the Johnstone Street garden in Point Chevalier with its seemingly endless torrent of cooking apples, just when we needed them most? But the joy of a brand new house must have been real to my mother: a stove that obeyed its row of switches, water that flowed hot from the tap, and a lavatory at the end of the hall, rather than the garden path or more recently the dungeon-like depths of the Symonds Street shop. Best of all, as the fences went up and the roads took shape, we discovered that a community was being born, and that we were part of it.

First, the neighbours. It was several years since we had lived anywhere long enough to get to know nearby families. This was to change. One day my mother happened to look out a side window, only a few feet from the house next door, in time to witness a small drama. 'Dorothy!' she screamed (I must have been nearest). 'The baby next door — its pram has tipped over!' To reach the scene, I had to run out our kitchen door on the opposite side of the house, back across the garden and hurdle the new wire-mesh fence. There I encountered an overturned pram, half-concealing a thrashing bundle of blankets from which arose outraged if muffled shrieks. Obviously, the unknown baby was concealed therein. Heart in mouth, I snatched up the bundle, managed to find and uncover a head and began jiggling the whole, making what I hoped were soothing noises. (This was my first close encounter with a baby.) Revealed was a furious, red little face embellished with dark eyes and wisps of brown hair. The mouth, opening for another roar, astonishingly widened on sight of me into the loveliest smile I had ever seen, while a small fist, wrenched from the constricting blanket, banged me on the head in a friendly fashion.

This was the only experience of love at first sight that I have ever had. Beverley, for so the baby proved to be called ('Bebbie', at her own insistence, as soon as she started to talk) was a revelation to me. I had not imagined before that a baby could be a person, as this one undoubtedly was. My mother reported that Beverley — aged six months — had engineered the upending of her pram by standing up, clutching the hood and rocking the whole thing with feverish enthusiasm. A child of early initiative, clearly, and a cheerful, outgoing one, at that. By the time her mother and mine arrived, she was looking to build on the fortunate circumstance that had — however dramatically — liberated her from the confines of the boring pram. We all, with the baby's older brother Denis, adjourned to our kitchen, where my mother put on the kettle.

It is impossible for me to exaggerate the difference that getting to know the Beuths made to my life. It seems likely that all young adolescents (an unused term, in those days) would benefit from having another family, living very close, in whose house they could feel utterly 'at home'; a family whose faces always lit up when they appeared. This is how it became for me. Mrs Beuth (it would have been unthinkable to use her Christian name — in fact, she and my mother would not have taken such liberties) treated me as a friend, rather than a child, obviously enjoyed my company and trusted me completely to look after Beverley. She was a tiny, sturdy woman, shy, but with a wry sense of humour. Mr Beuth, by contrast, was a large, bear-like man with an easy, friendly manner and a ready laugh. His eyes twinkled behind round spectacles; he seemed pleased with his life, and worked long hours as a bricklayer. He had met and married his wife in England and, after the birth of their first child, Denis, brought his family home to New Zealand to live. This had all taken place in Nottingham. Nottingham! Did they know Sherwood Forest? Of course! I was dazed by

this information. The wonder of Robin Hood and Sherwood Forest had
become part of me during my primary school days. And now, someone who
had lived near the fabled forest was living next door to us!

Sherwood in the twilight, is Robin Hood awake?
Grey and ghostly shadows are gliding through the break . . .

It was almost too much to believe.

I liked everything about the Beuths and I adored Beverley. I loved
Mrs Beuth's accent, and her cooking (her scones were almost as good as
my mother's, and she called them 'sc-oh-nes', to rhyme with stones). She
taught me how to knit all over again — I had supposedly learned when I
was about eight but had never persisted with the art. Denis, two years
younger than Val and a quiet, biddable little boy with a sweet smile, became
her devoted slave. They set up house in the tiny garden shed in our
backyard and were seldom seen apart.

At first our trip to the main road from our house resembled an
obstacle race. For what was left of the winter, we stumbled up to Richmond
Road through and around piles of shingle, clambering over wooden
footings and sliding in patches of mud. We children thought it was fun;
and progress on our fine new roads and footpaths was being made steadily.

The daily tram journey to and from school replicated that of the year
before when we had shuttled between the city and Point Chevalier. Val,
with no experience of the long, settled school life Ross and I had enjoyed
in Stanley Bay, must have wondered at all this incomprehensible junketing,
but she did not complain. To add to the marathon we walked an extra half-
mile, morning and night, at the Ponsonby end of the journey, in order to
save a ha'penny a day each. The fare from the section was a penny — as
against a penny-ha'penny — from our corner. Mum always made sure that
we had the extra money in case we were late, or it rained heavily, but we
very seldom used it. Looking back I recall the sensation of *knowing* that
the weekly sevenpence-ha'penny saved in this way by the three of us
mattered. I suspect that children understand and co-operate in economy
measures if they are confident of their parents' support and know that the
need is real. And we didn't know anyone rich to compare ourselves with.
Most working-class children in those days were used to using their legs to
save money.

The occasional treat was all the more heady for its rarity. There was a dilapidated tin shed near Richmond Road School in which a delectable boiled sweet called, mysteriously, 'American Boss' was made, and, presumably sold on to shops. All the local children knew about it. For a penny you could get a good-sized handful thrust into a paper bag at the door. We Norgroves were not slow to learn, and occasionally managed a visit. Am I wrong in thinking that I have never since tasted any sweet remotely like this one? Insert a jagged piece in your mouth and the flavour seemed to invade your very being . . . No, not like toffee, not like coconut ice (which Mum made in good times), not like jubes nor jelly-beans nor marshmallows. American Boss: Confection of the Gods!

Stirrings of an approaching, faraway war invaded our schoolroom at Grafton, for this was 1938. The headmaster, an old man called Andrews, took to coming into his senior classroom every morning with news of the latest developments in Europe. It was quite unreal, and his almost tearful announcement of Mr Chamberlain's bringing back 'peace with honour' from Munich at the end of September left us, if anything, with a sensation of anticlimax. What a lot of fuss about nothing.

Extraordinarily, Mr Manning kept me back after school one day and talked to me about something that he called 'your future'. No one in our family concerned themselves with the future. Mum was strong on the past, and *today* was certainly important. But the future involved planning, implying some sort of control over what happened or was likely to happen. I suspect that our mother, concerned to feed, clothe and keep us happy on a daily basis and feeling herself to be embroiled in 'the fell clutch of circumstance' (not to mention the 'bludgeonings of chance') did her best to avoid unprofitable reflection on the future. I had no contribution to offer on this subject, but I gathered from Mr Manning's remarks that he did not think I should go to Seddon Tech. As it was clear that Ross, who had been champing at the bit for some time, was about to gain his freedom from this unattractive institution without even completing his first year, I made no protest. I simply accepted a sealed letter addressed to my parents, and delivered it. Mum opened it, wonderingly, on my arrival home, and willingly divulged its contents. Mr Manning considered that my interests would be much better served by the Auckland Girls' Grammar School than by Seddon Tech. He pointed out, cleverly, that Grammar was quite close to my home now that we lived in Ponsonby and craftily, that I could even 'do commercial' if that was what my parents wanted. What did I think,

Mum asked? It sounded all right, I said . . . I didn't much like the sound of Tech anyway. Mum remembered that my cousin, Irma Brown, was at Grammar, and seemed to be liking it. We had seen very little of our Brown cousins since Grandma had deserted us to care for them two years before, but now we lived within walking distance of one another. This was to prove a bonus for us all.

In this off-hand way my 'future' was decided. Dad, being informed, seemed pleased. I think he was flattered by Mr Manning's unexpected attentions.

❦

On a January day in 1939, I and an intermittent stream of other girls, all accompanied by mothers — with a sprinkling of fathers — made our way up the Auckland Grammar School drive to present ourselves for enrolment. My carefully tended curls must have gleamed and bounced in the sunlight on this bright summer day. I realised years later that I was always recognised and remembered for these curls, which I thought nothing of at all. I was not even embarrassed by their inappropriateness on me, an athletic, outspoken, distinctly un-ladylike example of my species. But they were Mum's pride and joy. I was obliged to stand still every morning while she twisted innumerable pieces of my over-abundant hair into springy appendages which would then hang in a double row around my head. At least this achieved a reasonably neat effect. Mum had tried equipping me with the fashionable 'bob' when I first went to school as a small child, but my hair simply stuck out wildly around my head in spikes. The attempt was abandoned and the curls instituted. Not even a cyclone would have dislodged them. I suppose it was a sensible solution. Ross had the same problem but its resolution was simpler; he was simply shaved almost to the scalp. If attention to this necessary operation was ever delayed, as it seems to have been at the time the school photo was taken, he ran into the same problems.

My 'future' was about to begin. The drive that led into the Auckland Girls' Grammar School from Howe Street was lined on one steep side with fine old trees and gave a splendid view of a wide lawn and, suddenly, the sort of school buildings that I thought existed only in books. There were the tall, narrow, leaded windows, the massive doors, the obligatory ivy on the old brick and — unbelievably — a square fortress-like tower rising Norman-style from the ground through two floors to finally rear above the school. *Tom Brown's School Days* (in tiny print on cheap thick paper) had recently come my way and I had been fascinated by the view it gave of English Public School life. And here before me was the prototype building. Surely this was the right edifice in which to pursue one's 'future'? The whole idea of school, other girls, uniforms, and games (someone had told me they played *cricket*!) seemed suddenly, dazingly, attractive and within reach. When, inside the front door, I was confronted by a colonnaded hall, an imposing chamber that rose through two storeys to a distant roof, I was ensnared. Three sides were lined with galleries, which were reached by a handsome double staircase. The third side, behind a platform and lectern, was hung with large *real* oil paintings. 'I dreamt I dwelt in marble halls . . .' carolled Gladys Moncrieff in the back of my mind. This was the closest I had ever come to a marble hall and I was enchanted. Good old Arthur Manning had contrived to arrange an appropriate future for at least one of his pupils.

My mother and I were interviewed not by the headmistress, Miss Johnston, who was absent on leave in England, but by Miss Edgerley, a handsome though rather gaunt-looking woman who smiled kindly at me, welcomed us both, consulted my progress card, and with brisk but not patronising economy talked Mum *out* of 'commercial' for her daughter, and *into* 'academic'. My mother's faint reluctance on this score resulted in a compromise: I was to do 'academic without Latin'. I suspect that I kept grinning cheerfully. I liked this place and I liked Miss Edgerley. 'What a nice woman,' said Mum as we walked back up the drive, 'but she didn't look well.' Kate Edgerley had indeed been much less well than her colleagues realised; she died in February 1939, only a month after rescuing me from a life of typewriters and shorthand notebooks. She had taught at AGGS for thirty years and was Second Mistress. I have never forgotten her.

Providing me with a uniform must have posed a financial problem, but Mum did not mention it. Dad was still jobless, but Ross was now working as a message-boy for the Standard Optical Company, and the ten shillings he paid Mum every week will have augmented Dad's meagre unemployment allowance. (And Mum's financial strategies were always remarkable.) So she and I walked the length of Karangahape Road from the school, I finding it hard not to skip, to the George Courts department store. Here we bought a school hat (navy blue serge, badge to be provided at school), a white blouse (I would need three but Mum could copy the

style and make the others cheaply), a blazer (the cheapest one available —
Mum was apologetic about this but I didn't care — and the school badge
would later emblazon its breast pocket and render me gloriously
distinguishable as a Grammar Girl), a pair of navy blue cloth gloves, three
pairs of capacious black bloomers, two pairs of long black woollen stockings
and a pair of black leather lace-up shoes. Like almost all schoolgirls, I
already owned the obligatory gym tunic which, while rather worn, would
do until Mum could afford to buy good woollen serge and make me
another one. (This was achieved in my fourth form year along with a
beautifully tailored blazer.)

I watched with interest as the pound notes Mum counted out
carefully and paid over to the shop assistant were installed, with our
account, in a small bullet-shaped container, which was then snapped on to
an overhead wire. Along this, the little craft travelled at a dignified pace to
a lofty office, where it was disengaged, unpacked, refitted with the correct
change and documents, and dispatched on its journey back to us by a godlike operator in her cage under the roof. Other people's transactions could
be seen advancing and retreating along a network of similar lines. I could
have watched for hours. We very seldom shopped in department stores, and
it was a fascinating sight.

Mum and I walked all the way home, I clutching my string-tied
parcel. Mum produced a string bag from her purse to accommodate my
shoes in their bulky box, and swung this happily — she was thin and girlish
our mother — and we looked in shop windows and congratulated ourselves
on a job well done. It would not have occurred to either of us to imagine
that we might have a cup of tea or a cool drink in a shop. The point of
walking was to save money, not squander it.

On the way, we walked down Howe Street and along Hopetoun
Street to have another look at the school. The prospect from this viewpoint
was even more alluring. The school grounds sloped from the road, and at
intervals through old trees one could see the school, with the harbour
sparkling in the distance. Clearly visible from this angle was another,
smaller tower, a narrow fairy-tale structure . . . I clutched my parcel to my
chest in rapture.

That night I donned my new clothes right down to the gloves and bloomers, and paraded proudly for my own family, and then for the Beuths. Everyone was suitably and seriously impressed. The new leather schoolbag that had been provided for Ross's aborted career at Seddon Tech would now be mine and I slung it on my shoulder to complete the effect. Girls at Grammar, I had learned, might carry their bags in this way — an unexpected and dazing dispensation. All my life I had resented having to carry a suitcase, while Ross slung a leather satchel over his shoulder! I was certainly on my way to becoming a Grammar School Girl.

SIXTEEN

Only third formers — all new girls — attended AGGS on the first day of the first term each year. The whole day, in 1939, was given over to an Entrance Examination comprising English Grammar, an essay, Arithmetic and what I later learned was an intelligence test. On arrival, we were divided alphabetically into manageable numbers and herded, with an efficiency that was to become familiar, into form rooms. ('Classes' and 'teachers' were for primary school kids. We were now to enjoy the dignity of 'forms' and 'mistresses'.)

My group was housed for the day in a basement room which, being bisected on its only window wall by a steep flight of stone stairs that was bounded on the other side by the cavernous, ancient lavatory block, enjoyed no natural light at all. This, my first experience of a form room and a mistress, might have dimmed my eagerness for Grammar Girl status; it is certainly a wonder that it did not engender a total incapacity to write, compute and think among the twenty or so hopefuls there assembled. Perhaps it did, among the more faint-hearted. For Miss Smith ('Smuts' as she was always called) was not a reassuring figure. Tall and thin, with hair severely confined in a bun, she was given to ethereal, enigmatic smiles and utterances that seemed to have no relevance to anything earthly. Swathed in an ancient, positively greening gown, she was a dismaying figure —

though we found in time that she was relatively harmless. (Heather Northey, in her superb history of AGGS, *The First Hundred Years*, confines herself to one mention only of Miss Smith. 'Miss B. E. Smith, affectionately known as "Smuts" retired in 1952 after thirty years' service. She did much for the Christian Union and the hospital Choir.' Poor Smuts: to have mention made only of one's departure, after all those years . . . though 'affectionately' reveals compassion on the writer's part, if not a strict regard for truth.)

Between papers, we had short rest periods, which Smuts converted to her own bizarre use. She taught us to sing 'Lead, kindly light, amidst the encircling gloom . . .' leading herself in quavering but resolute tones. 'The night is dark, and I am far from home . . .' Far from home, indeed, were we all. I decided that she was merely barmy, and probably not representative. The other mistresses had seemed healthily normal; and the acting headmistress, Mrs Ward, who had welcomed us in the hall, had been kindly and encouraging.

I found the tests well within my capabilities, wrote a flamboyant essay on a topic long forgotten, and decided that the IQ test, which seemed like a set of entertaining puzzles, had been provided, generously, to relieve the serious nature of our ordeal. I walked home at the end of the day happily content, and reduced my own family and the Beuths next door to gales of laughter with my vivid description of the day's events.

Next morning, we reassembled. All papers had been marked overnight and the results correlated. Names were read out and we were marshalled into our form rooms. I was to be in III A 2; but only for a day. I was given a note to take home. I had done especially well in the entrance exam, and with my parents' permission would be moved into III A 1, where I would add Latin to my subjects. Mum and Dad were bemused but agreeable, and in characteristic style I was happy to comply. I didn't care what form I was in; I was simply enchanted with the whole place.

The girl who was moved *out* of III A 1 so that I might be moved *in* was the close friend of two girls who later became my good friends. They had, all three, with quite a few others in this form, come from the innovative Kowhai Intermediate School, one of the first intermediate schools in the country. My insertion into III A 1 and this other girl's ejection was not appreciated by her Kowhai colleagues; and it does seem, on reflection, to have been a callous way to manage a delicate adjustment.

I was simply escorted in by a mistress and the other girl escorted out. Her friends were outraged.

'You grinned at everyone, and we hated you on sight. And as for those Shirley Temple curls . . .!' Only the Kowhai girls paid any attention to the substitution, fortunately. One girl was as good as another when everyone was brand new. I didn't sense any antipathy, and was soon on cheerful terms with the rest of the form. Within a few weeks I had been elected form games captain, largely because of my prowess on the cricket field, I imagine — a skill arising from the years of practice with Ross and his friends. Very early in the year I was christened 'Curly', a name that has never been abandoned by friends made at that time, and later in my school life.

We became, in III A 1, almost immediately a family. We each had our own desk, in which we could leave all our books and personal possessions. We had our own form room, which opened off the hall, and our own form mistress, who was in our room before school each morning, and could be consulted on any subject. I think we were fortunate. All too often new entrants in large, modern, inevitably impersonal high schools seem to have no place to call their own, and no one to appeal to if in doubt. To a certain extent we were sheltered. Mistresses came to us, lesson by lesson. We left our form room only for specialist subjects such as Science, Music and Art, to all of which classes we went together. Our room was our own, and our form mistress appeared at the end of each school day, with advice, warnings and reminders in general, and personal words for miscreants in particular. ('Be sure your sins will find you out' seemed to work at AGGS. Did they *never* talk about anything else but *us* in the staff common room?)

Our form mistress in III A 1, Miss Haslett, also taught us Latin. She was a gracious, scholarly woman, near the end of her long teaching career. Her sweet smile in no way reduced the strength of her expectations of her pupils, but she was easy to respect, and she 'took us on' as her own. (I needed rather more of her support than most, as the year wore on. As a subject of complaint from other mistresses, I must have tried her patience.)

On our first day, we were all issued with a sizeable pile of exercise books, each in a different colour, with the school crest on the front. Blue for French, green for Latin, brown for History . . . and a larger book, a scribbler, for private use. In our scribblers, we were expected to record every instruction given, all homework set and anything else we wished. You could plan an essay, try out different spellings and tricky computations, 'doodle' or draw — in fact, do anything that took your fancy. I wish now that I had kept some of my scribblers. I used to write doggerel verse if I was bored, often illustrating it in my own crude cartoon style. Sometimes I would tear a relatively safe example out and pass it round the class. (I found one of these, miraculously preserved among old papers recently.) Others, of a more libellous nature, I would preserve for private exhibition.

I was carried away with delight at all these books. I had fallen in love with paper at an early age and had always loved a pristine exercise book on sight, regardless of the unattractive requirements the blank pages might later make of me. Never had I envisaged such bounty! We received also a small number of textbooks, and two exquisite little volumes about four inches by six, with spines embossed in gold. These I examined immediately, with wonder and a surge of joy. They were both from a series called *The King's Treasuries of Literature*. One was blue, and was entitled *A Shakespeare Progress*. The other, *Longfellow's Evangeline*, was green, and contained not only the long story-poem of the title but also *The Courtship of Miles Standish*. I have both of them still. I couldn't believe that we were being *given* these books, but it was true. We wrote our names and forms and the date in them immediately.

Other books we were expected to buy, and this was a problem. How could I possibly ask at home for money, when I knew there was none to spare? But things were looking up again, if only temporarily. That very week, the same butcher who had taken Dad on for a short time during our reduced days in Point Chevalier again offered him a fill-in job. This was a young man who had worked for Dad in his Auckland Meat Company days of glory, and had since, with his family's help, set himself up in a small shop in Mount Albert. By a lucky chance, Dad's employer lived with his parents in Ponsonby, and travelled back and forth daily in a little old van. It was easy for him to pick Dad up and deliver him home; and the best possible safeguard against the ever-present danger of Dad's defection to the pub at night. It even saved on tram fares. I could see Mum's spirits lifting, overnight.

By an almost unbelievable piece of good luck this man's young brother had just left Auckland Grammar after only one year. A message came, through Dad. Would I like to come and look through his discarded books? I went at once, list in hand, filled with hope that all my books would, like magic, appear. Alas, only one was on my list: a science text, I recall. But the boy's kind mother not only plied me with tea and cake, but produced a Grammar School jersey and a navy-blue gaberdine raincoat, both of good quality. Certainly, the coat had a long tear from one of its side pockets, sustained in the course of a spectacular spill from the young brother's bike, his mother told me, with graphic and bloody details. This was no worry; the tear would be mended at home with speed and skill.

In the event, Mum was giddily relieved at what she saw as the miraculous appearance of essential additions to my uniform, provision of which would have daunted if not defeated her. I, with my usual lack of concern for such mundane affairs, was pleased but not ecstatic. You could do without the odd garment; books were another matter entirely. I was nonetheless only too happy to be engulfed by the over-large jersey once temperatures fell, and the raincoat, shortened at hem and cuff, was as fine as any at school. Both garments lasted me for all my years at Grammar.

Books remained a problem. Most were available secondhand at school, and everyone except me seemed to have money to buy them. By the time Mum had managed to rescue a few shillings here and there for me from family funds, I was managing on a knife edge with recourse to other people's books and a certain amount of subterfuge regarding what I had, or had not done, and why. But I was a child of steely resolution, and some pride. I had no intention of revealing my penury. I would tell lies — or skirt the truth, perhaps — rather. As the secondhand books got fewer, they fortunately got cheaper (and scruffier) but I had them all, in the end. And I knew that, before the next year started, I must, myself, have accumulated enough money for books, *somehow*.

Meanwhile, the Casey Estate, as it was still called locally, was yielding up yet more agreeable facets. The roads and footpaths were completed, and we were getting to know more families. Next door, on the other side from the Beuths, lived a young couple called McDonald. Their second child was born just after they moved in. As their kitchen door was exactly opposite ours, and only a few yards away, we were talking to them in no time. Both Ross and I used to have interesting conversations with Mrs McDonald, and I often played with the children. (As a dispenser of wild horsey-rides I was in great demand.) Several years later Mrs McDonald told Mum that she and her husband 'hoped that Heather and Roddy would grow up to be just like Dorothy and Ross'! She cannot have been more than ten years older

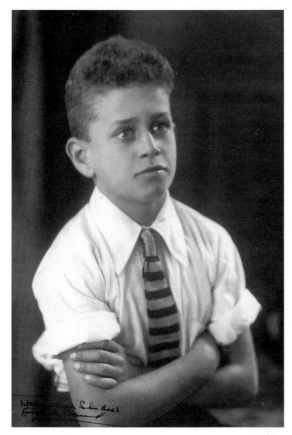

Ross, aged 9 years.

Valerie, aged 4 years, 1933.

Dorothy and Ross, aged 10 and 11.

Mr Watson's Standard 5 class, 1935. Dorothy on right of teacher, Ross seventh from left, back row. (Ken Stacey, our friend who was killed, second from left, back.)

Beverley, aged 15 months, '. . . a child of early initiative'.

New Grammar uniform! With Val, February 1939.

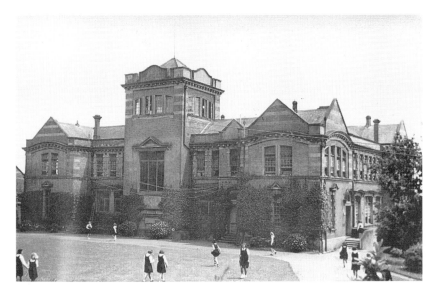

Auckland Girls' Grammar School, 1940.

Above left: *Val Parker and Nancy Laird, 1939.* Above right: *Avis Robson (Tweet) 1940.*

When third forms play a netball match,
There's riots everywhere,
And boots & fists & frightful yells
Go sailing through the air!

By Dorothy Butler, III A I, AGGS, 1939.

Dorothy, aged 14.

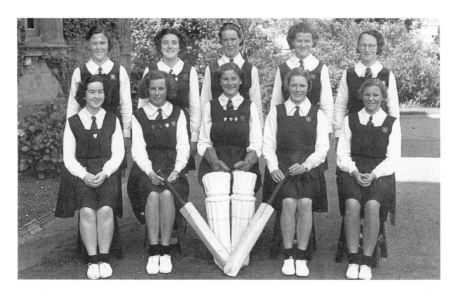

AGGS First Eleven, 1941. Dorothy second from right, back row. Pen (Win Penman) second from right, front row. Bro (Isobel Brodie) first on right, front row. My cousin, Irma Brown, second from left, back row.

Me, Bro and Nan at the old Newmarket 'Olympic Pool' after school, 1942. (Contrary to school rules, but great fun, with illicit ice cream to follow.)

Pen, Bro and Curly, '. . . an inseparable threesome'. Sixth Formers, 1942.

Prefects, 1943, while I was banging pots and pans in the cookery room! Second from left, front row: Avis Robson (Tweet) and second from right, middle row: Margaret Brand.

Front left: my father with New Zealand friends at the Victoria League, London 1940.
Middle front: Jimmy Simpson, who went down with his ship shortly afterwards.

Dad, Lance Corporal Derry Wray and Sergeant Wilf Wray, Cairo, 1941.

than us, but we both saw her as relatively elderly: a contemporary of our mother, we thought.

We instituted nightly cricket games in the middle of the now beautifully paved road, using our rubbish bin as a wicket, and recruiting all the kids in the street. Tawariki Road swept gently down and round from the main road, and we could always hear when a car started to descend. We had about ten seconds before the approaching car posed a threat. Our evasive strategy — which must be implemented instantly, regardless of the state of play — involved clearing the road, the nearest player grabbing the rubbish bin. This worked, though it certainly disturbed the tenor of the game. On one notable occasion, the lid of the rubbish bin, becoming separated from its other half in the scramble, suffered the fate we all so nimbly avoided and was squashed flat. Mum looked faintly aggrieved at this eventuality, but she could never resist our hilarity, and anyway, the time had passed when outlawing the practice would have prevented the damage. We had the same old battered rubbish bin with the squashed-flat lid for years.

Ross must have been the most cheerful, enthusiastic message boy in Auckland. He earned fifteen shillings a week. Of this, ten shillings went to Mum for the housekeeping and one-and-six to the Farmers' Trading Company as 'time payment' on his bike, a 'Monarch Special'. This sturdy black vehicle was his pride and joy. He had always longed for a bike, and now he had one. From the three-and-sixpence left after honouring these commitments, Ross gave sixpence each to Val and me every pay day, and was left with two-and-sixpence for his own use. Val and I were delighted by this munificence, but not surprised. Good fortune was to be shared, we all believed, without even discussing the subject. I started saving my sixpences immediately, my eye on next year's books.

At fourteen, Ross was still a boy. No one had so far identified the teenage state, and he simply went on wearing his school clothes (minus the giveaway cap) to work. Neither he nor I was tall at this time, though Ross later grew to six feet and I to five-feet-six. There was still more than a year to pass before he could begin his apprenticeship as an optical mechanic, but meanwhile he enjoyed himself. He used to regale us every night with tales of his interactions with the opticians in the city to whom he made deliveries. Ross was obviously (and unsurprisingly) everyone's favourite. Once, a well-known optician gave him a pound note in thanks for some extra effort. Ross told me, several years ago, that he could hardly wait to get home to give it to Mum. He knew that her only shoes had holes in both soles, padded with cardboard but no proof against winter rain. His remembered joy at Mum's delight — she went straight off to George Courts the very next day — shone from my brother's eyes after sixty years.

Taken up with the exciting developments in my own life, I registered this event only dimly. I have experienced some shame — disbelief, almost — that I could have been so unseeing of the real problems in our family at this time, except as they affected me. I know now that Ross *knew* he must leave school and get a job so that he could help Mum. It was perhaps just as well that he was finding Accountancy at Tech not to his taste; he'd have left anyway. (His only regret, Ross told me later, was that had he stayed a few more months he would certainly have won the school lightweight boxing championship!) I think that he was also becoming more aware — and judgemental — of our father's weakness, and its devastating effect on our mother's life. My love for my father somehow kept my mind trained on his good points: his charm, his understanding, his humour. These things were ceasing to impress his son, in the face of what Ross increasingly saw as his father's irresponsibility. Ross had Mum's quiet determination to make things work; to a certain extent, her stoicism. But a great deal of his father's magnetism, too: different, but of the same quality.

What did I have? Not Ross's looks. He developed a kind of Errol Flynn, devil-may-care attractiveness which, with his superb build and outgoing ways would have marked him out for attention anywhere. I had a good mind, I suppose, given to reflection, and a love of reading. Increasingly, discernment about friends; I've always loved being alone, and in the face of a noisy, well-packed household, developed a capacity for inner retreat. At thirteen, I still had the body of a younger child; hard, and thin and quite undeveloped. My mother always said that I was the healthiest of her children. From the time of the nose accident at six, I never saw a doctor until my compulsory 'medical' for Teachers' College. I think I was equipped for life as I wanted to lead it, and simply ignored any limitation perceived by others.

The things I wanted were blissfully available, now that I was at Grammar: books to read in hitherto unimaginable profusion, other girls who seemed, surprisingly, more like me than those I had known before, games and general good cheer — and an atmosphere of scholarship which

I enjoyed, sampling it shamelessly in terms of my own interests and abilities, and coping with less attractive subjects with an eye to evasion, as avoidance was clearly impossible. I saw the sense, always, of actually *passing* exams, but a narrow margin seemed adequate. Economy of effort provided plenty of time for the pursuit of my favourite occupations.

SEVENTEEN

*R*oss and Val made friends on the Casey Estate in record time. Val and Jacqueline Buffett down the road became bosom companions, as did Ross and Mervyn Olson, son of the local policeman, and these friendships endured into adulthood. Ross and Merv joined the Cox's Creek Sea Scouts together and were soon fanatical collectors of badges. I was pressed into service in the signalling field; Ross claimed that I learned the Morse code in a single night (willingly abandoning Latin and French 'vocab' in the cause, no doubt). Thereafter I spent at least an hour every night in Ross's blacked-out bedroom, tap-tap-tapping out invented messages on a small battery-operated machine complete with blinking light provided by the Scout troop for the boys' practice. We then moved on to semaphore, with flags, and I once again proved a fast learner and a smooth operator. I begged to be allowed, occasionally, to receive and transcribe messages instead of always 'sending' but this privilege was granted infrequently, and grudgingly. The boys needed me for *their* receiving practice. (I was something of an expert in the end, albeit a lopsided one.)

My life seemed to be divided into two very different halves. Ross's friends became my 'home' friends — though their interests and activities were not mine — and Val's younger friends seemed to be always underfoot.

'Bebbie', now astonishingly athletic and voluble for one so young, was a constant, loved distraction. I was happy, but there was a problem: I needed a modicum of peace and solitude at regular intervals, and this was well-nigh unachievable.

Our government house had three bedrooms, but was not large. Almost all our living was done in the kitchen, where we sidled between bench and table. The sitting room was at the front of the house and was overcrowded with our chesterfield suite and large sideboard — both well suited to the gracious proportions of the rooms in old Devonport villas, but too bulky for this small, square room — plus the piano, and sundry other family possessions for which there seemed no appropriate home. In the early days I often found peace to study or — more usually — read, in the depths of the old couch, but then we acquired something called a 'radiogram' (a cabinet with a radio below and a turntable, or 'gramophone' on top) and my refuge was lost overnight; Ross's friends, increasing in number and size all the time, invaded, joyfully brandishing records. (A cowboy singer called Gene Autrey springs to mind and ear — and Marlene Dietrich with a throaty rendition of 'The Boys in the Backroom'.) How we managed to afford this luxury I cannot imagine. It came with half-a-dozen free records of diverse and doubtful taste, and Mum managed before long to buy a recording of her favourite tenor, John McCormack, whose songs we all loved. Mum's favourite was 'Somewhere'.

> Somewhere, somewhere, beautiful isle of somewhere,
> Land of the true, where we live anew . . .

Living anew must often have seemed attractive to Mum.

It occurred to me at intervals that there must have been lashings of peace in the homes of Ross's friends, but this, of course, was not transferable. And anyway, I *liked* Ross's friends, and usually just gave up and joined in the revelry. Mum, as ever, simply smiled serenely and dispensed tea and scones, and was often found in friendly converse with one of the boys in the kitchen. I don't recall any loutish behaviour, though there was noise and larking and laughter in plenty. All these boys were apprenticed and worked long hours at trades. Ross was the ringleader, and his increasing interest in sailing and boats gradually became theirs. There was to be no drifting in Ross's life; he always applied himself purposefully to the matter in hand and seemed to ignore setbacks. This certainty of intention, along with his infectious personality, pulled other boys into his slipstream almost automatically.

The kitchen table as a place to do one's homework had limitations. I had to share it with family meals, the ironing cloth (Mum remained an indomitable night worker, and almost everything was ironed in those days) and a multitude of other domestic activities. Preparing our packed lunches for the next day was one of these. Ross's lunch became a legend; Mum would slice, by hand, a whole loaf of bread and turn the resulting pile into bulky sandwiches for his lunch alone. On several memorable occasions Ross went off with my modest repast as well, claiming that he had thought it was his morning tea. (My enraged threats of retribution soon cured him of this quaint notion.) Of necessity, I became adept at working in the midst of other people's noise and activities, a capacity that has stood me in good stead ever since; but one could hardly call this 'study'. Getting by on a shoestring was my real talent. (And that has stood me in good stead ever since, too.)

Inadvertently, I had established a reputation for divergence on my second day in III A 1. Our English mistress told us to read Longfellow's *Evangeline*, as homework. I didn't start it until quite late (we Casey Estate cricketers were out in full force on what was a balmy evening) and then, having read a few pages, decided to have a look at *The Courtship of Miles Standish*, the other half of the handsome little volume. This was more to my taste, and I read on until a late hour, finishing *Miles* but neglecting the virtuous *Evangeline* altogether.

The next day, we were tested on *Evangeline*, and I was obliged to admit that I hadn't read it (everyone else had). I was soundly reprimanded for this omission, but then — more as an afterthought than an excuse — mentioned that I had read *The Courtship of Miles Standish* instead. No, I hadn't misunderstood the instruction. I had simply preferred the beginning of *Miles Standish* and gone on reading it. Being instructed to prove this assertion, I embarked on an enthusiastic and detailed account until stopped. I received a very strange look from the English mistress. She told me that I would be in deep trouble if I did not in future do *exactly* as ordered, and that, as I would get no marks for *Evangeline*, I was already lagging in the English stakes. (Every piece of work in every subject was marked so that we could be ranked every term, and our honour or shame divulged on our reports.) I was mildly surprised at the fuss engendered by this — I considered — minor transgression, and read *Evangeline* the next night (doubtless neglecting vital French vocabulary and heaven knows what other set tasks). I was unconcerned, on the whole. Marks, and one's place in the form, were simply not among my preoccupations.

The school itself appealed to me more and more. We were introduced to 'three-wall fives', a game adopted from the great Public Schools of England, we were told. (There was also one-wall fives, played in the courtyard under the school — useful for wet days but altogether inferior, we felt.) We loved the old, weathered concrete structures at the back of the school, bounded by our furthest fence. Here, there was privacy; we used even to take off our shoes and stockings, and tunics, and lie in the sun, sometimes; and always held our end-of-term feasts within the sheltering walls. Three-wall fives can be played competitively by two people, or for practice — and fun — by as many as like to join in. The ball, hit by the hand, must strike two, or three walls before bouncing on the ground, each player taking her turn as it comes round. Long queues of girls could be seen joining in at morning interval — even unlikely, usually unsporting girls. Wonderfully inclusive and non-competitive when played in this way — and furiously competitive when two players were well matched — fives was a splendid feature of school life. (Three years later, in the Lower Sixth, my friend Win Penman and I vied for the school championship. We had a practice match in the lunch hour, and I won. Later the same day, we played the final, and I lost. But it was a fair win; and Pen, as we called her, *was* school games captain.)

Sliding down the banisters was a noble tradition at AGGS, and most of us aspired to master the art immediately. Not everyone succeeded; this was no reckless sling-your-leg-over-and-let-go operation — it was a ladylike, side-saddle balancing act. All the banisters in the school (except a rail that divided the wide staircase from gallery to hall and was always under official eye) were attached to walls. These were splendid, moulded mahogany structures, but were mounted very close to the walls. One's first few attempts were bound to fail. The knack was not unlike that of riding a bike: one minute you *couldn't*, and then suddenly, you *could*. As a means of swift descent, the banisters were incomparable, our shiny Italian-cloth bloomers imparting both speed and comfort. The only danger lurked at the bottom; one was virtually catapulted off — occasionally into the arms of a mistress. Fortunately, banister-riding was not a sin of the first water. An 'impot' (imposition) would be issued: lines, or a poem to learn by heart — a useful addition to an already impressive repertoire for most of us, though we groaned in protest privately.

Miss Johnston's absence abroad for the first two terms of 1939 lent a softer flavour to school life, had we only realised it, than was usual. We were coached for her return: unspeakable retribution would follow mispronunciation of her name: Johnston, with a 't'. (Northey in *The First Hundred Years* claims that EMJ would actually send back mail if her name was *misspelt!*) We had mastered AGGS protocol, which the staff would not have dared abandon, but none of us could have anticipated the chill that would invade our formerly friendly environs with the return of the bona fide head. The very air was colder, it seemed, in Miss Johnston's presence; even a distant prospect of her slightly hunched figure passing through or around or beyond, inside or out, was enough to induce, if not actual fear, a sort of rigidity of spirit.

We met Miss Johnston, formally, on her first day back at school. The entire third form was assembled in the hall for her inspection. We had been suitably prepared, and were more silent than silence itself. Johnny, on the platform, appeared to be fumbling inside her gown, in the region of her lean bosom. When she withdrew her hand, she was seen to be holding a lorgnette, the better to identify the features of her 1939 crop. We were transfixed. I had thought that such optical curiosities, along with monocles, existed only in comic strips. One hundred and fifty of us managing not to laugh was a feat that only the temporary effects of mass fear on mirth could have achieved. She seemed to peer at us individually through the quaint appliance, with intentness, but no sign of enthusiasm. Then she addressed us.

We would profit from our schooldays, we were told, if we were obedient, quiet, of clean habits, hardworking and punctual, always changed into our sandshoes indoors, and disposed of apple cores in the receptacles provided. (She had a fixation with apple cores. Once she found one 'beneath the Honours Board!' and made an impassioned speech about the iniquity of the culprit who, being invited to confess, sensibly did not.)

We had all been at school for two terms already, under the strict but kindly eye of the acting headmistress, Mrs Ward. Some of us had managed to evince none of the virtues listed, and had even trodden the hallowed halls in our outdoor shoes and fired apple cores into the bushes, without the wrath of God descending upon us. Perhaps the wrath of EMJ was of a different nature entirely. There was room for unease; justifiable unease, as we soon discovered.

Before and after school and at lunchtime a queue of girls could be seen, arms rigidly at sides, lining the wall outside EMJ's study. The girl at the head of the queue was obliged to stand to attention, just visible to 'Johnny' through a glass panel in the door, but under threat of death to look in. As the incumbent victim came out, Miss Johnston would tap a bell on her desk, and the next would enter. There was an immutable formula. 'Good morning, Miss Johnston. I'm Dorothy Norgrove of III A 1.' Northey relates the tale of a nervous, 'over-rehearsed' fourth former who mangled the formula into 'Good morning, Miss Bentley. I'm Doris Johnston of . . .' 'The reception,' Northey reports, 'was icy.'

We might have been more forgiving of 'Johnny' had she occasionally given a sign of humour, but, like Queen Victoria, she seemed to be chronically *not* amused. There was a cutting edge to her interactions with us which seemed to mock her own insistence on politeness and consideration for others. She was never as polite to *us* as she required us to be to *her*. On one occasion, I — in the toils of some strife, no doubt — got no further than 'Good morning, Miss Johnston. I'm . . .' to have her bark at me, 'I know who you are!' Unreasonable, since this was her formula, not mine, *and* ill-mannered, I thought. A few years later my friend Avis Robson — by this time a sixth-former and prefect — entered the holy precincts exuberantly one day, with good tidings of some sort, to be met with, 'How dare you fling wide the door and sail in!' This occasioned enormous mirth when reported by the deflated victim of the attack to the rest of the Lower Sixth, and was much quoted then and later.

Remorselessly, we collected Johnny's utterances, most of which described our vices and inadequacies, real or imagined; with delicious satisfaction we lampooned her mannerisms. We longed for a repeat of an incident of the year before we came, when the old tyrant had mounted the platform at assembly, her skirt and gown both hitched behind and tucked into her bulky bloomers. Was it true? Oh, why couldn't it happen again? Those of us who were religious prayed that God might grant us this delight . . . He never did; but Miss Johnston herself kept the supply going. When, only weeks after her return, I was sacked from the post of form games captain (for skipping assembly in company with my friend Isobel Brodie

(Bro) — we simply took a book apiece and read, sitting on boot boxes in the 'dungeon' cloakroom), Miss Johnston made me the subject of a public peroration. 'You are,' she declared, 'a disgrace to your form, your school, your country, and indirectly, the Empire!'

This wonderful piece of grandiloquence has been passed down for generations. It was quoted by Bernice Stevens at a function to launch the Jean C. Webster Trust, of which I am a trustee. Miss Webster, who spent many years at the school, teaching English under Miss Johnston and two subsequent principals, could not have been more different from her. Well able to maintain Grammar-style discipline without spreading terror, 'Webbie' contrived to dispense a mixture of humour and sound sense which left no doubt as to her humanity. Miss Johnston's humanity, by contrast, was always questionable. It was simply not possible to imagine her engaged in the earthy, ordinary activities of daily life as we knew it. The fact that she lived in a private hotel in the city — where she doubtless struck chill into older hearts than ours — increased this impression. Ordinary people lived in *houses*.

Aileen Roberts, an attractive and popular girl in my form, was appointed games captain in my place. I approved of this move in the circumstances, and Aileen gave no sign of minding. When it happened all over again next year in IV A 1, one might have expected her to protest, but she took over once again with no more than a resigned sigh. We were a cheerful, accepting lot on the whole. I don't recall any nastiness or resentment in the years we were together, though we did tease one another about personal eccentricities. Strangely no one made an issue of my curls, which were not cut off until late in my second year. 'Curly' endured as a nickname, but I never experienced it as anything but fond; and ultimately, so much part of me that it registered only if another girl, in a formal situation, felt obliged to use my right name. And of course, mistresses always called me Dorothy.

EIGHTEEN

There were girls in the class who were to become my lifelong friends. In front of me sat a slight, dark-haired girl with glasses called Margaret Brand. Certainly, my attention was first caught by her immaculately covered textbooks. Her father, Margaret told me on application, had wrought this miracle; he had used 'blind holland' in place of the whatever-was-available that the rest of us were obliged to use. The covering of textbooks was compulsory, and in this area I had fared reasonably well, having discovered a cache of leftover wallpaper in one of our wardrobes. But Margaret's books were beautiful!

Margaret was one of a small clutch of very young, very intelligent girls — children, really — who had passed through their early school years in record time, and now found themselves with classmates who were in many cases two years older than them. This disparity probably mattered less at that time, and at that school, than it would today. In III A 1 at AGGS, school was all. If any of our number had interesting outside lives these were, if not concealed, at least not flaunted. And 'interesting lives' 1939 style were a far cry from those of today! Margaret and I, though always on good terms, were not to become close friends for some years; but once forged, the bond between us endured. Margaret told me once that my spirited opposition to injustice in our first year at AGGS provoked her earliest suspicion that resistance to tyranny was possible. As Margaret grew up to be a prodigious resister of tyranny, I was pleased. In fact, no comment has ever given me more real pleasure. I didn't know I was resisting tyranny; I merely always liked things to be *reasonable*.

Nancy Laird and Val Parker, friends of the unfortunate girl whose place I had usurped, forgave this transgression, and we became good friends, in time. And Avis Robson — 'Tweet' — a very clever girl indeed, whose general roundness and fairness reminded one of a Dutch doll, and who seemed, constantly, to be laughing at *something* was a very early friend.

But my true soulmate, as the year wore on and we all settled in, was Isobel Brodie — 'Bro' to us — a girl from a background as different from mine as either of us could have imagined had we been given to such contemplation. We were not. Being at Grammar was like being in the army: it didn't matter where you came from — and our homes were dispersed over the whole of the city — what you *were* was the sole consideration.

Bro was a short, stocky girl with hair as curly as mine, but always arranged in plaits. (Why hadn't my mother thought of *that* solution, I wondered?) In Bro's case, it wasn't a solution to a problem; her family were Exclusive Brethren, and in this sect, long hair was obligatory for girls and women. I was scarcely conscious of this, and would not have appreciated its significance had I known. Bro's wit and humour, her casual, cleverly evasive approach to unreasonable authority and her love of books — even without her passion for cricket — would have commended her to me as a kindred spirit. She was simply such good company. Win Penman had been Bro's close friend during their primary school years. She had been placed in III B ('the dungeon', where I encountered Smuts and 'Lead Kindly Light' on my first day) but was promoted to our form at the end of the year. Win, whom we always called Pen or even Penman, came from a family that was strictly religious, but she had a well-developed sense of humour and no capacity at all to judge or label. One couldn't fail to like her; everyone did. She, Bro and I became an inseparable threesome, and remained so through school.

My fourth form expulsion from office, while more privately conducted than that of the previous year, struck a note of farce which was widely relished. I had been summoned to The Presence, and must obey the call. The signs were ominous, though my offence on this occasion evades my memory utterly. Perhaps it was simply a build-up of discerned subversion. I and my friends were playing fives when the appointed time came. I had recently been awarded a gold drill badge, a school honour bestowed on those who excelled in sport or 'drill', though more usually given in the Fifth. Win Penman (she had a gold drill badge, too) eyed the new badge on the front of my tunic, anxiously. 'She'll have that,' said Pen. 'You'd better wear your blazer.' My blazer was miles away in the cloakroom. 'Have mine,' said Pen, picking it up off the ground. Off I went, buttoned securely into Pen's blazer. Johnny wasted no time. After a highly colourful description of my iniquity, with examples, she produced from a drawer a small pair of scissors and ordered me to unpick my school badges — all of them. My hat badge must be fetched from the cloakroom as soon as the unpicking was complete. My blue and gold striped school tie was impounded immediately. I thought momentarily of confessing my reluctance to deface Win Penman's blazer, but quelled the impulse; my disinclination to disclose yet another crime was stronger. It might even have qualified as one of the 'dirty and disgusting habits' Johnny was forever attributing to us. (This expression also, we had made our own.)

Everyone's delight knew no bounds at this entertaining turn of events. Somehow, compounding our complicity, we managed to convince the sewing teacher that one of us had had a respectable clothing mishap, the repair of which required the instant application of needle, navy blue cotton, and scissors. Still collapsing occasionally into helpless laughter, we transferred my blazer badge to Pen's blazer. I went home devoid of AGGS label, and entertained my family with the details of the fiasco. No one considered for one moment that any of this could be my fault; they all 'knew what Dorothy was like', and could not imagine anyone taking such exception to her. Anyway, I didn't seem to mind, so why should they? And I didn't; it all seemed inexpressibly silly. I had wonderful friends, I was leading the sort of life I knew suited me, I was conscious of the affection and trust of those whose opinion mattered to me, and could simply laugh at the rest.

Heather Northey, who was at school in the mellower days of the sixties under Rua Gardner, wrote in her *History*: 'EMJ's strict control practically eliminated the possibility of those deeds of bravado which might have taken place earlier.' As one who suffered — and survived — EMJ's regime, I know that those venturesome spirits in the school who were not to be subdued by tyranny simply exercised a degree of cunning. Rigid subjection inevitably renders 'deeds of bravado' even more attractive to the truly intrepid.

Before the first term was out, Bro and I had found a way — through the dungeon — to the nether regions of the school and explored them thoroughly, with a torch. In almost total darkness, we unearthed nothing more exciting than a few old bottles, a boot or two and several ancient tobacco tins; but it was fun, and certainly illicit. We emerged looking like chimney sweeps, which discouraged us somewhat, but we had other subversive entertainment in mind. (Absenting ourselves from assembly — which led to my first demotion — was one.) Thereafter, in company with other miscreants (who in many cases later became prefects, and in all cases, later still, pillars of society) we made our way across the school roof to the tiny, enchanting, out-of-bounds tower which had no internal access. We had learned quite early that access to the roof was available through a cleaning cupboard halfway up the other 'official' tower stairs — and discovered with great joy on our arrival that there were simply *hundreds* of autographs written on, or carved into the tiny tower's posts, balustrades and walls.

We constantly flouted the 'straight-home-from-school-unless-authorised-by-letter-to-visit-dentist-or-doctor' rule and descended rejoicing to the city, often making dishonest use of the Farmers' Trading Company free trams and buses. Here we would spend an enjoyable hour in Whitcombe and Tombs' bookshop, where one of us might even, occasionally, be able to buy a book. I was steadily collecting Dickens in Collins Classic editions, at three shillings each; and that year, four of us combined to present ourselves with a Classic apiece at Christmas. Three shillings each, and you could choose your title. We did it the next year too. My original copy of *Silas Marner*, on the desk beside me as I write, is inscribed: 'To Dorothy, From Avis, Winifrid and Isobel.' We were well taught enough to know that inscriptions in books should strike a note of formal dignity: in real life Avis was always 'Tweet' (her name in Latin meaning 'bird'), Winifrid 'Win' or 'Pen', and Isobel 'Bro'. (The staff must have got wind of this unlikely scheme, as Miss Webster mentioned it to me many years later, when we met — and she had not taught us until the Sixth.)

Less innocently, by the time we were in the Fifth, we took to sneaking

into an occasional five-o'clock session at a Queen Street cinema, equipped
with delectable hot pies which we would eat once the lights went out. On
one notable occasion, in the general confusion of standing up for 'God Save
the King', someone contrived to drop a hot pie into someone else's hat —
a contingency provoking so much hysterical mirth that it was remarkable
we were not evicted. As a final extension of these depravities, in the Sixth,
we would take a delicious plunge into the Civic Fun Park where a huge
wheel with tiny carriages attached (the 'Octopus') would whirl us,
shrieking, through the night sky with the stars and the lights of Auckland
— reduced for the war, but never totally extinguished — reeling around
our dazed but delighted heads.

I suspect that several of our number were obliged to fabricate feasible
excuses at home for their absence on these exhilarating excursions. I, of
course, had my family's blessing always. There was never any necessity for
me to deceive them. Having fun was positively encouraged. Extraordinarily,
we were never caught. The possible repercussions do not bear contemplation. Expulsion might even have resulted from the exposure of such vice
— in which case the school would have jettisoned several university
scholarships, not to mention assorted honours and much distinction of one
sort and another as the years rolled by.

Most of our mistresses were strong, scholarly, hardworking women
who almost invariably remained single and devoted themselves to their
calling. They were otherwise as different from one another as any other set
of workmates or colleagues. Miss Gorrie was young, and beautifully dressed,
always. Her hair and makeup were those of a magazine model. Several
enthusiasts in our form actually kept track of the number of her stylish,
high-heeled shoes. She was an inspired teacher of History and Geography,
and ultimately lectured at the University of Auckland. I came top in
Geography in III A 1 mainly because I desired Miss Gorrie's approbation
— not my usual style, certainly — but also because I loved drawing and
colouring maps, and decorating work, and in our Geography books we had
free rein. At one point Miss Gorrie inscribed my book with 'Your work is a
pleasure to mark', and I thought I might die of the joy of it. I also came top
in Art, but this was purely accidental and had nothing to do with the Art
mistress, whose name I cannot recollect. Winning the 'Thrift Day' essay
prize was no great surprise either; I had won several at my earlier schools. I
by now had a rare line in sycophantic blather about the wisdom of 'saving

for a rainy day'. Still, a book voucher was a wonderful thing.

Miss Blond, who taught us History in IV A 1, was English, and memorable. She had a way of clamping her mouth shut at the end of sentences which was intimidating in the extreme. It was rumoured that she was a pacifist, and we were wide-eyed at this aberration. (She was fierce enough with us; perhaps it was only soldiers she was not prepared to shoot.) But we cherished her un-maiden-lady-style remarks, always delivered in a *very* pugilistic manner. 'Never judge a man by how clean his shirt is, girls!' was a delicious, slightly shocking piece of advice, we felt. Unfortunately, Miss Blond's socialistic sympathies did nothing to soften her distaste for contradiction (or even questioning) so she and I could never be comrades. Before long, I was obliged to spend every History period standing in front of the class, where, presumably, she could watch me and prevent any interruption. As this was the exact location of the somewhat inadequate heater, and winter was upon us, I did not really mind. I always felt that Miss Blond and I were sisters under the skin. But I was her match, and she didn't care to be matched.

Frances Powell — I never thought of her as 'Miss' — taught us History in the sixth form, and treated us as people. One could imagine *her* conducting her life normally out of school. Some of this endearing normality was explained when I read, in Northey's *History*, that Frances Powell (later Haughey) began her working life as a kindergarten teacher and later worked with the intellectually handicapped. No chance of losing touch with reality in either of these two spheres! We also enjoyed her tales of her frugal existence during her Teachers' Training College days in the Depression. She used to walk all the way from Ponsonby to Mount Eden, she told us, in company with another student who padded along in bare feet, carrying his only, irreplaceable, pair of shoes. Northey describes Frances Powell as 'particularly gifted with Upper Sixth Scholarship candidates', and I'm sure this was true, but I remember her as a person one might have encountered anywhere. (Most mistresses only 'looked right' in gowns, with a backdrop of blackboards.)

Miss Warnock, our form mistress in 1940, was a small, robin-redbreast-style figure with black hair in a twenties 'bob', plump pink cheeks, and small, round dark eyes which sparkled with enthusiasm: for mathematics in particular, and the brilliance of several Upper Sixth girls whom she was schooling for scholarships, in particular. Her passion for this project was so intense that we, her 'own' form, became her confidantes, and were caught up in the fervour. It was irresistible. Even those of us who had no passion for maths were swept along.

Miss Virtue, who taught us English in the fourth form, was a larger-than-life character whom we all loved. We harboured a notion that she was rather 'faster' than she should be, though no evidence for this exciting suspicion was ever forthcoming. But she read aloud to us, often for a whole period at a time, and we were entranced. She would even let us lean our heads on our arms while we listened. In the August holidays I forced Val and Denis, nine and seven respectively, to listen to the whole of *Silas Marner* read aloud, and they did, without protest. Gloomy and moralistic in the best Victorian tradition it had, at least, a lost-and-found child in it, and was all I had to hand. The experience — and Val's begging me for more each day — set me on a course from which I have never diverged. Someone, or something else, might have inspired me later, but Miss Virtue got me going, then and there. All one needs is a child and a book; and both of these have always been to hand, for the last fifty years.

Late in our fourth form year, Miss Virtue asked me if she might keep a piece of my work: a story we had to write, the opening paragraph of which was provided. I remember having enjoyed this exercise enormously and being astonished when I received full marks for it. It hadn't seemed hard to produce. Miss Virtue kept me behind the others, and told me that I wrote 'well enough to *write*'. I must have looked at her blankly, for she said, almost angrily, 'You could be a *writer*.' I had no idea what one should do to become a writer, and anyway, why me? Lots of people in the class got consistently higher marks than I did — I did well only when, as now, no preparation was required and I liked the assignment. The rest of the time I was either under-prepared, or worse still, hadn't even read the required book. Getting through all Dickens's novels, which I did by the end of the fourth form, not to mention *Wuthering Heights*, which I kept re-reading with ever-increasing fervour (I was in love with Heathcliff for years), *Gone with the Wind*, which my mother, astonishingly, bought me for my birthday, and a steady stream of film magazines, which appeared from somewhere (Mrs McDonald, perhaps?), plus a positive avalanche of ripsnorting westerns from Ross's friend Peter Arnott, ensured that I would have little time for any homework, even English. I was, if anything, embarrassed by Miss Virtue's assertion, and very pleased that she had not made it publicly. I thought about it briefly though. Here was someone else concerning herself with my 'future'. (Miss Warnock told me, many years later, that she had once, during this year, stomped into the staff common room saying, 'That Dorothy Norgrove will drive me mad!' Miss Virtue, who was marking books, had looked up, smiled and said, 'Ah, but she writes like an angel!' No review I have ever received since has pleased me more than this tribute. Miss Virtue must *really* have believed that I could 'write'!)

Apart from expecting, some day, to be grown up — and not too soon, I hoped — fourteen was the best age I'd been for years — I simply had no idea of doing anything except going to school. Of course, I would have to get a job some day; Ross had one already. Speculation was unprofitable — and anyway, I was in trouble again. Staying late at school for some purpose, and walking home as I often did along Ponsonby Road, I had been overtaken by Ross on his bike. Of course I accepted a lift on the bar — 'a double' we called it. Could anyone contemplate refusing such an offer? And who was the miserable sneak — a prefect, no less — who witnessed this innocent spectacle and reported it to Johnny? And what right did Johnny have to accuse me of lying when I asserted that 'the young man' was my brother? In no time at all I was guilty of an even graver sin than riding, in Grammar uniform, on the bar of a young man's bike (which I would have considered a fair cop): I had contradicted Miss Johnston by refuting her assertion that I was lying! Silliness to the nth degree, it seemed to me. I don't recall the consequences, but I know that I accepted 'doubles' from Ross on several future occasions, running the gauntlet without detection each time.

In September 1939 the long-delayed war between Britain and Germany began. Miss Johnston's editorial in the school magazine told of the distribution of gas masks and the digging of air-raid shelters in the London she had left to return home. She urged us all 'to be ready and willing to help if the call comes', and spoke of 'the principles of truth and justice which are, and ever will be, the guiding principles of the British Common-wealth of Nations to which we all belong'. None of us took much notice; we were always being urged to greater virtue and industry, and the avoidance of anything that smacked of levity and self-indulgence (or fun). And anyway, nothing much seemed to be happening here. All that fuss was on the other side of the world. Much was to happen, to our family and to others, before it was all over, and the world was to start up again. Meanwhile, nothing was as important as the onset of the cricket season, summer, and the long holidays.

NINETEEN

The AGGS school magazine was an impressive publication, and appeared annually. I was astonished in my first year to hear that one of my poems, written under orders in class, had been selected for the 'Literary Contributions' section. It was called 'Cricket'.

Its subject was, of course, dear to my heart. I had thought that cricket, as a topic, was probably not poetic enough to qualify for this particular assignment, but typically was unconcerned. I didn't aspire to publication anyway, and I *felt* like writing about cricket.

> Oh! Here is for cricket, with pad, bat and wicket,
>   And not forgetting the ball,
> And the cheer of the crowd, and a shout free and loud,
>   At the bowler's victory call.
> And the click of the bails, and the sighs and the wails
>   When the batsman goes out for 'a duck'
> And the crack of the bat, and a cry of 'Howzat?'
>   And the batsman bewailing his luck!
>
> Oh! Here's for some fun, in the rain or the sun,
>   If this is the game we are at,

With a thrill in the air, and a hush everywhere
    When the next man goes out with his bat,
And his heart leaping high for the fun that is nigh
    When he takes up his stand. Then a pause —
And he'll hit and he'll run, and the day, it is won!
    And he thrills to the sound of applause!

And so here's for cricket with pad, bat and wicket,
    And not forgetting the ball,
And the thrill of the cheers, ringing loud in your ears;
    Oh! This is the game for us all!

A very *manly* poem, it now seems to me; but the days of protest about the implied gender of pronouns, and the use of the generic 'man' were still far in the future. We thought — indeed we knew — that 'he' and 'his' used in this way applied to the *genus* 'man', and that *this* meant either sex.

Most aspiring poets in III A 1 penned odes to the seasons, the sea, and natural phenomena of one sort and another (bloody daffodils again). One of my friends, Val Parker, distinguished herself with a flurry of literary passion for cobwebs, which began: 'Oh Cobweb, you gossamer thing . . .!' and, being invited to read her poem aloud to the class, delivered this line with such passionate ardour that she reduced her unfeeling friends to gales of quite unfair hilarity. We never allowed Val to forget this fervent tribute to cobwebs. (I reminded her of it recently, sixty years after the event. We have been friends ever since.) Miss Ward glared at us, I recall, and accused us of lacking literary sensitivity. We all tried to look chastened.

Next year, Val used her undoubted gift for rhetoric to win the Fourth Form Speech Competition, and we all applauded wildly. There was a place for everything, we felt. Miss Roseveare, our elocution mistress, tried to persuade me to enter this competition, but I demurred, and ultimately escaped. 'You have a very good voice,' she told me. (I think she meant *loud.*) 'But do you have a slightly older brother? Perhaps . . .' I ignored her well-meant advice that I consider refining my tone and mode of expression; I had no intention of going down the 'How-now-brown-cow' road. But I liked Miss Roseveare, and merely employed my proven method of defence: smile cheerfully and take no notice.

In England, they called the first three months of World War II in 1939 'the phoney war'. Not a single British soldier was killed or wounded during this time, though children were steadily evacuated from London, and feverish preparations made for 'the real war' which would surely come.

In New Zealand, adults glued their ears anxiously to the crackling reports that came nightly on the wireless from the BBC in London. Men and mere boys presented themselves in large numbers at recruiting offices, many with little idea of the real issues involved, but anxious 'to serve', as their fathers and uncles had twenty-five years earlier. 'Where Britain goes, we go' was still the guiding principle. When, just before Christmas 1939, news came that the German pocket battleship *Admiral Graf Spee*, badly damaged by Allied warships including our own *Achilles*, had been sunk by her captain to avoid certain capture, we all rejoiced. Here was proof indeed that Britain still ruled the waves, as she always had; and of course, always would. How little we knew of what was really happening! I wrote a poem in Henry Newbold style:

> Achilles, Ajax, Exeter —
> Here's to the bold and free!

❧

School went back in February 1940 and we learned that henceforth we might change out of our black woollen stockings, once at school, into white cotton socks. (Naturally, we could not be seen in the *street* thus under-clothed.) Joy unparalleled! The dispensation arose from the difficulty in procuring the wretched stockings, and in no way conceded the unsuitability of wool for encasing schoolgirl legs in the summer heat. Soldiers' uniforms must come first, we were told. Our agreement was heartfelt.

Before long, we were mobilised to knit. (Mrs Beuth's tuition stood me in excellent stead, here.) Vast bundles of khaki wool were dispensed, with patterns. I began with a scarf, but found it so boring that I moved on to a balaclava, and then to a pair of mittens — gloves that left the tips of the fingers uncovered. After a bit of fumbling, and much dashing next door for help, I learned to produce a wearable mitten, and stuck with this item for the duration. I was very proud of my accomplishment; I had always admired practical skills. Anyone could write an essay, I thought, but to turn out a useful garment, build a set of shelves or repair a mechanical contraption — there was talent for you!

Life went on in its well-ordered, predictable way at school. One of its most regular features involved my descent into trouble of one sort or another, due mainly to my propensity for insubordinate argument and a tendency to be engaged enthusiastically on projects that had definitely not originated in the classroom. I think I must have been a maddening pupil in some ways. Most of the girls were frightened of getting into trouble; terrified, in some cases, of being reported to the headmistress, with inevitable repercussions at home. I had no such anxiety, and found it hard to take Johnny's outbursts seriously. I simply did not believe that we were the reprehensible specimens of our kind that she painted us; nor that anyone in her right mind would aspire to the heights of painful and humourless virtue she proposed.

At home, we were in for another shock, and it came. Dad announced that he had 'joined up'! He and Mum had discussed the possibility in private, and now it was an accomplished fact. New Zealand was recruiting men in ever-increasing numbers, and they must all be fed whilst in training. A call had gone out for skilled cooks, butchers and bakers to volunteer and 'do their bit'. Dad needed a job; he was thirty-eight, and would not be expected to go overseas. He would be based in a New Zealand camp, subject to army discipline, with regular leave. We were astounded. Our father in uniform! A *soldier*! Would he have to learn to march, to shoulder a gun, to *shoot* a gun? Dad had no answer to these questions, but he told us that this would be a real, secure job; and an important one. Mum would have a regular income, which would come straight to her, every fortnight. His own accommodation, food and clothing would be provided by the army.

Both our parents seemed pleased. Mum had feared that Dad might not pass his 'medical'; he had never been robust, and the years of drinking had taken their toll. Before the news was broken to his children, however, he had passed this test and been declared 'fit to serve'. He was to report to the Narrow Neck Camp in Devonport, less than a mile away from our next-door-to-the-Camerons house in Old Lake Road of ten years before.

Everything seemed to happen at once. Next time we saw Dad, he was resplendent in uniform: the long, belted, much-pocketed jacket as worn by New Zealand soldiers in World War I (the Great War, we still called it) and the famous 'lemon-squeezer' hat. We thought Dad looked wonderful in his uniform, and told our friends proudly of his gesture. It must have pleased Dad to see renewed respect in Ross's eyes; and I suspect that the enforced part-separation was a relief for Mum. Day-to-day anxiety about the extent of Dad's drinking was removed from her shoulders overnight. When he was made a corporal, we knew that Dad had found a niche in which he could succeed. The rigid structure of everyday army life was exactly what he needed. And of course, he was quickly popular with the other men. We would have expected that.

We waited eagerly for Dad's first leave and greeted him with hugs and cries of joy. When we heard that he *had* been obliged to march, and drill, and carry a gun, we were wide-eyed. Dad assured us that this instruction was simply army routine for all soldiers, including the men of the Army Service Corps. 'I won't be shooting anyone, thank God,' he said. It was impossible to imagine anyway; but then war itself was impossible to imagine in peaceful New Zealand.

There was no doubt about it; the army was good for Dad. He was clearer of eye and fitter of body than he had been for years. Regular meals and sleep — the latter dictated by exhaustion as well as regulation, he told us ('We work like slaves!') — had even put a little flesh on his spare frame, and he was jaunty and confident.

We still listened nightly to the news from London, and in the early summer months of 1940, it was sobering. Among our elders, we detected unease. It was unthinkable that Britain could be erecting barbed-wire barricades on her southern coast, mining beaches with holiday names like Bognor and Folkstone, but it was true. Hitler intended to invade. Britain expected him to. If British factories had worked feverishly before, they were now working round the clock in a frantic effort to turn out anti-aircraft guns, rifles, tanks and, above all, fighter aircraft.

On his next leave, Dad told us that he had been asked to go overseas with the Second Echelon (the first had already left) and that he had agreed. Mum was pale, but did not protest. We three children were impressed. Many of our friends had older brothers in the forces, but few had fathers who were young enough and fit enough to 'go away'. And of course, it wouldn't be for long. Everyone knew that the war would be won quite quickly. Anyway, the Americans were sure to come in on our side any minute . . .

Dad left New Zealand with the Second Echelon, destination unknown to the public, in early May, 1940. The Auckland contingent paraded down Queen Street, and we all went to watch. There were thousands of men, all fit and eyes-front, but smiling as the military bands played and the huge crowd of onlookers cheered. Our eyes ached, watching for Dad — and then there he was, with his rifle on his shoulder, slim and straight and smiling. We cheered until we were hoarse.

A week before they finally left, there was an 'open day' at Papakura Camp, where the 'overseas' men had been assembled. We all went by special, free train from Auckland station. It was a fine, Sunday afternoon; there was an air of informality and fun about the event — almost like a gala — with throngs of relatives and friends, from babies to old men and women, bands playing, and tea and cakes for all in a big tent. Dad introduced us proudly to his friends, and showed us where he ate, and slept. Such a skinny, hard little bed, we thought, with nothing but a pillow and a few grey blankets in a pile on one end. But Dad was his old self, making us laugh, and listening eagerly to our news.

We could only feel happy as the train bore us back to Auckland. And we would see Dad again before he left. Certainly, only on the railway station, as the men boarded the train for Wellington, and embarkation; but still, we hadn't had to say a final goodbye on this lovely summer day. And the afternoon tea had been wonderful!

❧

It was almost dark, a few days later, as we presented our special tickets for admission to the platform where men of the Auckland contingent who were to be part of the Second Echelon awaited their train for Wellington, and their last contact with their families. Dad found us quite quickly. The men were all wearing their new, more comfortable 'battle dress', with waist-length 'lumber jacket' and soft, Scottish-style cap, and I thought how handsome my father looked. The party flavour of the open day was entirely absent; people were smiling resolutely, determined 'to give the boys a good send-off', but few smiles reached the eyes. Many of 'the boys' were truly boys, looking as if they might be off to Scout camp, rather than war.

The men's high spirits kept the tone of the huge gathering intact until the command for them to board the train. Then final, frantic embraces were snatched. Dad hugged each of us in turn, speechlessly, and then he and Mum were clinging to each other, and I could see that Mum was crying. I felt wooden, and Ross was expressionless. It was quite unreal. I knew I should feel something, but I didn't; only a frozen detachment. Val, only nine, looked small, and forlorn and frightened, and Dad tried to cheer her up with a laugh, and another hug, before he disappeared into a carriage.

Departure was accomplished army-style: all to orders, no fuss. The crowd waved, unidentifiable khaki-clad figures could be seen waving back through windows . . . and then there was nothing; only silence.

What can the wives, parents, brothers and sisters, and children of men who have just left to be swallowed up in a war say to each other? We all filed through the barrier, and into the station. There were a few, insistently jovial voices, mainly those of older men. The complaining murmurs and cries of tired, uncomprehending small children lent an air of normality to the procession, but we were a bleak band.

Mum, Ross, Val and I walked in silence through the echoing vaults of the big station, up the ramps into the forecourt, and out on to the street. Then we walked to Queen Street, where we caught the tram home. Mum would make cocoa for us all, we knew, and Ross and I would make hot toast in the wonderful new electric toaster he had bought for us at Christmas.

Dad was to be gone for three and a half years. His few months in camp in New Zealand had accustomed us to his daily absence from our lives, but this was different. It was as if he had simply disappeared.

TWENTY

My mother died in 1982 at the age of ninety. Among her effects was a bundle of letters, tied with a ribbon. All were addressed to Mrs W. V. Norgrove, in my father's handwriting, and bore the label 'On Active Service'. Most also bore the censor's stamp which became so familiar to servicemen's families during the war.

I had not considered reading these at the time of my mother's death. My father wrote separate letters to each of us and often included these in our mother's envelope. But we never read Mum's letters; indeed, she would keep ours for us to read ourselves, always. Example is clearly more effective than instruction. Reading letters intended by Dad for Mum's eyes alone was not to be considered. And so they stayed in their package, in a box in the top of one of our wardrobes and, in time, were forgotten; until a few days ago, when I faced the fact that I might — perhaps even should — after nearly sixty years, read them.

I have done this. I have read every letter, enclosed each one in a new, larger envelope, marked it with its date, assigned it a number, and arranged all in a suitable sized box in old-fashioned catalogue style. I thought this would take me a few hours, but in fact, it occupied my total attention for almost three days. Of course I did other things during this time, but my father was seldom out of my mind. He seemed to be alive again; a thirty-nine-year-old man (younger than either of my sons!) cast suddenly in a role he could never have imagined, and exiled from family, home and country for an unknowable length of time.

I had not realised, or had forgotten, that Mum had written to Dad the day after we farewelled him from the Auckland railway station. Relatives must have been given a special address for this purpose; the letters were delivered to the men on their first day at sea. We did not receive Dad's first letter to us for some months after he left. Although we had expected this delay, it seemed like an eternity. Dad really *had* disappeared. No information at all was given out by those in power about the movement of troops. The silence was complete.

And then, the letter, with enclosures for the three of us. Sixty years later I am glad to know that Dad received Mum's first letter so promptly: the only one, during all his war service, to be read shortly after it was written. We had embarked, had we only known, on a frustrating period during which letters could be lost entirely (when ships went down), sent to the wrong 'theatre of war' (because troops had been dispatched elsewhere without notice) or suffer indefinable casualties of a thousand kinds. Sometimes, letters would arrive in the wrong order; often, the writer would presume knowledge that the recipient did not have — a clear and tantalising sign of lost or delayed mail. One seemed always to be casting letters into a sort of limbo from which they might, or might not, ultimately flutter down into the hands of the addressee. This could hardly be called correspondence; one simply churned out a sort of monologue interspersed with questions, the answers to which would probably never be forthcoming. Dad's letter to Mum, written during his first few days aboard ship, arrived in company with others written either at sea, or after his arrival in England. For the Second Echelon — christened 'the glamour boys' by less 'fortunate' New Zealand soldiers — was diverted to England, instead of joining the First Echelon in Egypt. Britain's state was perilous at this time. Her army had been driven out of Europe, and France had surrendered to the Germans. Invasion seemed inevitable; a large force of colonial troops, however incompletely trained, was more than welcome.

Dad's first letter, once I had arranged the clutch in correct sequence, was seen to have been written in stages at sea, long before the troops suspected they were bound for England. (They were never told, but one of

Dad's subsequent 'somewhere at sea' letters mentioned a rumour, and the censor for once left this piece of information intact.) After 'My Dearest Em', and the hope that we were all well, Dad told us of the Echelon's departure from Wellington:

> We left N.Z. on a dull grey morning — the departure was kept very quiet . . . It was an experience I will never forget — the bustle on the wharf — the casting off of the ropes — our ship slowly drawing away from our berth — the churn of propellers — the little tug always at hand if needed — the boys all singing in one voice 'Now is the hour, for us to say Goodbye' — then the realisation that I had left you and the kiddies for perhaps a long time . . . Dearest, my greatest thrill was yet to come — lunch is on, I am sitting in front of a goodly helping of roast beef, vegetables etc — one of our N.C.O.'s handed me a letter — your letter — I cannot write what I felt and how happy I was to hear from you . . .

My father wrote in what used to be called 'a fine hand', strong and flowing; a page of his writing is good to look at, all these years later, and this is a seven-page letter.

Dad described life aboard a huge liner with thousands of other men, and then mentioned his three children, in turn: 'How is our big son?', and then, after asking about Ross's work at the Standard Optical Company: 'If Ross is not satisfied and wishes to go elsewhere, let him, as I have a lot of confidence in him and know he will get on if given the chance . . .' Then me: 'Let her have her third year at Grammar if everything goes well . . . although I know she is very headstrong, she has brains and knows how to use them . . .' Headstrong? What a quaint old word. I suppose it described me. I overheard Mum tell someone, about this time, in her cheerfully patient way, 'Dorothy will always do exactly what she *wants* to do,' and I remember reflecting that she was right. On to Val: 'Is Val still as methodical as ever? How is she getting on with her dancing?' (Auntie had started another dancing class, and Val was attending — and Mum played the piano and earned a few extra shillings every week.) 'Are she and Denis still as pally as ever . . .?'

I feel, reading these sixty-year-old comments, that my father, whose devotion to us I have never doubted, was making a real effort to play a role in our lives, however remote. It is impossible to know how Dad

contemplated his own poor performance as breadwinner in the recent past
— to mention only one of his inadequacies — and retain his self-respect,
or even if he did. Was he apprehensive that we three, as we grew older,
would start to judge him? For Ross had *not* had the 'chance' Dad now
hoped for him; he was certainly to 'get on' as his father predicted, but this
was solely due to his extraordinary energy and determination. Ross's lack
of secondary education did not, in the end, prevent his realising his
ambition (which increasingly involved boats and the sea) but would
certainly have handicapped, if not defeated, a boy of lesser intelligence,
cheerful good humour, and capacity for hard work. It was everyone's good
fortune that he had no capacity at all for resentment, or grudge bearing.

Meanwhile, Dorothy was to be allowed a third year at Grammar . . .
As if Mum would have forced me to leave, or prevented me from doing so
had I been so inclined — or Dad, either, had he been at home! All these
years later, I feel guilty that I, 'headstrong' as I was, never even considered
leaving school to help the family economy. I can only plead that Ross, in
particular, always seemed to approve of me, and what I was doing. And
Mum, of course, desired only that we should all be happy. (These factors
may have explained my nonchalance, but hardly excused it.)

Before long, a way of contributing fell into my lap, so that, at least, I
was never again obliged to use family money for school books. Mr Beuth
worked longer and longer hours as a bricklayer, now that so many young
tradesmen had joined the services. Both our houses had large back lawns
and smaller front plots, which sloped steeply to the road. Ross mowed our
lawns. I remember him, with Mervyn's help, taking our ancient hand-
mower to pieces and reassembling it with much earnest cogitation. When
Mr Beuth suggested that I should mow his lawns — for half-a-crown a
time — my joy knew no bounds.

The Beuths' mower was new and shiny. I learned quickly how to oil
it — the only attention it ever required — and thereafter kept the lawns
next door in excellent order, clipping the edges with a new pair of shears
and enormous satisfaction. If I had been given to introspection, I might
have felt guilty that Ross mowed our lawns without payment. Alas, no
such thought assailed me, though I did notice, as the months rolled by,
that the Norgrove lawns fell further and further behind the standard
maintained by the neighbouring Beuths. Not only did our old mower
present constant problems, but Ross's enthusiasm for things nautical

tended to get in the way — and Mum was not one to fuss, inside or out.

I have never forgotten the Beuths' lawns. In the summer, I would get up very early on a Sunday morning. No worry about waking the neighbourhood; this mower emitted only a soft purr. In term time, I would usually prop a book up on the revolving clothesline. From this I would (supposedly) learn French or Latin vocabulary, or attempt to imbibe some of the appallingly boring and incomprehensible scientific facts without which, we were assured, we could not safely face life. I was obliged to face life, in the end, under-equipped. The properties of acids, bases, salts and oxides were inextricably muddled in my reluctant mind and remained so. They served one purpose, however. I had been conceited enough to believe that I could learn anything, if I wanted to. I discovered that I couldn't learn the properties of acids, bases, salts and oxides and retain them even if I *had* wanted to. In the end I *did* want to. I still muddled them, hopelessly. Science, reputedly supremely logical, never seemed so to me. A smidgeon of humility invaded my soul. After all, there were girls in my form who, while clearly bound for a 'science' future, still passed in English and History, my subjects.

The Beuths' lawns not only, in time, increased my 'book money' cache to a size that allowed me to contemplate buying an occasional book that was *not* a textbook, but provided my first stirrings of satisfaction in a job neatly and precisely done, and *finished*. My mother's lack of interest in housework, while it certainly provided a background against which almost any childhood game or activity was possible, began to annoy, and occasionally exasperate me, as I grew. I took to making sporadic attacks on the drawers in the kitchen, the cabinet in the bathroom, the unclassifiable mess in the wash-house . . . but it all seemed futile. No one *wanted* their mess cleared up. (Understandably; the air would be rent with cries of 'What happened to the . . .? Where's my . . .?' after one of my sorties.) I gave up. I didn't really mind . . . well, not much, and not all the time.

Before long, another modest but regular source of income surfaced. Dad's only sister, Auntie Maud, asked me if I would help her son, my cousin Lloyd, with his French. Lloyd was only a year behind me at school, and was fortunately 'on' the same French textbook series as we used, so this was easy. I simply worked through his book with him, giving him the individual attention he needed, but was unlikely to get at school. He was a quiet, rather shy boy, but by no means slow.

Fortunately — perhaps surprisingly — Lloyd seemed to be agreeable about this project, and all went well. He had been born when his mother was no longer young, and his father had died when he was only six months old. Auntie Maud, with baby Lloyd, had moved back home to live with Grandma and Grandpa Norgrove in Westmere. Lloyd, a handsome boy with, to quote my mother, 'a lovely nature' was thereafter cherished and sheltered by his mother and grandmother, and repressed by his autocratic grandfather. There was not a lot of fun in Lloyd's life, Ross and I thought. He would always stay on for a while after his French 'lesson', his admiration for Ross and his activities apparent to all. Poor Lloyd. In the end, he would have to go. (Lloyd's schedule was carefully monitored.) He would depart, wistful, over-clean for a Saturday morning, thanking my mother politely, his books under his arm.

Auntie Maud was kind, but starchy. She was always beautifully dressed, and smelled of lavender. (At least, I imagined it was lavender.) She had been converted by a preacher called Dallimore, a sort of early Billy Graham, who held 'revival' meetings in the Town Hall, and, according to his converts, affected miraculous cures. He used mass hypnotism, and used to purvey 'blessed' handkerchiefs, which he claimed would cure their owners of any illness or disease. Auntie Maud frequently pressed one of these on me. It, also, would smell of lavender, and be so dainty and decorated that I could not possibly use it for the vulgar purpose of blowing my nose. Anyway, you never knew.

I had not envisaged being paid for helping a cousin whom I liked anyway, but Auntie Maud always sent Lloyd equipped with sixpence for me. Lloyd's French improved spectacularly, and the Edmonds Baking Powder tin in my bedroom, repository of my wealth, grew heavier by the week. One day I would own a real bookcase, with books on every shelf.

From the other side of the world, news of the heroism and horror of the Dunkirk evacuation came crackling over our wireless. The drama of the rescue of 340,000 Allied soldiers from death or capture on Belgian beaches by hundreds of little ships (private yachts, fishing boats, tugs, colliers and pleasure steamers, as well as naval vessels) lent a sense of triumph, even romance, to an event that was in reality a disastrous defeat. 'Wars are not won by evacuations' were Churchill's stark, admonitory words. A few weeks earlier, only one week after Dad's departure with the Second Echelon, Winston Churchill had replaced Neville Chamberlain as Prime Minister of Great Britain. We heard Churchill's first speech in the House of Commons as Prime Minister a day later. 'I have nothing to offer but blood, toil, tears and sweat . . .' We could not know that these words would be handed down the decades — centuries, probably — but we felt their grandeur, sensed that a new passion had invaded the scene. Churchill gave the public *words*, glorious apposite words, arranged in surprising ways to stimulate and inspire. He talked about 'trackless ocean wastes' when lesser souls would have made reference to wide seas; he told the people of Britain that 'We shall fight on the beaches, we shall fight on the landing grounds, we shall fight in the fields and in the streets, we shall fight in the hills . . .' and you could almost hear them saying, 'Yes, by God we will!' In an extraordinary way Churchill, a son of the nobility and an aging man — he was sixty-six when he assumed office in 1940 — achieved a degree of intimacy with the ordinary people of Britain that was unprecedented. His words took root in the hearts and minds of people who were facing the horrifying possibility of invasion and defeat, and warmed them.

Our elders in New Zealand may have been truly conscious of this cliff-edge situation in the distant 'motherland', but it occupied small space in the minds of the young. Even those whose brothers or fathers had departed for the fray still, at this stage, saw 'the war' as a somewhat exciting, unexpected occurrence in their lives. What we today know as 'the media' (comprising, in those days, newspapers, the wireless and the 'news-reels', which preceded 'the big picture' at the cinema) dwelt on the 'gallantry of our fine forces'. The announcers used a jaunty, brisk style, even when delivering bad news. The populace was to be at all costs kept happy; that way, energy would be maximised, morale boosted.

Meanwhile, at school, a diverting exercise had been introduced: air-raid drill. We were all required to wear small bags round our necks, under our blouses, containing an identification disk, cotton wool to stuff in our ears, and a cork to bite on, during the expected attack. Expected? None of us believed that anyone would ever rain bombs on *us*. It all seemed farcical; an entertaining diversion to rescue you temporarily from Maths, Latin, History, Science (depending on the luck of the day) and provide opportunity for a bit of fun. The operation involved abandoning our desks at the clanging of the school bell, and proceeding 'in orderly file' out of the

school and into Western Park, just next door. Here, we would lie prone on
our stomachs, under the huge old trees, stuffing mouths and ears according
to plan and shrouding our heads with our gym tunics. This manoeuvre
exposed five hundred sets of voluminous black bloomers encasing nether
regions of a variety of amplitudes, and one thousand black-stockinged legs
from matchstick to tree-trunk model — a startling contemplation for
casual park strollers, or pedestrians in Howe Street. A head (or perhaps
bottom) count would be made by mistresses, and the tableau maintained
for several minutes. Then, at the signal of a piercing whistle, we would
restore our rumpled selves, consign cork and cotton wool to our little bags
and return 'in orderly file' to school.

A further development involved the appointment of 'runners' to
convey information to 'Air Raid Precaution Headquarters', which had been
set up in Pitt Street, in those days accessible only by way of Karangahape
Road. Runners were chosen for their fleetness of foot and (I suspect) their
general pushiness: a quality not encouraged in our ranks ordinarily, but
likely to be of use in the event of an enemy attack. It is perhaps unsurpris-
ing that I was selected as a runner. There were about six of us, and we used
to conduct our own private race, once equipped with imaginary statistics
of the dead, dying and wounded among us and dispatched on our heroic
mission. Naturally, strict school protocol as regards uniform applied if we
were to be seen outside the gates. The ludicrous sight of a posse of
Grammar girls, hatted and gloved, with blazers firmly buttoned, thundering along Karangahape Road — even in those days amply peppered with
pedestrians and traffic — must have convinced the populace that there
really *was* a national emergency, or that these unfortunate girls were fleeing
from some unspeakable horror at school. (Grammar was known to practise
uncompromising discipline.) I enjoyed a private fantasy of the other
runners all falling to enemy fire, while I alone, hatless, one arm dangling
useless, my face streaked with dirt and blood, staggered into the
headquarters to report total carnage in Western Park . . .

We were used to regimentation by bells at school; *real* heavy, brass
bells, rung by prefects. Every year on the 25th of April, Anzac Day, we were
summoned to rise for two minutes' silence in honour of the fallen men in
World War I. And there was always fire drill. Intended as an orderly
evacuation, this usually resembled a stampede, and was enjoyed by all. My
cousin Irma, ahead of me at school, recounted a delicious fiasco which had

resulted from a teacher mistaking the Anzac Day call to silence for a fire drill. It is hard to believe that all thirty girls in the form were similarly deluded, but at Miss Whatever's urgent instigation they sprang enthusiastically to their feet and pounded down the stairs to the tune of her shouted encouragement: 'Hurry along girls! Hurry along girls!' The din, in the silent school — the silent *city*; all traffic stopped, factories switched off their machines, and people stood still in the streets — must have been tumultuous. In the hall, the rabble faltered to a sheepish stop, confronted by the outraged figure of Miss Johnston. She who could not bear the most infinitesimal divergence from protocol (and had no sense of humour whatever) must have been in danger of spontaneous combustion.

Apparently, nothing was said to the girls. No one dared enquire what was said, in private, to the luckless Miss Whatever. She was reported to have 'looked pale for a week or so'.

TWENTY-ONE

I have always taken comfort from the thought of my father's sojourn in England, with the Second Echelon. Despite later experiences in London during the worst of the 'blitz', I know that he enjoyed it. There can be no doubt that the Second Echelon — 'the glamour boys' — were infinitely more fortunate than any of their peers in this unexpected diversion. It was, of course, none of *their* doing, and a great many of them were later to be killed or wounded in Greece, Crete or the Western Desert.

Trying to assemble the details of Dad's travels before he and the rest of the Echelon arrived in Egypt has been difficult; his letters are full of anxious questions and touching remarks about his separation from us: 'What I would give to see you all, just for a few minutes . . .', apologies for writing what he calls 'much ado about nothing' as censorship was so strict, and his longing for mail. 'Seven weeks at sea, without a line from those I love best . . .' And in August, still, 'I have not had any mail from N.Z. as all our mail went to Egypt and it has not arrived here yet — also, I have heard that some of our mail has been sunk near England and some went down on the *Niagara* . . .' Again, in a letter dated 8th September: 'I have not had one letter from New Zealand and it is nearly five months since we left . . . still, I'm not the only one — all the boys are longing for news from home . . .'

It seems likely that this dearth of mail was one of the few drawbacks to being part of the otherwise fortunate Second Echelon. Fifty-eight years later, I can hardly bear to know that my father was bereft of any contact with us — with *me!* — for so long. I know that my mother wrote regularly, and urged the three of us to greater effort when we might have flagged. It is almost too much to bear . . . But halfway down page six of this eleven-page letter I am rescued from total anguish: 'Great Rejoicing — I've just been handed eight letters from NZ . . .!'

Eight letters? Where were all the others? (In Egypt, or at the bottom of the ocean with the *Niagara*, one can only surmise.) Among the eight letters was one in which Mum had enclosed the addresses of Mrs Beuth's mother and sister, with Mrs Beuth's earnest plea that Dad get in touch with them — even visit if he had leave. We didn't hear until after the Christmas of 1940 that Dad had actually visited and been invited to stay with the Races, Mrs Beuth's relations in Manchester, and that the visit had been a huge success. (This was confirmed by letters from the Races to the Beuths, but civilian letters also, in those days of uncertainty, could take months.) Well, of course we knew they would like Dad, and he reported that Mrs Race was 'just like Mrs Beuth, but a little stouter' so we knew how welcoming she would have been. And Dad had been equipped with reasonably up-to-date news about 'their' Millie, who had been borne off by a New Zealander called Lionel Beuth, complete with little Denis, and of baby Beverley, whom they had never seen. And Dad, being Dad, actually *knew* these children, in a way many men in those days (and perhaps these) would not have.

I recall that both we and the Beuths were vastly amused by Dad's account of himself with the Race parents, their grown son and daughter and a stray aunt all sleeping, between three double beds, in the Races' basement-cum-air-raid-shelter. 'In No. 1 Bed,' wrote Dad, 'Mr and Mrs Race, No. 2 Bed, Doreen and her aunt, No. 3 Bed, John and myself . . . I am having such a good time, and such a change from camp.' Dad went on to tell us of the Races' wonderful hospitality, and the 'conducted tours' they had given him around Manchester.

This was in late October 1940, exactly six months after he had left New Zealand. Reading this letter now, I find solace not only in Dad's enjoyment of England, but also in the knowledge that he had received at least some of our mail in the previous month. Several more letters had arrived since, he told Mum, including 'one from Dorothy telling me how well she did in her exams . . .' (a certain amount of selective reporting is evident here) . . . and then, 'We have been very lucky to be blest with such wonderful kiddies. Ross, Dorothy and Val are always with me, and you know I am longing for the day when we (You and I) will be united as never before . . .' He was an intensely loving man, my father; and conscious of our love for him, I think.

Earlier, in letters written before any of ours reached him, Dad had told us of the troops' twenty-four hour long train journey from their unspecified port of arrival, to their undisclosed destination. 'Everything you ever read about the English countryside is true. I love England, and some day I hope to bring you here. I feel selfish that I am seeing it without you . . .' Later, the typical New Zealander's shock at the overcrowding so common in older countries comes through: 'Cities where people are herded together in rows and rows of brick tenements which are all alike — built right onto the road and some of them with very small and sometimes no backyards . . . how these people bring their children up healthy is beyond me.' (Mum's point exactly, of course, when she campaigned in her quiet way to get us out of Symonds Street!)

But he told us, too, of lanes and hedgerows, fields of clover and wild-flowers, glimpses of ancient castles almost lost in 'bush', women and children working in fields waving a welcome as the troop train went by, tiny villages 'each with a beauty of its own', old churches and little streams . . . and then arrival at their final station, and a two-mile march to their camp, 'under canvas'. 'If only I had a gift for description,' said Dad, 'I'd be able to convey things to you better . . .' (For a boy who was turned into a butcher at thirteen, Bill Norgrove managed to document his doings and describe his surroundings remarkably well, it seems to me. Why hadn't *he* been offered 'a chance'?)

Dad's cheerful enthusiasm — his sheer well-being — comes through as he describes their living conditions: '. . . good meals, comfortable tents — fairly long hours but favoured with wonderful weather . . . a pleasant time. During the last couple of weeks we have been away from camp on manoeuvres. We have been all over a certain county — a different camping site every day — the country and scenery we have passed through beggars description. To mention only a few of the wonderful sights — an old church built in 1280, a paddle mill 1816 . . . old castles with wonderful grounds ... At the present moment we are in a grove of tall old oaks with a small stream only a few yards away — children are fishing and romping on the banks — everything peaceful.'

Then, a day later: 'We had word to shift camp in the early morning, so I had to leave your letter. We had a wonderful trip, with just as good weather and scenery ... At the moment we are camped in a great grove of beech trees. We went for a walk this afternoon. The fields are still a carpet of wild flowers and we found blackberries, hazelnuts, elderberries and hawthorn berries ... Wilf and I had a really good time.'

Dad had mentioned Wilf Wray on numerous occasions, and I find myself as I read growing fond of Wilf. He was certainly an army friend; we had not known him earlier, and never met him after the war. Perhaps he lived elsewhere in New Zealand, and Dad simply lost touch with him. I am gripped by a feeling of unease. Did Dad's friend Wilf come back? Unlike my father, he was not stationed at Headquarters, but was 'up in the desert' once they arrived in Egypt. Dad told us later about numerous friends who were killed or wounded. Was Wilf among them? I cannot remember.

Why do I feel, reading these old letters, that Wilf was good for my father? There is a photograph taken in Cairo in 1941 (or 1942; it is undated) of Dad, with 'the Wray boys', Wilf and his brother Derry, who were 'down from the desert on leave' and had, to quote Dad, 'looked me up'. He gave a few details on the back of the photo, and assured Mum that they were drinking 'Ginger-Ale — that's the truth ...' Was he trying to reassure her, without exposing his weakness to the world (or the censor), that he was *not* 'drinking'? Certainly, Dad's eyes are clear, his half-smile in the photograph utterly natural. We knew that he had been made a sergeant in England, and been promised further promotion. Didn't this mean that he was not only working hard and with initiative (he always did that) but staying sober? Mum must have hoped — even prayed, in her own way. Ross may have wondered; I, by contrast, did not even reflect. I simply missed him; but less and less, I suppose, as time went on and my own concerns obtruded.

Dad was to see a little of England, and something of Scotland and Wales, too, before Egypt seized him for the rest of his war service. He managed a tour of Oxford, his father's birthplace, where he was enchanted by 'the ancient colleges, the whole atmosphere of the place ...' and spent a fourteen-day leave in Glasgow, Chester, Manchester and Liverpool as the guest of families who had offered hospitality to Commonwealth servicemen. Dad spoke glowingly of the warm welcome these people gave him; leaving each family when the time came was like parting from *real* family, he told us. 'If only I had your and Dorothy's gift for description — what I could write,' he said in one letter, but I doubt either Mum or I could have done better.

In September 1940, in a letter from Aldershot (the first time he had ever named the camp) Dad told us that he had been chosen as one of ten A.S.C. men to take a catering course at Lyons, in London. He sounded excited, exhilarated even, at the prospect. Lyons, he told us, were the biggest caterers in England — they employed 40,000 people in their London factory alone; many more at their famous 'Corner Houses' and throughout the country. 'Over 250,000, all told,' Dad had scribbled in the margin. He described this posting as 'a wonderful opportunity . . .' and looked forward to living in London, away from his unit 'in spite of air raids'.

We were to learn from later letters of the terrifying nature of life in Central London in late 1940, when the Battle of Britain was fought out in the sky overhead by day, and German bombers dropped their lethal cargo by night. Dad and his mates became very used to air raids; once, the Victoria League Club where they lived suffered a near miss and every single one of its hundreds of windows was shattered. A year later, we learned from Dad in Egypt that the Club had suffered a direct hit by a bomb shortly after the Echelon had left England, and had been completely demolished. 'The manageress and secretary who were both wonderful women were killed, along with a lot of soldiers and airmen,' my father wrote, asking Mum to be sure to keep the photo of the Club, which he had sent earlier. The photo is still in its envelope . . . 'I felt it very much when I heard of it . . .'

❧

Meanwhile, back in the sagging old sofa in Ponsonby, Auckland, New Zealand, I am lost in the salons of Regency England as seen through the eyes and pen of Georgette Heyer. The sofa itself has now assumed the contours of a hammock. Every afternoon, Val and her friends practise circus gymnastics over its back and arms. Bebbie and I regularly demand our turn for 'bouncy games' (Bebbie is a manic bouncer; I merely stand by to avert catastrophe) and nightly, Ross's friends, by now all gruff voice and muscle with a sprinkling of acne, cast themselves on to its creaking springs and drooping arms to enjoy Roy Rogers ('The Wheel of the Wagon is Broken'), sultry 'vocalists' of the South Seas persuasion ('The Royal Hawaiian Hotel') and of course, Gene Autrey ('South of the Border'). Mum has bought a Vera Lynn. We squeeze in renditions of 'I'll See You Again' and 'The White Cliffs of Dover' whenever we can.

In and around this cheerful maelstrom, I continued to read my way through Georgette Heyer. One Friday night after I had just reached the top of the school library queue for *These Old Shades* and taken ecstatic possession, I arrived home to find that I had not, after all, consigned the book safely to my schoolbag. I recall the pain of this realisation as physical; I could almost not bear it. I considered returning to school and imploring Mr Rodgers, the caretaker, who lived with his family in a cottage in the grounds, to open up the school for me. Good sense prevailed, and I abandoned this wild plan. Mr Rodgers (a splendid man, who ran the practical mechanics of AGGS for thirty-eight years) was no doubt as scared of Johnny's wrath as any fourth former. I gave myself up to grief instead, and retreated to *Wuthering Heights*. *Vanity Fair* had also become entrenched among 'my' books; the ones I kept by me for regular forays. At school we had 'done' Byron's *Eve of Waterloo*, and I knew every word . . .

. . . and bright

The lamps shone o'er fair women and brave men;
A thousand hearts beat happily; and when
Music arose with its voluptuous swell,
Soft eyes looked love to eyes which spake again . . .

. . . and book and poem were inextricably linked. Thackeray's *Vanity Fair* simply flowed on from Byron's 'Eve' . . .

Darkness came down on the field and the city; and Amelia was praying for George, who was lying on his face, dead, with a bullet through his heart.

This seemed to me the saddest, most achingly romantic sentence in English literature, equalled only by David's discovery of Steerforth's body in *David Copperfield* . . .

> But he led me to the shore. And on that part of it where she and I had looked for shells, two children . . . among the ruins of the home he had wronged — I saw him lying with his head upon his arm, as I had often seen him lie at school.

These deaths — George Osborne's and Steerforth's (both of them cheats, if not scoundrels) seemed infinitely more real to me than any relating to the contemporary war, notices of which were appearing regularly, now, in our newspapers. Deaths of brothers (no *fathers* so far) were always announced at assembly, and we regularly sang appropriate hymns. 'O God Our Help in Ages Past' and 'For Those in Peril on the Sea' were staples. It occurred to me that there must be *German* relations of soldiers and sailors singing the same or similar hymns of supplication; certainly, Italians. And couldn't God, if he existed, have prevented all this unreasonable mayhem from happening in the first place? As it was, he wasn't making much of a job of saving anyone.

> From rock and tempest, fire and foe,
> Protect them whereso'er they go . . .

. . . we carolled earnestly, once a week. No help was there for young Jimmy Simpson (Petty Officer James Simpson) whom I remembered as a boy about five years older than me, and whom Dad had met, and been photographed with, in London. Jimmy may have avoided rock and tempest, but the foe — and probably fire, too — got him when he went down with his ship in the North Atlantic. My early, implicit faith in the reasonableness of things and people, including God, was suffering constant erosion.

But I loved the hymns for their *words*, and sang them with gusto at prayers every morning. I have always been grateful for my exposure to this tradition (from which the young are now preserved in our state schools). Where else would I have heard 'Gold of obedience, and incense of lowliness' or 'Truth in its beauty and love in its tenderness', or the promise in: 'Mornings of joy give for evenings of tearfulness. Trust for our trembling and hope for our fear'? 'Truth in its beauty, and love in its tenderness' seemed to me then, as now, the essence of all that might cure the world of its human woes. And the Bible readings. I suppose I might, in time, have encountered Psalm No 121, but one could not count on it. 'I will lift up mine eyes unto the hills, from whence cometh my help . . .' From the verandah of our house in the Kare Kare valley, in bright morning or darkening evening, the stark and beautiful hills offer comfort and hope, and the wonderful words stir in my mind.

From Waterloo to the American Civil War, with its terrible loss of young life. (Why did I not connect this slaughter with what was going on in Greece and Crete?) *Gone With the Wind* — my own copy! — had me in thrall. I was in love with the spineless Ashley, who now vied with the scowling Heathcliff and the treacherous Steerforth for my affections. Or was it Leslie Howard who had my heart? For I had seen the picture (never 'film' or 'movie' in our vernacular), and Clark Gable had *become* Rhett Butler; Scarlett O'Hara, Vivien Leigh; and Olivia de Haviland, the saintly Melanie (whom I regarded as a pain in the neck, in both book and film. Perhaps, like Scarlett, I was simply jealous of her).

With some ingenuity — if lack of regard for safety — I had encased the centre light in the bedroom I shared with Val with a piece of dark-coloured cloth, so that most of the light was directed in my direction. This meant that I could now read on for hours after Val was asleep, and start again an hour before I had to get up in the morning. I seemed to need little sleep, and was prepared to forgo much of that for the greater pleasure of reading.

Dickens had been joined by Jane Austen and the other Brontës (Emily, of course, had been entrenched for years in *Wuthering Heights*) and a succession of accidentally encountered titles: Scott's *Kenilworth* and Charles Reade's *The Cloister and the Hearth* come back with a surge of pleasure.

A girl at school, astonished that I had never even *heard* of *The Wind in the Willows*, lent me a copy, and I was instantly, and forever, captured. This borrowed copy was illustrated by Arthur Rackham and became, for me, the definitive edition; years later, when I was able to buy my own copy, it was Rackham I chose. Ernest Shephard is exactly right, I believe, for A. A. Milne's engaging little animals and their friend Christopher Robin, but Toad, Mole, Ratty and Badger come alive in all their dignity, humour and humanity in Rackham's pictures.

I had by now made the acquaintance of the 'Bear of Very Little Brain', the lugubrious Eeyore, the irrepressible Piglet, the irresponsible Tigger, and Rabbit and All his Friends and Relations; I had spent some of my precious book money on a copy of *Winnie the Pooh*, and read it nightly to Bebbie. A. A. Milne's brand of humour seemed just right for *me* at fifteen, I discovered. Bebbie, in the way of loved children who listen to stories, enjoyed it whether she understood it or not, and was soon chanting the rhymes:

> It's very very funny
> 'Cos I *know* I had some honey
> 'Cos it had a label on, Saying Hunny . . .

Our joint favourite was 'Piglet meets a Heffalump'. (Help, help . . . a Heffalump, a Horrible Heffalump! . . . Help, help, a Herrible Hoffalump! Hoff, Hoff, a Hellible Horralump! Holl, Holl, a Hoffable Hellerump!) Val and Denis were often part of the listening audience, and we all rolled around in an ecstasy of enjoyment.

To say that I enjoyed these sessions is to understate my reaction. Reading aloud to young children seemed, and *felt*, the most natural and satisfying occupation in the world.

TWENTY-TWO

*J*n real life, I was in love with the school games captain who once smote me on the shoulder after an inter-school cricket match and said, 'Well played!' — which remark sustained me for weeks. This obsession was called a 'pash' and was acceptable, provided you didn't go on about it. Some people developed pashes for mistresses — Miss Gorrie-of-the-shoes *must* have been aware of her horde of breathless followers — but I was not afflicted in this direction. I was, however, in love with Professor Horace Hollinrake of the Auckland University College (as it was in those days) who coached and conducted the Secondary Schools' Combined Choir for yearly performances in the Auckland Town Hall. This was, of necessity, a seasonal passion; we learned our songs in our separate schools, and came together for only one rehearsal prior to the big night. My devotion was shared by a high proportion of the great choir.

Prof Hollinrake, baton in hand, flicking pages of music with the other, was an electrifying force, and we sang our hearts out for him. Tall, thin and English, he had hair that flopped alluringly over his eyes and seemed to me like an eagle, wings flapping. By sheer force of spirit he got his sopranos spectacularly to the top note in 'My God and King', the altos (including me) holding their note determinedly and the newly metamorphosed basses from Auckland Grammar and King's thundering

173

away below. Any one of us would have died for him, at that moment, I believe.

There were several staples in the yearly programme: 'Jerusalem', and 'I Vow to Thee, My Country' always, with a piece from the *Messiah*, which might vary from year to year, and a few 'new' but always classical items. The huge Town Hall organ, behind and above our heads, accompanied our most stirring numbers and seemed to shake the very earth. The thrill is with me still. I could never remember, next morning, having come home in the tram. None of us noticed the lack of original New Zealand music. Our songs were British because *we* were British, we had been brought up to believe.

❦

Somehow I fitted in a modicum of homework around my reading (which by this time had become compulsive), time with Bebbie, who was increasingly dear to me, the few domestic tasks I undertook voluntarily (I always did my own washing in the weekend — Mum had no capacity for regularity in such matters), mowing the Beuths' lawns, Lloyd's French (mine improved too), sports practices during the week for Saturday cricket, and later hockey, and the comings and goings and *stayings* of a horde of boys whose feet and hands and voices all seemed over-large for their human condition, and other people's comfort.

Ross, and a few of these friends, being now sixteen, had joined the local social scene, and even went to dances whenever they could afford to. Entry to these public functions required them to wear jackets and ties, and these were acquired somehow; often borrowed from fathers, older brothers or any willing lender. I remember Ross's first *bought* 'sports coat': a showy checked affair, which he wore with panache and a colourful tie, his hair subdued temporarily with something called 'Brylcreem'. This doubtful substance imparted a dull shine, considerable stickiness, and a powerful smell. As Brylcreem was *de rigueur* this year, all dance halls must have reeked of it.

As if our house were not noisy enough, Ross had acquired, from somewhere, a concertina (he called it a squeeze-box) which he played with robust enthusiasm and some skill. I became adept at learning French and Latin vocab, English figures of speech, and geometry theorems while strap-hanging in the tram. If you were lucky you might begin your journey in a seat, but no Grammar girl might *ever* be seen sitting while an adult, male or female, stood. As ordinary mortals paid full fare at fifteen, and school pupils in uniform half fare until eighteen, you could find yourself standing for a passenger, male or female, who was younger than you, by the time you were in the sixth form. Often, the commotion caused by your struggling out of your window seat, bulky bag and all, caused more general discomfort than it eased. Not to do so, however, would have been a cardinal sin.

Once, a sheaf of papers I was holding while strap-hanging was wrenched from my grasp by the stiff breeze from a suddenly lowered window, with near-disastrous results. One athletic young man captured several pages as they were escaping out the window. Other passengers snatched and grabbed the rest and restored them to me triumphantly from hand to hand. What might have been an embarrassing fiasco turned into a cheerful romp. Everyone seemed suddenly to be talking to one another — and me. I abandoned any further attempt at serious study in the tram.

Disconcertingly, Ross and his friends seemed suddenly to have cast themselves in the role of 'lads of the village' and were seen to be perpetrating, if not atrocities, at least questionable pranks. These were invariably funny — though marginally unlawful — and fortunately involved no (intentional) danger to other people's life and limb. The development was, I suppose, understandable; these were boys who had never been allowed the subversive, childish fun that secondary school pupils and university students claimed as their right. They all worked long hours at their various trades and accepted adult responsibilities which boys who were still being 'educated' could not have imagined. One last fling before 'the years bring the inevitable yoke' must have seemed not only desirable, but justifiable.

Several of the more sensational of these antics have been savoured in our family ever since: the night, for example, that Ross and his 'cobbers' greased the tramlines on Richmond Hill and lay on their stomachs in Warnocks' paddock to witness the predictable results. They knew there was no danger, they assured us later, propping one another up as gales of mirth engulfed them in our kitchen — the tram could only fail to get up the hill and finally slide back to the bottom, where it would immediately be stopped by the slope upwards in the opposite direction. There would be no other tram along for at least half an hour . . . Mum made an attempt at disapproval, but soon joined in the laughter, which gained momentum next day when it was discovered that Ockie, bound innocently homeward from the city, had been on the tram! 'I knew very well who the likely young rogues responsible were,' he claimed, providing a graphic description of the passengers' consternation, and the mystified tram driver's repeated attempts to scale Richmond Hill. 'Each time, we got a bit further up,' Ockie reported. 'And then just as we all thought we were going to make it, back down we went!' (Obviously, they 'made it' within the prescribed 'safe' half hour.)

On another occasion the boys all behaved so badly ('loudly' is probably a better description of their boorish antics) at a local dancehall that they were offered their admission money back and requested to leave. They complied so meekly with this edict that the management must have been puzzled. Of course, the management had no way of knowing that the riotous bunch had not actually paid to get in; one of their number had noticed a window with a broken catch in the gents, on their last visit . . . Our mother was never told this shameful tale, but it was rapturously celebrated in appropriate circles such as my formroom at school, the Beuths' kitchen next door, and various workplaces around Auckland. And of course, Ockie had to be told. Ockie relished Ross's pranks. I remember him removing his rimless glasses to wipe away tears of pleasure at the revelation or retelling of some improbable — but all too real — excess of my brother.

Ross himself used to claim, generously, one might almost say, that the real author of all the outrages was Pinky, who did seem to have a capacity for divergent and original behaviour which left ordinarily equipped mortals open-mouthed. Pinky really rates a book of his own, and certainly merits a mention in mine. After all, he was an exciting, if unnerving, feature of my life for years.

Peter Arnott — 'Pinky' to all except our mother ('No one should distort a fine name like Peter') — slept so often on the floor in Ross's bedroom that in the end we invited him to live with us. Peter's widowed mother (she who had held him so tightly after the earthquake of '31) had sent him from Napier to be apprenticed in Auckland, and wrote to him faithfully every week. Peter had been boarding with an uncle and aunt and their young family when Ross met him, and was chafing at the control that these relations (who later had our understanding if not our sympathy) attempted to exert.

Letters were exchanged, and Peter joined us, beaming with delight,

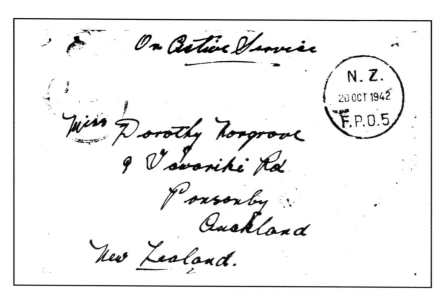

Letters from Egypt, 1942.

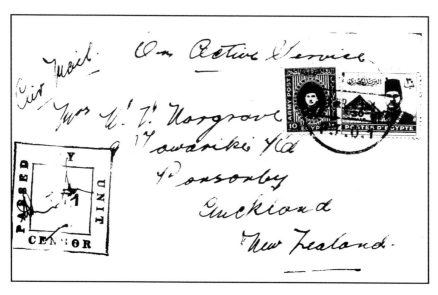

'. . . a fine hand, strong and flowing.'

My father, taken on his return from the war, 1943.

Ross, aged 16. 'One of the lads of the village.'

'Boomerang' on her cradle by the sewer. Ross, left, Ginge right.

Above left: *Ginge (Roy) 1943*. Above right: *Ross at the tiller, 1943*.

Ginge, Dorothy, Val Parker, Pinky. Front: Jacq Buffett, Val.

Valerie, aged 12.

Val and Pat, both aged 16, in 1940s teenage uniform.

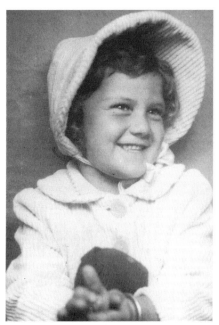

Left: *Beverley, '. . . a sturdy, articulate four-year-old'.*

Grandma Brown, front with Ross. Back: Val, Dorothy, Irma, Shirley and Maurine Brown.

Val, 14, Ross, 19 and Dorothy, 18.

Dorothy 'Miss Norgrove', assistant domestic science mistress, 1943.

and pink to the roots of his dark, spiky hair. (Peter's propensity to blush prodigiously in response to situations pleasurable as well as embarrassing had given him his nickname.) We must have looked respectable on paper, as Peter's mother agreed readily to his joining us. If she had been hoping for a degree of 'control' in her son's life, she might have done better not to assign him to the Norgroves; my mother had no notion, ever, of trying to control anyone. But she beamed, in her vague fashion, upon Pinky, and gave him love and creature comfort, and that seemed to do as well as, or perhaps better than, control, in the long run.

Together, Pinky and Ross hammered together a 'bunk' from timber acquired 'from behind the soap factory'. 'Just junk — they really *want* people to cart it away . . .' Our mother looked doubtful, but did not protest. Certainly, we could not have afforded to *buy* another bed. (My father's army pay was eight pounds a fortnight; welcome, as it was so regular, but little enough.) Peter's board might have been expected to help financially, though feeding both Ross *and* Peter might well have defeated a less determined provider than my mother.

But Peter 'took us on' as his family, fixed things for Mum (albeit often with bizarre results), became a friend and ally to me, and adored Val. He belonged to the London Book Club, and read two or three books every week: novels by authors as diverse as Maurice Walsh and Mickey Spillane, as well as westerns and marvellously fanciful yarns about a gentleman cat-burglar called 'The Saint', and — bliss! — requested extra Georgette Heyer titles for me *and* paid for them. (He became addicted to G.H., too.) Reading Peter's books before they had to be returned became a positive duty. Homework edged yet another rung down the ladder.

Peter idolised Ross, but was nothing if not his own man. He was never swamped by Ross's personality and predilections the way most of the boys were. He combined a sharp intelligence with astonishing physical courage, to the point of recklessness. His strange mixture of confidence and confusion in social situations made him often a figure of fun, but there was always admiration in the other boys' amusement. Any one of them would back out of a hazardous spot before Pinky, they knew. And hazards, as well as potential disasters, seemed to seek Pinky out. He was prone to accident and misadventure of such a singular nature that 'Tell us a Pinky story, Ross!' became a frequent request among a wide circle of eager listeners. Of course, Ross's capacity for *telling* funny stories was famous, too; it just so happened that Peter, over the years, supplied him with a rich hoard.

I cherish the tale of Pinky, confined to the Thames Hospital after a (no doubt outlandish) accident aboard the small yacht they were sailing, finding that his bell would not function and (naturally) dismantling it for repairs. Subsequently, not only the faulty bell but every other bell in the hospital rang, and rang, and continued to ring. A scene of confusion and near panic ensued, doctors and nurses running in every direction and ambulant patients, imagining a fire, running or hobbling to exits.

Order was ultimately restored when the bell system was disconnected at source, and trembling patients restored to their beds. The patient responsible, predictably red to his toenails, received frosty treatment. The management must have been relieved when, overnight, he simply disappeared. He was kidnapped by his loyal shipmates, who '*had* to sail that night' and refused to abandon him. There was a conveniently open window . . . 'We left a note, and we looked after him . . .' A daunting task, apparently accomplished. The hospital, advisedly, seems to have drawn a decent veil over the whole affair.

It is worth noting that Peter's own versions of the quaint exigencies that overtook him almost daily were even funnier than Ross's. Always very earnest and slightly perplexed, he had even been known to fall off a wharf while trying to explain, if he could not justify, the latest setback in his life. But then, Peter always walked along the stringers at the edge when traversing a wharf . . .

❦

I am obsessed with my father's letters. Why did I not read them earlier? Did I really forget about them for the seventeen years that they lay in their box in the top of my wardrobe? Did my mother re-read them — occasionally, ever — during the long years that she kept them? She never mentioned them.

The recurring themes of these letters haunt me. My father's longing for letters, and joy when they came; his constant reference to 'when I come home', and questions about his children: 'They must be so much bigger — what I would give . . .'; his unrealistic hope that he might some day take my mother to England; the implicit anxiety about their relationship in his almost excessive expressions of devotion; achingly, 'When I come home we will be united as never before . . .'

These sixty-year-old letters would be interesting to anyone. But it is not interest that keeps me poring over them, handling them, putting them in and taking them out of their envelopes. It is anguish.

My father came home from the war after three and a half years, looking fit and well, if, like most returning troops, somewhat apprehensive; tentative really. My mother was noticeably nervous; I think, now, that she knew, or at least feared, what was to come.

For my father's hopes for happiness were not realised. He died three years later, when an untreated stomach ulcer burst. He had literally, and recklessly, drunk himself to death. He was forty-five.

TWENTY-THREE

'$\mathcal{B}$e sure to say,' says my friend of fifty-nine years, Avis Robson ('Tweet'), 'that no one *ever*, at home or at school, told us anything about sex.' We are having lunch together. Tweet has hardly changed, it seems to me; perhaps a round, cheerful face with straight short fair hair is an enduring combination. Perhaps, when I look at her, I see what I expect to see.

When we were in the fourth form Bro wrote in my autograph book (we all had them):

> From quiet ways and small beginnings,
> Out to the undiscovered ends,
> There's nothing worth the wear of winning,
> But laughter, and the love of friends.

— and I reflect now that Hilaire Belloc's modest but, I think, right-minded verse speaks a reliable truth. Both 'laughter, and the love of friends' were freely available commodities at AGGS, and have sustained me ever since. A surprising number of us are still friends.

Tweet reminds me, in support of her assertion about our sexual ignorance, that a volume of a certain encyclopaedia in the school library had had its section on 'Sex' (or more likely, 'Reproduction' — the fateful word was rarely used in those days) neatly excised. I hadn't remembered this, if I had ever known, but she is right about the close-over. We were to be kept in total ignorance of things sexual until we were safely delivered from the pristine halls of AGGS, apparently a plan in which our parents only too willingly colluded. Not that they would ever have conferred; the subject, at every level, was simply taboo.

A girl in Mr Manning's Standard Six at Grafton School had informed a group of us, expertly and with no furtive whispering, about the mechanics of menstruation. Her name was Isobel, and she had joined the school for only one year, as had I. In fact, she had actually only just joined the *country*; her mother was a doctor who had come here to practise. Her *mother* was a doctor? I was incredulous. I had never met anyone whose *father* occupied that godlike state. But it was true. They were Scottish; Isobel had lovely, golden-red hair and a strange accent, and seemed to know everything. She was the only other girl who went on to AGGS with me from Grafton School, but was placed in III B. I cannot think why; whenever I encountered her at school she *still* seemed to know everything about everything.

Isobel's instruction, however limited, in the mysterious workings of the female body was useful, particularly as it was all I (or the other wide-eyed listeners, I have no doubt) were ever to receive. Our mothers, as far as I have been able to ascertain, helped us — with as much embarrassment as we experienced ourselves — to cope with the practicalities of the unwelcome first visitation, making it very clear that it was 'not the sort of thing you *talked* about' and that henceforth we were on our own. As no one had invented any of the disposable appurtenances that grace the modern market, or, if they had, had certainly not brought them within the reach of ordinary mortals like us, and as laundering facilities were still relatively primitive, this posed problems. I was fortunate, I suppose, that I was a very slow developer; I was not faced with the need to cope until I was fifteen, and was never afflicted with the cramps and headaches that many girls experienced and, on the whole, endured in silence.

In books and magazines and on the silver screen, we saw plenty of romance of the anguished-eye and sanitised-embrace variety, but nothing more. This led to a great deal of starry-eyed adoration of male film stars, and much speculation but few conclusions. A small group of girls in our form who attended the Friday night ballroom dancing classes held at the

Mount Albert Boys' Grammar School were heard regularly to whisper about 'boys' on Monday mornings (in contrast to my ribald accounts of 'the boys' who plagued my life at home and treated me as if I were one of their number) but had no real revelations to offer.

But parents and teachers, those stern arbiters of our innocence, couldn't win, really. Shakespeare was full of lewd references once we escaped the carefully chosen excerpts in a neat little volume called 'A Shakespeare Progress'. 'What's a bastard?' asked an innocent in IV A 1, to everyone's delight. 'A child born of unmarried parents,' said Val Parker, much braver than the rest of us. 'But that's impossible,' said our innocent. 'You can't . . .' 'Yes you can . . .' said Val, prepared to defend her ground. She got no further. 'That will be *enough*, Valerie,' said Miss Virtue; and it was, for then. But not for later. We discussed the proposition at length in the fives courts, and Val did seem to have an agreeable fund of information on the subject. (I learned later that her parents had an astonishingly forthright way of delivering information on delicate subjects.)

Along with Shakespeare (and the Bible, which was a valuable if somewhat opaque source) we were immersed in Victorian novels, an extraordinary number of which seemed to rely for their heart-wrenching drama on wronged and ravished maidens, though detail was still short. George Eliot's *Adam Bede*, *Vanity Fair* (Becky Sharp's peccadillos were a great joy), Goldsmith's *The Vicar of Wakefield*, Hardy's *Tess of the D'Urbervilles* (a positive welter of male passion and female ruin), Scott's *The Heart of Midlothian* (for those with the fortitude to wade through the thicket of historical events, impenetrably convoluted relationships and obscure Scottish references) — even *David Copperfield*, with Steerforth's seduction of the stainless Little Em'ly . . . How could they believe that our imaginations thus stimulated were not working overtime?

And how deceive themselves that the Romantic Poets were not working their wonder? They may not have actually directed us to Ernest Dowson's 'Cynara', but it was there, in our *Golden Treasury*:

All night upon mine heart, I felt her warm heart beat,
Night-long within mine arms in love and sleep she lay;
Surely the kisses of her bought red mouth were sweet;
But I was desolate and sick of an old passion . . .

And what about Nelson's fall from grace in the arms of Lady Hamilton?

Or Charles Stuart Parnell and his Kitty — or Byron and his *half-sister*! — or Oscar Wilde? Omitting salacious details from famous people's otherwise worthy lives didn't fool us (or not for long) and the library was a fine source of information, especially for the dedicated readers.

Somehow, we all stumbled through our adolescence, coped with changes as they occurred, gleaned a little here, and a little more there, were swamped by unexpected sensations at inconvenient moments, and were required, always, simply to 'get on with it'.

※

I had the additional complication of living in two quite different worlds. The other girls in my street, Mervyn's two sisters, for example, were already at work, and seemed to have outstripped me, at least socially. They wore different clothes from me; some of them even teetered along on high-heeled shoes (looking like Minnie Mouse, I thought) and wore — imagine it — lipstick! A girl who lived opposite us, and had been part of the cricket regime several years before, was said to be 'boy-mad'. We still smiled cheerfully at one another in the tram though, she from her seat, and I from my strap. What form did her addiction take, I wondered?

In my hat-and-glove-and-blazered state, with my bulging bag of books, I stood out on the Casey Estate. 'The boys' knew I was different, too; I met them on their own ground in our kitchen, and spoke their language (different from 'school' language) in a way I suspect their sisters and the girls they met at dances did not. This was, of course, due to Ross's training; we were still 'close', though diverging in interest and activities — and we still laughed at the same things. Usually.

'Do you remember,' says Ross, 'sitting at the kitchen table in the morning in your pyjamas with a book propped up on the sugar basin and your school hat jammed on your head? I wouldn't have dared laugh. You'd have thrown the sugar basin at me.'

My sausage curls had finally been adjudged inappropriate by a range of people including, I suppose, me, though I don't remember feeling passionate about it. Accordingly, they had been cut shorter, and 'combed out'. The result was predictable. Bits sprang into curls with minds of their own — as against Mum's carefully organised assembly — and the rest settled into a fuzzy mop. I hadn't minded the sausages, but I didn't care for this. Action was necessary.

Every morning early I immersed my head in a handbasin of water (at least, in our government house, we had ready access to *hot* water), combed my hair determinedly downwards and jammed my school hat on my head. This subdued the hair, temporarily, but was not very good for the hat, which started to emit an unattractive stench. I don't recall the resolution. In the end, I arrived at the short, somewhat fuzzy hairstyle I've had ever since. But Ross was right. I'd have thrown *something* at him.

Irma told me recently that she and her sisters used to be amazed at the way Ross and I 'knocked one another about'. I don't recall this at all. I remember wild games from an early age, our patient mother putting up with widespread domestic carnage. Though she always claimed that we were not destructive, all sorts of things deteriorated or fell to bits in our cheerful ménage. But I suppose I was more accustomed to 'rough-housing' than the average girl, and that my nature, as well as my nurture had adapted me to such boisterous activity.

Tweet's mother, Mrs Robson, the matriarch of a much more ordered, but very warm and welcoming household, said once, when I stayed with her family at a beach house in Milford in the summer holidays, 'You might as well be a boy — you're just a taller version of Bob' (who was about ten, and with whom I liked to play in a way I suspect was not typical of fourteen-year-old girls). I could certainly climb cliffs and trees and throw things — balls, stones, shells — as well as any boy. I had a young boy's build, too, and voice, if Miss Roseveare was to be believed.

But I knew I was a girl. From the time I read *Little Men* (an infinitely better book than the rather sickly *Little Women*, I considered), I knew that I would like to look after children. I found Bebbie's development both mysterious and fascinating. I was already listening closely to her speech. How did she know that the past tense of a verb was usually formed by adding 'ed' to the present tense, which led her into understandable errors such as 'I eated my dinner' and 'I runned fast . . .', and when did she change to 'ate' and 'ran'? Why was she so confident, when other children I observed were fearful? (At three, she would cling like a limpet to Ross's back, close her eyes and hold her breath as instructed, and swim under the water with him at Cox's Creek.) I began to be critical of the treatment I saw children receiving in shops and trams. I was astonished and indignant to see people slap two-year-olds for behaviour that was only venturesome and inquisitive. Many adolescents start to be concerned at the injustice in the world; I reserved my outrage for the insensitive treatment I saw meted out daily to small citizens in a country that called itself civilised.

'Matric' was upon us, we were told almost daily; we should be working seriously, and steadily. I was spending every afternoon between home-coming and dinner time with Bebbie, who had caught whooping cough. Mrs Beuth had decreed that I should stay away, entirely; I had never had whooping cough and all would be lost if I caught it in my Matric year, she thought. Even Mum, never one to issue orders, tried to dissuade me, but she would not have expected me to listen, and I didn't. Bebbie's big brown eyes now looked twice their usual size in her pale little face, and her hair clung damply to her forehead between the terrible coughing spasms that marked this cruel childhood disease in pre-inoculation days. With true Bebbie spirit, she would try to play. But she could not stand alone once an attack came and needed to be held while she coughed and coughed and then struggled for breath through the long whooping spasm before she vomited. Mrs Beuth was exhausted. Once it was clear that I *would* be there every night, she simply handed Bebbie to me at the door, in mute relief. The whooping cough lasted for months and I didn't catch it. Nor did I get in much of the serious and steady work that was said to be essential for passing Matric.

At Grammar, we faced the University Entrance Examination (Matriculation) at the end of three years instead of four, in the top academic form. There was no choice of subjects: we sat three-hour papers in English, History, French, Latin, General Science, Arithmetic, Geometry, Algebra (separate papers) and, for good measure, something called 'Extra Arithmetic', which was actually designed for lower forms which did not take Algebra and Geometry. (The logic of this 'extra' for *us* was never explained. It was probably thought to be good for our souls.) I couldn't imagine having trouble with English and History, and would probably manage about a sixty-average mark in the maths papers, with a similarly unspectacular pass in Latin and French. Mercifully, our Science syllabus in the fifth form had been modified by the inclusion of something called 'Dietetics', a discipline dispensed by vigorous, hearty Miss Frazer, who seemed actually to like us. (I suspect that our male peers over in Mountain Road experienced no such comfortable adjustment to *their* science syllabus and would have seen the idea as an affront to their male dignity anyway.)

Dietetics was the science of food: the way in which the body processed sustenance in its various forms and was either enhanced or reduced by it. Miss Frazer preached wholemeal bread, fruit and vegetables, milk and Marmite, and liver once a week. She directed us to insist that our mothers buy dried peas — hitherto overlooked, and very cheap — soak them overnight and cook them gently into a tasty mush to augment our thin meat protein ration. My mother seized every piece of advice and acted on it avidly. No white loaf ever penetrated her kitchen again — and Mum's dried pea concoction with mint, parsley and a tiny knob of precious butter (by now rationed along with meat, eggs, sugar and tea) became a staple feature of our diet.

When Miss Frazer decreed that we must all begin saving the water we cooked vegetables in to use for soups and stews, I was able to announce that my mother had *always* done this anyway. Mum was pink with pride when this conversation was relayed to her.

Somehow, learning about chemical properties and their interactions and effects seemed different when applied to ordinary, everyday commodities, particularly an attractive commodity like food. I was not going to fail in Science after all. I would surely scrape a pass if my Dietetics was impeccable. (It was, and I did.) I have never forgotten Miss Frazer and her salt-of-the-earth pronouncements about all sorts of things, not merely food.

I don't remember worrying about Matric; Bro and I were anguishing over Vera Brittain's *Testament of Youth* which she had acquired from somewhere — probably from her much older sister. Elizabeth Brodie was a nursing sister at the Auckland Hospital and had her own flat in Grafton Road, a large, it seemed to me, *elegant* apartment, and entertained a group of us at intervals to a lovely, cake-and-biscuit-style afternoon tea. This was blissful. Both Bro and I resolved to become nurses.

I was seeing more and more of different styles of life from my own: the comfortable well-ordered ways of the Robsons, tea poured from a silver teapot, with table napkins, cake forks and good conversation at Elizabeth's, and, before the year was out, an introduction to the Lairds. Nancy Laird belonged to a Scottish family who had arrived from Glasgow as assisted immigrants just before she, the seventh child, was born. In fact, Nancy's mother's unexpected pregnancy, discovered while they were still applying to emigrate, was seen as a disaster. Mrs Laird's health, almost ruined by 'keeping up standards' in an unhealthy Glasgow tenement, might have wrecked the family's chances of acceptance. Somehow, she scraped through; Janet and Thomas Laird and their six children made the long sea trip to Auckland, New Zealand, and settled in Charlotte Street on the slopes of Newton Gully.

Nan and I became firm friends in our fifth form year. Both Bro and Pen lived in distant Mount Albert, in the bosom of families who were quite unlike mine. They would be 'school friends' only. I loved the Lairds and their cavernous old house in the respectable but working-class district off Eden Terrace at first meeting. The house was a larger replica of the old villas we had lived in in Devonport, with a wide hall down the centre, numerous rooms on either side, and front and side verandahs. Mr Laird, by now retired, had founded (the only possible word) a magnificent vegetable garden. Having lived and worked all his life in brick buildings surrounded by miles of stone and concrete, he had set himself to mastering the science and art of gardening, once the opportunity presented itself. He had been spectacularly successful; his kumara beggared belief.

All the Lairds appeared to like me as much as I liked them; they called me 'Curr-rrly' and pressed me, always, to stay to the next meal, and like as not the next. That they fell gratifyingly into the 'large family' category that I had always loved, since Cameron days in Devonport, was sheer bonus.

The comings and goings in Charlotte Street constituted entertainment of a high order. There were sons-in-law, boyfriends, grandchildren and a seemingly endless stream of miscellaneous characters whom Mrs Laird could somehow never quite turn away; there was laughter, and cheerful gossip in a soon-familiar accent which Nan, astonishingly, fell into at home and shed at school. I began staying the night occasionally and, being introduced to all and sundry as 'Nancy's friend Curr-rrly', felt utterly included, utterly absorbed.

Nan's oldest sister was nineteen years older than her, the other girls ranging in age down to the twins, Georgina and Jack — the only boy in the family — who were six when the sole New Zealand baby was born. It was apparent to me from my first meeting with the Lairds that Nan, a beautiful, happy baby, I was assured, had cheered them all in the uncertain days of their arrival, and continued to do so. Some of this radiant warmth seemed to extend to me.

Nan's only brother, Jack, had been young enough to receive the education his older sisters had been denied in Scotland; he went from Auckland Grammar School to Auckland University College, and emerged, as Senior Scholar, top of his year, with an MA in philosophy. I was at first told simply that Jack was 'away in the country' (which was true) but learned later that he was in detention as a conscientious objector to military service. For the first time, I wondered about nationalism, patriotism and prejudice. My mother's castigation of military pomp and heroics as 'men behaving like children' and my own innate requirement of 'reasonableness' in all things set me wondering. The casualty lists from the other side of the world, interspersed with photos of Private This and Lieutenant That — mere boys, smiling proudly in their uniforms, but dead now in someone else's cause — were longer and longer in our daily papers. It seemed never-ending; and futile, somehow.

I wondered about Jack Laird. A photo revealed him as like Nan: dark haired and round-faced, with a sweet smile. 'Jack's the one that got Mum's nature,' said Jenny; and after the war I learned that she was right. Jack Laird — Dr John Laird — was one of the kindest, most humorous people I ever knew.

One of Nan's sisters, Jenny, had a singularly beautiful daughter called Jeanette who was a few months older than Beverley, and Nan and I would often take the two little girls to a beach or park — once, on a ferry ride — or simply amuse them at the Lairds' accommodating home. Nan and I took to going to 'the pictures' together on Saturday nights, swooning breathlessly over James Stewart and Gregory Peck. I hadn't had an out-of-school girlfriend for years; my life at home was wholly taken up with the younger children, and 'the boys'. I hadn't felt deprived; but I loved this venture into a totally new environment where girls were meant to giggle hysterically about anything or nothing, needed the almost constant application of sustaining food and drink, and received approval from everyone — even dour 'Dad Laird', who would shake his head wonderingly at our frivolous chatter, but never protest. We were plunging deeper and deeper into war, with blackouts, rationing, and shortages of everything, but my life had widened a little, and I was happy.

TWENTY-FOUR

*R*oss had a boat. Ross *owned* a boat. My brother's smile, always wide, seemed likely to meet around the back of his head. He had bought it — this craft of undeniable antiquity and doubtful sea-worthiness — for five pounds, his life's savings. He was now properly apprenticed and earning thirty shillings a week. Unimaginable economies had been made in other areas of his life to make the purchase possible; five pounds was as much as our family had to live on for a whole week.

You might say that this was Ross's first move onto the ladder that would take him, once the war was over, into the harsh world of coastal fishing boats, then on to scows, first as deckhand and ultimately skipper, and then, by way of endless spare-time and on-the-job study and examinations to the navy-blue uniform and braided cap of a master of Auckland Harbour Board tugs: Captain Ross Norgrove, Master Mariner.

But all this was still far in the future. Further still was the day when he would sail his own sturdy thirty-three foot yawl *White Squall* to America, and then on to the West Indies, to become in the 1960s one of the top charter boat skippers out of the port of St. Thomas, in the Virgin Islands.

Ross's ultimate boat, called, loyally, *White Squall II*, was a magnificent seventy foot schooner but it is likely that his pride of ownership in the leaky, dilapidated *Boomerang*, sitting on her improvised cradle next to the

189

sewer outlet in the upper reaches of Cox's Creek, exceeded even his satisfaction in this final triumph. In the mid-seventies, when it started to become apparent that the mysterious disability which would progressively rob Ross of the use of his limbs would also wrench him from his beloved boats and the sea, he turned, with his usual good cheer and determination, to writing about it all. A succession of books published by Marine International in the US gave him, ultimately, international recognition. In a trial run for the first book, Ross tossed off an entertaining account of those long-ago days when the *Boomerang* held all his hopes and dreams for the future. Typed, and bound in cardboard covers, this 'book' is among my treasures. I have uplifted several photographs from it for this book.

Boomerang, purchased 'where is as is', lay on a piece of reclaimed land which was part of the half-finished Westhaven breakwater. She was seventeen feet long, five feet wide, and eighteen inches deep, with a deck that stretched about four feet back from the bow, and little side decks about eight inches wide. And, predictably, she leaked. This drawback was aggravated by a minor marine accident on the way to the proposed restoration site in Cox's Creek.

Here is Ross on the subject. As captain he is giving orders to his three regular henchmen, who are rowing:

> I knew a lot about the sea . . . I had read that when an order is given to a helmsman on a ship, he repeats it. If the captain or mate of a ship says, 'Steer northwest,' the helmsman says, 'Northwest, sir!' If he is told to steer southeast he says, 'Southeast, sir!'
>
> I decided to dispense with the 'sir' bit . . . However, after we had sorted out which side was port and which was starboard, I would call out 'Pull port!' or 'Pull starboard!', whichever was necessary, and the crew would repeat it as we rowed and bailed our way along.
>
> Oh, I could just see myself, square of jaw with a steely glint in my eye . . . gazing into the tempest as a dutiful crew unhesitatingly obeyed my every — CRASH!
>
> 'We've hit a rock!' I yelled.
>
> 'We've hit a rock!' my dutiful crew chorused back.
>
> 'You didn't have to repeat that!'
>
> 'You didn't have to hit a rock!'
>
> Insubordination! And on my first voyage, too.

The damage was not widespread '. . . and she couldn't leak much more anyhow,' as one of the aggrieved rowers pointed out. All hands and the captain bailed feverishly; and they made it . . . round the coast and into Cox's Creek, under both bridges — there were two in the creek in those days — and on up the narrow waterway, with mangroves closing in on both sides, to the appointed spot by the sewer, in triumph. 'It was a pity,' wrote Ross, 'that our only audience was a couple of birds squawking in the mangroves and the odd crab scuttling across the mud, because we had rowed a full two miles over the ocean, up a dangerous river, and we had only hit one rock.'

The significance of this prized position next to the sewer outlet — which was not a true sewer pipe but an antiquated stormwater drain which discharged questionable, foul-smelling material into the creek, and was always called 'the sewer' — lay in the fact that it was conveniently — miraculously — located at the end of our street, a mere five houses away. We all, down to Bebbie, traipsed down to offer our congratulations and to admire. Meanwhile, Ross and Peter were busy constructing a cradle for the precious craft, so that restoration could begin. The timber was, as usual, acquired from the back of the soap factory. Mum never enquired why, if she ever noticed, expeditions to procure necessary materials always seemed to take place during the hours of darkness; though she did take note on the night that Ross, with Pinky's help manhandling the enormous packing-case side which was to yield all the timber they would need for the construction of a modest boat cradle, slipped, and fell fifteen feet into the sewer outlet. 'Goodness,' said Mum mildly, as he stood in the back porch, dripping unspeakable sludge onto the floor, 'you smell as if you've been in a sewer.'

Everyone — family, 'the boys', even the neighbours — seemed always to be caught up in Ross's enthusiasms, and pressed into service in likely and unlikely ways. We all fetched and carried, anguished and exulted, and listened with fascination to his extravagant plans. Now nearly eighteen, he had tried to 'join up' and been rejected; New Zealand needed soldiers, certainly, but skilled optical mechanics were much harder to come by, and in wartime, indispensable. Dad had several times advised Mum in his letters (I know now) to do her best to keep Ross out of the services. 'One of us is enough,' he said in a letter received about this time. I doubt that Mum would have interfered with Ross's wishes had he been determined, but he was not. His mind was focused on the boat at the bottom of the road and he knew he was doing essential, skilled war work (if he thought about it at all). He simply joined the Coastguards, a voluntary service that was the marine equivalent of the Home Guard and much more to his taste.

The Coastguard training was an extension of skills already mastered in the Sea Scouts, and involved the manning of the flagship *Minerva* — a large launch — and a small cutter, overnight at least once weekly, and often at weekends. Ross obviously enjoyed this venture and, as usual, was voluble about his experiences. Tales of near-disaster, from the hilarious to the horrifying, abounded, and though the waterfront pie-cart was reported to be responsible for a degree of dereliction of duty, he was in deadly earnest about the vital nature of the Coastguards' work. As in peacetime, the sturdy little vessels answered emergency calls from small boats, and ferried urgent medical cases from the islands in the gulf to the mainland. Additional wartime duties involved 'standing watch' on both wharf and boat, with the understanding that, in the event of enemy attack (not as far-fetched an idea as all that, as the Japanese advanced through the Pacific 'like a wolf on the fold'), the Coastguards would act as messengers between the city and North Shore. There was no radio aboard these boats, and the electronic wonders of fifty years ahead could not have been imagined. Ross's Morse and Semaphore, augmented with the flags of the International Code, had him cast in the role of signalman almost immediately.

The Coastguards yielded another treasure: a soulmate who, also kept from active service by his apprenticeship (to the engineering trade), proved to live within walking distance of our home, and expressed lively interest in the restoration of the *Boomerang*. Known as 'Ginge' by reason of a thick thatch of gold-bronze hair, this new friend proved to have constructive skills of a high order (according to Ross) and had even expressed willingness to 'go halves' in any future boat-ownership. *And* he was musical, with a good singing voice, and appeared to share Ross's latest enthusiasm, which was to acquire and play a guitar. I got sick of hearing about him. In the flesh, Ginge was yet another set of long male legs to trip over in the kitchen and another loud and clear voice in the boys' interminable arguments. Oh well. (Mum, in true form, refused to call him Ginge 'when he has a perfectly decent name like Roy'. Nor would she call Stan 'Irish'. . .)

In V A 1, we all 'got' Matric. I suppose one could say that we were programmed to do so. The exhortation, pressure and threats to which we were daily exposed at school, and to which we responded according to our dispositions, were designed to ensure that the most industrious, if not necessarily the most intelligent, of us were set on the path to academic distinction. My expectations of my own performance were roughly realised; high marks in English and History, mediocre passes in everything else.

By the time results were published in the newspapers in early January, I was about to start three weeks' work in a local factory which devoted itself to bottling or otherwise packaging manufacturers' goods: talcum powder, lotions both medicinal and cosmetic, and unidentifiable substances of a pungent nature. This was boring but not arduous, and served the purpose of reinforcing my early decision to avoid factories and shops as places of employment. (I read furiously at the tea breaks and lunchtime, and managed to last out the time.)

The *Boomerang* by this time *looked* spruce and seaworthy. She had been re-ribbed. The boys boiled the new jarrah ribs for hours in our copper, and then Ross tore down the road to the boat with one rib at a time swathed in sacking, to preserve the heat. Here, he and Ginge (the supposed expert) riveted each rib in turn into place. This was a major operation, triumphantly accomplished, but a serious problem remained. The boys knew that their ex-lifeboat craft needed a centreplate which, lowered as necessary, would act as a keel, if they were to rig and sail her. Reluctantly, they agreed that this required the services of a *real* expert.

Ross scraped up two pounds to pay for this operation, describing himself as 'completely broke' after the event. The construction of a small, open cabin was accomplished smoothly, they thought, though unexpected leaks required the later application of strips of half-round beading, which, the crew explained to casual enquirers, were intended to 'give her a bit of class'. Finally, painting *Boomerang* brought joy all around, in both process and product. (I was naturally recruited at this stage.) We all agreed that she was 'a handsome little craft', and indeed she was. In no time at all, it seemed, the mast was stepped, the necessary ballast to keep her steady loaded aboard, and the heady prospect of *a cruise* contemplated.

My mother's willingness to allow Ross to store hard-won accessories — spars, bowsprit, gaff and boom — in his bedroom astonished Ginge, whose family exerted unyielding discipline over its young. The fact that the boom protruded six feet or so out the necessarily always-open window and could deal unwary visitors a dazing blow on their way to the back door did not worry her. 'Where else could he keep his gear?' she would have asked if challenged. Ross, of course, expected such reasonableness from his family, and got it. (So did I; though my needs, rather harder to meet, were mostly not even mentioned, let alone met. I didn't grumble; what would have been the use? And anyway, everyone's devotion to me was total. It wasn't *their* fault that I seemed to be 'different'.)

That the spruce little ship *floated* on her historic launching day, and *sailed* — in a gentle breeze inside the bay — was enough to have the boys feverishly loading her with supplies and equipment for the trip to Waiheke, twelve miles away across the waters of the Hauraki Gulf. Bathed in glory, they set out. That water poured in through the top of the centrecase once the little boat, heavily loaded, was exposed to a brisk wind, and a sea of several feet was an unforeseen and near-total disaster. The *Boomerang* was rescued by the police launch *Lady Shirley*, which its crew managed to hail, and towed halfway home; unfortunately, up the wrong side of tiny Watchman Island, where they were left on a mudbank. The cold and disgruntled crew — Ross, Ginge, Irish and Frank — walked home in chest-deep water, pushing and pulling their boat, and munching their way steadily through a two-week supply of cakes, biscuits and scones provided in tins and jars by my mother. Every last crumb had gone by the time the haven of Cox's Creek and home was reached.

The conclusion was irrefutable: the centrecase should have been constructed at least six inches higher. (So much for real experts.) Modification was possible, but not in time for a summer cruise. In their minds, halcyon holiday delights beckoned; they simply could not wait to get at least a toe into the water of famed yachtie dissolution at Waiheke. If they couldn't sail, they would camp. The steamer *Tangaroa* offered a daily service. Mum got out her mixing bowl, and the boys addressed themselves to the frantic assembly of makeshift camping equipment. Exactly why ours was the only mother involved in provisioning help, I have since wondered. Fortunately, Mum never concerned herself with rights and wrongs, only needs. And now that we had a steady if modest income, I think she enjoyed the role.

My appointed task, while the crew partook of their land-based Waiheke holiday, consisted in traipsing the mile and a half to Cox's Bay

each day, and the mile and a half back, to check on the prized craft, and if
need be 'bail her out'. This proved always to be necessary. The boat was
anchored some distance out in the bay, and I was obliged to go at lowest
tide. There was a bung in one side of the hull,

as befitted an ex-lifeboat, and I used to pray, always, that the craft
would be lying on that side on the mud, so that I could simply (well, with
a bit of a struggle) remove the bung and let the water run out. When I
was out of luck, the *Boomerang* would be lying with her bung facing the
sky, and I would either have to bale her with the 'billy' I carried back and
forth for the purpose, or invoke any available help in the task of pushing
her over.

I made the acquaintance, that summer, of a group of boys, all about
eleven or twelve, who played around the creek and on the mudflats, as we
had, years before in Devonport. They were unfailingly willing to help, and
even offered to 'do the job' if I wanted to miss a day. I didn't; I seemed to
have a stake in the gallant little craft. My brother's precious lifeblood had
been invested in her, after all.

TWENTY-FIVE

We went rejoicing into the Lower Sixth with a few exceptions. Several 'science' girls left to pursue pharmacy qualifications, an innovative step in 1942. Encountering one of them, white-coated, in a chemist shop several years later, I was impressed. Val Parker's father decreed that she should leave school and start paying her way, and found her a job with an insurance company. By a stroke of good fortune, a severe shortage of teachers resulted, later that year, in the Teachers' Colleges opening their doors to any applicants with Matric — an assurance, in those distant days, of considerable academic accomplishment — and Val made haste to apply, commencing her training in the following year. As she became an outstanding, lifelong teacher of young children, this deliverance was fortuitous.

For the first time in our lives at Grammar, we were offered some choice in the subjects we would study, though care had to be taken to keep within the bounds of university requirements. Those of us with an eye on an Arts degree must keep a foreign language and, of course, English. The form divided neatly into those who were still at school only to get something called Sixth Form Certificate, without which they could not apply for Teachers' Training College or entry into hospitals as student nurses, and a smaller group which would return to the Upper Sixth in the following year and sit for university scholarships. My friends Avis Robson and Margaret Brand were numbered among these; Bro, Penman, Nancy and I were bound for a primary school teaching career whether we liked the idea or not. The alternative, nursing, had taken my fancy the year before but my mother had said, 'Nursing! You'd have to do *exactly* what you were told, all the time. You'd hate it. And the discipline is *terrible*,' and for once I had believed her. It was never a serious idea anyway.

It was announced that there were two awards available for needy senior girls, from something called The Costley Bequest Fund, and Nan and I applied, and were both successful. This, while a modest grant, solved blissfully the problem of books, new shoes and the endless oddments without which life could not, it seemed, be sustained.

Bro, Pen and I were all nominated to contest election as prefects, and Pen and I as school games captain. Johnny dealt summarily with any aspirations I might have harboured. I was summoned, and informed that she had grave doubts as to my suitability for either of these august roles. She was, however, honest. She told me that my nomination as school games captain had been widespread enough to suggest that I would probably be elected. Would I give her my opinion? I did so without rancour. I was quite sure that I would find the job tedious if saddled with it, and was happy to bow out. Pen was duly elected (she might have been, anyway) and proved her worth as an excellent games captain. I had faint feelings of guilt as I observed her wrestling with lists and scurrying about in her official capacity, but at least she was good at it. I, by contrast, have carefully avoided office all my life and have no capacity for such toil. I am happy to *work* in a good cause, but cannot abide the minutiae of organisation according to bureaucratic rules. (There are plenty of people who have talent, and *enjoy* it, I have always claimed, in my own defence . . . a selfish rationalisation perhaps.)

This was a good year. We had no outside exams to face, and every expectation of earning our certificates without too much trouble. Reading still occupied a great deal of my time, both officially and unofficially. I recall that we were all in VI B bowled over by Richard Llewellyn's *How Green Was My Valley* (Tweet went to the lengths of calling one of her daughters *Bronwyn*; but who am I to talk? By the time my first daughter was born I had had *Catherine* stored up since I first read *Wuthering Heights* in the fourth form . . .). Howard Spring's *My Son, My Son* had me in a state of anguish for weeks; and Bro and I managed to get hold of Vera Brittain's tribute to Winifred Holtby, *Testament of Friendship*, almost hot off the press; extraordinarily, as the war was still on, and new titles almost unobtainable. I think we saw — or wanted to see — some of the quality of our own friendship in the devotion of these two women a whole world away from us in background, age and experience.

Winifred Holtby's novel *South Riding* must have come from the same source (surely not the school library?) and I recall that we were both swamped by it, too. Re-reading *South Riding* a few years ago I found myself wondering how two long-ago schoolgirls, utterly inexperienced in the ways of the world, could possibly have been drawn so irresistibly into its complex plot and unlikely setting, let alone have persisted through its considerable length. But we were, and we did. I still think *South Riding* one of the finest books I have ever read; but my response to it must have been very different then, surely. I am surprised, in retrospect, that it affected me so strongly. (Equally surprising, on reflection, is the fact that Winifred Holtby wrote it not long before her early death in 1935, when she was only thirty-seven.)

Val and Nan had by now both become out-of-school friends, a welcome new feature in my life. (Hereafter, my sister was always called 'Young Val'.) We were welcome in one another's homes, and though Val and Nan have both since admitted to finding the Norgrove household unconventional, they attest to having been fascinated by its general air of libertarian, but welcoming chaos. I had added Margaret Brand, also, to my small band of occasionally visiting-and-visited friends. By a lucky chance, Margaret lived within walking distance in Westmere. She, too, has recalled her attraction to my noisy well-frequented home, as against the quiet solitariness of her own. (I, by contrast, remember the orderly peace of hers!) Margaret was the only child of intelligent Scottish parents who were determined to give their clever daughter the education they had never had themselves. Scottish austerity and expectation, softened by the humour and companionship of a practical, cabinet-making father, ensured her excellent work habits and high principles; Margaret's essentially kind and humorous nature seems to have been inborn. Along with these qualities, there developed, as she grew, a surprising gregariousness. Margaret's own subsequent homes have always been open day and night to friends, relations, friends' friends, children's friends . . . simply *people*. I like to think that our small, overfilled Tawariki Road house may have been one of her first models.

Beverley, now a sturdy, articulate four-year-old, ran in and out of our house at will, and gave me constant pleasure. With Val and Denis, she now attended a local Sunday School, and provided my first experience of the young child's capacity to make its own sense of the incomprehensible: 'The Lord is my shepherd, I shall not want. He makes me lie down in the green parsnips . . .' Soon, she would start school. It seemed an age since she had overturned her pram and become a vital part of my life.

I had made a new friend, too, in the previous year: one who was destined to become increasingly dear to me, and to my future family, as the years passed. Betty O'Dowd came to Grammar, into the Lower Sixth, when I was in V A 1. In the ordinary way of things, we might not have become friends, but our route to school in the morning brought us both along Hopetoun Street, a less-used route than the Howe Street hill. One could not fail to note another Grammar Girl — particularly one who seemed to have, and indeed, *had*, joined the ranks at an unusual level. (I learned in due course that Betty had spent her earlier years at a small convent school, which could not, ultimately, provide the preparation she needed for university.) One could also not fail to notice *Betty*, in particular. She was tall and stately, amply built, with dark-rimmed glasses and what I thought was a somewhat imperious air. Beside her, I felt scruffy and gangling; not a sentiment often wrenched from my cheerfully self-accepting person, and one that didn't last long. For we were soon talking on our all-too-short way to school each morning, and I discovered that Betty had a highly original sense of humour, and was unusually interesting; intriguing, really. (I tried to describe her to Mum and Ross at home, and felt that I hadn't captured her *being* at all. Betty was different from anyone else I had ever met, but I couldn't put my finger on the key points.) I came to cherish our brief morning exchanges, but had little opportunity to get to know her any better until my Lower Sixth year, by which time she was in the Upper Sixth. That we both went to university in the following year — Betty on the wings of a scholarship and I by the skin of my teeth — was my good fortune, and cemented a friendship that has never wavered through all the years of our very different lives.

My future, casually disregarded for so long, was almost upon me; and I knew that I wanted to go to university. I did not want to be drummed off to Teachers' Training College, the solution for those who aspired to some form of higher education but must ensure an income as well. I was not repelled by the notion of becoming a teacher; far from it. It was simply that I did not want to become entrapped and beholden, as teachers were, to the government, in the form of the Department of Education, which bought you body and soul, it seemed: two years at Training College, another as a probationer, and then three years' compulsory country service. Only a very small number of primary school teachers enmeshed in this system ever completed university degrees. I knew myself well enough by now to realise that I would find this control irksome, and that I would have to find some other way of 'earning my keep'. I needed a job that would allow me to enrol as a full-time university student.

This, of course, posed problems. I knew that my brother and his friends worked for forty hours a week, fifty weeks of the year; at least Training College students had the regular school holidays, amounting to ten weeks yearly — and the college did release their students for the limited university lectures they allowed them to take.

There were times when I thought that Training College was my only option. But I didn't stop pondering the problem . . . and hoping. Like Mr Micawber I was simply waiting for something to turn up.

Something did.

Twenty-six

As little third-formers, we had clattered down the stairs once weekly to the cookery room, which stood on stilts against the lower boundary of the school grounds. This was the school's one nod in the direction of domestic training for its 'academic' students, and we relished it. Clad in white aprons and caps made by our mothers, we banged about with basins and measuring cups and produced questionable concoctions such as sago pudding, lemon blancmange and scones which in no way resembled our mothers' fluffy offerings. Miss Finlay, the cooking mistress, was kindly, upright and well-starched, the cooking room itself scrubbed and well-ordered, with white walls and shiny brown linoleum.

We had been vaguely conscious of a 'helper', a young woman who seemed to be in charge of the large, shelved pantry, and who ticked our names off a list as we demonstrated that we had indeed produced the day's required dish, washed up our utensils, scrubbed our tabletops, and displayed our well-washed bowls and dishcloths in a tasteful manner thereon. We would then stand to attention like soldiers during kit inspection. Any shortcomings, and the operation must be repeated.

All this was by now far in the past. What we did not know was that this 'helper' was always a Grammar Girl, straight from a senior form, who traditionally pursued a science degree at the university, and was paid at approximately the same rate as Teachers' College students. The information that the cookery room incumbent had finished her degree, and that a replacement was being sought for the following year was calmly delivered to us at assembly one morning.

I recall that my head swam, and my heart beat faster. Did it have to be a *science* degree? Had I absolutely cancelled out any chance I might have had for such a position by reason of my well-established reputation? I had no idea; but I knew I could *do* the job. The older I became, the more I realised that I *liked* order in things; this job would require deftness and efficiency but hardly intense intellectual application. I would have only university work to occupy my *mind*; the school was close to both home and university, I would have school holidays and school hours, and an income.

One applied simply by handing one's name to Miss Johnston's secretary. I, and several others, did this, and waited. Finally, Johnny sent for me. Was this, once again, to suggest that I stand down? No, it was to offer me the job. A science degree was not obligatory, she told me, while I was still trying to prevent my mouth from either hanging open in incredulity, or stretching into a grin of disbelieving delight; it was just that most Arts students went to Teachers' College if they were unable to pursue full-time university work. She felt sure that I would not have applied had I not seriously wanted the position and that therefore I would apply myself to it with suitable industry. She even smiled faintly, a contortion that did not suit the lines of her thin, austere face and was, I thought, rather frightening in its unfamiliarity.

I needed to sit down, once dismissed. I could simply not believe it. I could now contemplate enrolling for a full-time university course. In those distant days, all Arts lectures were held between 4 pm and 8 pm; it would be a tight squeeze getting to 4 o'clock lectures when school did not close until 3.30 pm, but I would manage, I felt sure. There was, of course, some risk involved, as against the 'safe' course of Teachers' College enrolment: if I failed to pass at the end of the year, I would have achieved nothing. But I did not propose to fail.

※

'After all these years, I'm still astonished that she gave me the job.' I am talking to Tweet, wondering how to make what has always seemed unbelievable look credible on paper. 'Rubbish,' says Tweet, who finished a near-lifetime of teaching as deputy principal of a large girls' high school, 'she knew you were intelligent, and energetic and *purposeful*. Of course she'd give it to you.'

As Johnny's prescription for her pupils had always seemed to involve meekness, obedience, application and extreme conservatism, none of which qualities I had ever exhibited, I was to be forgiven for surprise at the time. But endless speculation was fruitless. Unconfined joy was the only sensible response, and I wallowed in it. I had been saved.

Our last, special assembly was upon us.

> 'Lord dismiss us with thy blessing,
> Thanks for mercies past received,
> Onward be our footsteps pressing . . .'

There we all were — well, most of us — at the end of four years; a handful of the favoured, ten, perhaps, going on to the Upper Sixth, where they would actually have their own *sitting room* — a narrow, cupboard-like chamber equipped with a 'gas ring' on which sausages were traditionally cooked — most of the rest of us proceeding, like-it-or-not to training as teachers or nurses, and I to return, not really on the staff, but not in the schoolroom, either.

> 'May our seedtime past be yielding,
> Year by year a richer store . . .'

we sang heartily.

I think I was conscious that my years at Grammar had been my salvation, though I had only a vague idea of what they had saved me *from*. Perhaps I'd have found a way, as Ross did, to provide a life for myself that suited me. I knew I was resilient — there had been plenty of evidence in my life so far to support that assurance — but merely to survive is not to flourish, and I knew that Grammar had allowed me to flourish.

I might have felt in the circumstances that I was not *really* leaving, but I was firm on that point, in my own mind. My cooking room job was intended to support my new life as a university student. I might still be *in* the school for the next few years, but not *of* it. 'Look up, not down, look forward not back . . .' Perhaps Dad's wall texts had borne fruit after all.

This had been the year when we had whirled around the night sky in the Octopus at the Civic Square and eaten pies in picture theatres; when the city had started filling up with American soldiers and sailors in immaculately tailored uniforms, putting our rough-clad boys to shame and charming our young women with their soft accents and gracious manners; the year when my wristwatch arrived from Dad, in a battered package which had spent nine months making its hazardous way from Egypt to Ponsonby. The watch was to celebrate my passing Matric, Dad's note said, and it was the most wonderful present I had ever received. I cried, uncharacteristically, when it was revealed in its slim, velvet-lined case, but I was crying for Dad, whom I seemed no longer to know, and who had saved his meagre personal allowance for months to buy my watch. I wore it for years, and still treasure it.

This was also the year when blackout regulations ceased to be casual and began to be policed. We stumbled about in unlit streets, while out on the waters of the Waitemata, Ross and Ginge learned to navigate 'by guess and by God', often with only the dark outline of North Head and Rangitoto against an inky sky to guide them, trusting the feeling in their bones to help them find the gap in the boom defence which stretched between St Heliers and Devonport and was intended to prevent submarines from entering the harbour.

It was also the year when Dad sent Mum one silk stocking in one letter, and the other in a different letter (two together would have been overweight) and they arrived half a year apart, a stream of non-stockinged out-of-sequence letters separating them, while we all held our breath; when Dad received in January the Christmas parcel from Grammar, which I helped pack, with all the others, and was one of the few recipients who wrote to send his thanks, though no one wondered about that — some parcels *never* arrived, and some brothers and fathers were either not where we thought they were, or not alive. I was proud of him, though.

'Life here is very monotonous,' wrote Dad from base camp in Maadi, Egypt on March 20, 1942. 'I very rarely go out and am trying to save up for a trip to Alexandria . . . I saw Claude and Ray Cameron [our Narrow Neck neighbours!] the other day when their crowd camped with us overnight. They were OK and wanted me to go to Cairo, but as Wilf Wray and his brother Denny were also here I had a quiet night with them . . .'

Good old Wilf again! 'When something does happen, I can't tell you so my letters must be very dull . . .' says Dad, and he goes on to talk, as usual, about us. 'Dorothy, Val and Ross are always in my thoughts and I wonder how long it will be . . .' He is obviously concerned about what he calls 'Japan's temporary successes' in the Pacific, and wishes he were at home with us.

Then, 'I feel Jimmy Simpson's loss very keenly — he was a great boy, and very attached to his wife and worried as she was to have a baby. I wonder how she is, poor girl . . .'

This is a sad letter, which Dad tries to brighten at the end, and I am again overcome with the feeling that I had forsaken him. Shouldn't I have written more often? (How often *did* I write? I can't remember.) 'Old, unhappy far-off things and battles long ago' crowd in on me as I read this fifty-eight-year-old letter from my father to my mother. Why do quotations always spring at me, unawares? 'Man, that is born of woman, and hath but a short time to live, is full of misery . . .' So much suffering everywhere . . .

But these are seventy-, not seventeen-year-old reflections, and uncharacteristic, anyway. I have been reading not only my father's letters, but details of World War II battles and casualties. Mum had always reassured us about our father's chances of survival. At the base camp in Maadi, where he and others worked long, hot hours at a new factory, providing food for the troops in the field, he was not involved in actual combat. I know now that he was exposed, constantly, to what must have seemed an ever-flowing stream of young New Zealand men on their way to the terrible desert battles, many of them — 2,700 by mid-1943 when the North African campaign ended — never to return, another 6,000 to be brought out wounded, and a further 3,600 to disappear into German prisoner-of-war camps. Dad never told us any of this in his letters; only, regularly, 'There are things happening which I can't tell you about . . .' He must have been able to see his own son in the faces of the jaunty, eager young soldiers, newly arrived and anxious to be part of it all. He told us of heat, sand, flies, bed-bugs and exhaustion, but not of the sickness of heart that must have engulfed him often.

I'm glad that Mum didn't tell us about Jimmy Simpson's unborn, now fatherless baby.

A few of us — Tweet, Nancy and I as I recall — managed to get a holiday job in a factory near the bottom of Queen Street, close to the wharves. It made children's shoes. Most of the time we were busy at a huge table cutting out linings by hand from patterns stamped on cloth, with plenty of opportunity to chat among ourselves, and with the other girls — some of them younger than us — who were permanently employed. They, but not we, would in time graduate to the machines where the shoes were stitched together, but we all had a turn at an appliance that attached buttons to the tiny straps of baby slippers. One simply inserted the strap appropriately positioned, pressed a foot pedal firmly, and the machine did the rest.

Despite early fears of accidentally attaching a button to the end of one's finger, we all mastered this technique, and enjoyed the change from cutting. But one day, while one of our number (not I) was operating the machine, there was a loud unfamiliar rattling noise, followed by a series of deafening reports, and thousands of tiny buttons, awaiting their turn for attachment in a 'hopper' above the working plate, flew skywards in a wild eruption, to descend like hailstones on heads, tables, and floor. The consternation of the innocent operator and — after the initial shock — the hilarity of the whole company cemented the episode firmly in my memory. For the rest of our tenure, buttons kept turning up in unlikely spots — even in someone's pocket.

A serious older 'girl' persuaded — almost *forced* — our small band (which she doubtless considered frivolous) to attend a Women's Temperance meeting one Friday night after work. Here, we all signed The Pledge, an act of dedication to abstinence from the vine and its products, which I have only just, and far too late, recalled. Everyone at the gathering was very humourless, but there were several 'testimonies' from women who had fallen and been subsequently saved, which brightened things up considerably from our point of view. Veiled reference to depravity of a startling (but unspecified) nature had us longing for more, but detail was withheld. We ate thick fish-paste sandwiches and drank tepid sweet tea and astonished the assembly by lustily singing every word of 'Who is on the Lord's Side?' without ever looking at the word-sheet. Obviously, Grammar had given us *something* with which to face the world.

This year, Ross and the boys managed a real sailing holiday, and the peace at home was golden. With the boys' bedroom empty, I was able to invite Nan to stay for a few nights — there was always room for me at the Lairds' and I was anxious to return the hospitality. We walked across to the Herne Bay beaches to swim, went to the odd film, and talked, and read. One morning Mum and Auntie, with Val and Pat, departed on foot for Point Erin Park. Here they would picnic, and the children swim in what were then known as the Shelly Beach Baths. Nan and I had been invited, but declined in a lordly fashion. By afternoon, however, we were hot and bored, and thought we would, after all, join them, at least for a swim.

We found their picnic spot with its familiar checked rug and bags in the park, and were surprised, and rather disapproving, to note that they had left their possessions, even the leftover food, lying carelessly about. Self-righteously, we packed everything up, propping the bags against a tree, and went in search of them. We found Auntie and Mum sitting on a seat in the bath house, watching Val and Pat swimming. Their blank faces when we related, in rather admonitory tones, how we had packed up their picnic for them, told all. Beside them were their sacking picnic bags, packed neatly with rug and provisions . . .

Contemplation of the bewilderment of the owners of the (wrong) packed picnic, not to mention their response if they had caught us in the act, was convulsing and sobering by turns. Nan and I made our speedy way home by a route that did not take in the park.

My mother's efforts to 'get Dorothy ready' for her sortie into the working world — even though it was in the bosom of my old school — occupied her fully for the last few weeks of the long holidays. Mum decreed that I must now have something called a 'suspender belt' to hold up my stockings, as against the home-made elastic garters which prevented our black woollen hose from collapsing around our ankles (and made sure we all developed varicose veins later). This was a fearsome affair; each stocking had to be anchored at front and back, attention being given to the fact that when one sat down, considerable strain was placed on the rear supports, which had a vicious habit of giving up the struggle and popping open. As, in the civilised world, young ladies could not be seen to be groping at their nether regions in public, you were obliged to shuffle around with one sagging stocking until retreat was possible.

None of this would have been necessary if we had been able to buy stockings that fitted us. I never owned any that reached more than six inches above my knee and I have long legs. Later that year, I bought some 'easies' (always in the plural), a tubular elastic affair that stretched from one's navel to one's thighs, with suspenders attached, and was designed to give more flexibility, as well as keeping one's contours firmly confined. I had no need of this second facility and must have bought an over-large size for my bony frame, as the whole wretched thing persisted in sliding down, pulled by the suspenders, which were pulled in turn by the stockings, until I was obliged to walk with my upper legs clamped firmly together, my lower legs operating scissor-like, until I could find a dark corner in which to hoist the whole lamentable structure up again. Perhaps shoulder straps, to hold the easies up, might have helped . . .

I have often thought, in recent years, that in no area has women's liberation been more truly *freeing* than in that of clothing. The sight of young — and old — women today shopping in comfortable trousers and jerseys, their feet encased in socks and flat-heeled shoes, gives me profound satisfaction.

There had been times, during my life at Grammar, when I had had no clothes to 'go out in' except my school uniform, but the situation had improved since the advent of Dad's regular army pay. Still, one would not have expected more than one set of 'going out' clothes at the best of times. Now, I would need several changes, as well as shoes, a supply of the despised stockings, and a jacket. I had already discovered that university students almost without exception wore fawn cotton gaberdine raincoats, and that these were meant to be grubby. I was saving steadily for this badge of office, and expected to be able to buy my raincoat before winter, though arranging grubbiness in a hurry might be problematical.

Mum made all my new clothes: several skirts and blouses, and a dress, mostly out of material that she already had stored away. My most handsome skirt was made from a years-old light grey serge skirt of her own mother's, 'turned' and beautifully tailored. My mother had great skill 'with the needle'. A blue tweed jacket, made from *new* material, was a great joy, and lasted for years. As each garment was finished, I donned it and dashed next door to show Mrs Beuth and Bebbie. I hadn't changed much, in some ways, since I had paraded in my Grammar uniform, years earlier. When Mum arrived home, triumphant, from a sale at Smith and Caughey's with *two* new, light woollen jumpers, one a soft rose and the other pale blue, I could hardly believe my eyes. I would be royally apparelled, it seemed to me.

It was obvious that my mother enjoyed this outfitting exercise. Even though all clothing and materials were rationed, we were not short of coupons as we seldom bought anything new. I had shown little interest in what I wore previously, but 'things are different now', Mum decreed, and I had to agree. For her part: well, there was some evidence that I was turning into a normal girl after all, and this was gratifying.

TWENTY-SEVEN

*I*n February 1943 war raged throughout the world. In North Africa, after two years of fighting over 1,600 miles of desert between Tunis and El Alamein, the Germans were facing imminent defeat. In eastern Europe the Russians were struggling desperately to repel the German armies, and in the Atlantic, the battle to stop the Germans preventing American supplies from reaching Britain was waged continuously, on the sea and in the air. In the Pacific, February was the month in which the Americans finally drove the Japanese from the island of Guadalcanal lessening, but still not banishing, the possibility of a Japanese invasion of Australia, with New Zealand the next obvious step. In retrospect, it is possible to see that the tide was beginning to turn in our favour on all war fronts, but casualties on land, sea and in the air reached horrifying proportions for all involved nations, in early 1943.

In Auckland, New Zealand, the sun shone and I put on my new clothes and advanced if not bravely, at least determinedly into my future. Fortune favoured me, this year. Its first manifestation appeared in the person of Rachel Woodward, Bachelor of Home Science, aged twenty-two, straight from a southern university to her first job: as Domestic Science mistress at AGGS. *And*, she assured me, her assistant, 'terrified at the prospect'. Rachel didn't look, or sound, terrified; she looked attractive and all-of-a-piece (as against my fragmentation) and sounded cheerful, confident and *pleased*, not only with the conditions she encountered, but with *me*.

I had been practising a style of quiet unobtrusive dignity (which was difficult, because alien to my nature) and here we were, Rachel and I (not 'Miss Woodward' as I had expected), actually *laughing* together, in no time at all. 'We'll just have to help each other, as we're both new,' said Rachel. I was overcome with the realisation that she had no idea how new — how *green* — I really was, but my fears were soon reduced. I could see, at our first encounter with the new batch of third-formers, that Rachel had an easy, natural authority, and that the girls liked her as much as I did. I simply did whatever she told me to do, and, to my great joy, this involved reading aloud to each form in turn during the first week, while Rachel, having talked to the girls about her plans for their year's work, busied herself with the necessary organising and ordering.

I did prove to have one positive and outstanding capacity, fortunately: I was much better, or perhaps merely more *courageous* than Rachel at the daily lighting of an antique gas water-heater which had a tendency when lit (after a heart-stopping minute of total silence) to blow its unfortunate attendant backwards out of the cupboard in which it was housed, often singed about the eyebrows, and always anointed with a sprinkling of ancient dust and soot. (The girls so enjoyed this spectacle that we used to delay lighting the evil contraption until the first class of the day was in. It would have been a shame not to have had an audience.)

Under Rachel's tutelage, I not only learned to cook, but to sew, for she was the 'clothing' expert as well. I learned that discipline need not involve oppression, and (if I had ever doubted it) that laughter was good for all, and need not be equated with disruption. I had almost a whole month to settle in before university began, and by that time I knew that my decision to apply for this job had been a fortunate one, my appointment a piece of almost unbelievable good luck.

Val, Bro, Nan, Pen and I enrolled in due course at Auckland University College, as it was then. There were four colleges, one in each of New Zealand's four cities, in those days. Together, they comprised the University of New Zealand. As Teachers' Training College students Bro, Pen and Val were doing reduced courses, while I enrolled, as I had planned, for full-time study: English I, History I and French I. Betty, and most of the other very able girls from the Upper Sixth, enrolled for four subjects, but I had no hope of passing, or even attending lectures for, more than three. Still, I could fit my degree into three years, I knew, if I passed everything.

Nan had been obliged to find other employment, as she was still too young to apply for Training College, but, like me, knew that her family needed her to start 'paying her way'. News of her job in the office of the Pig Marketing Association in Eden Terrace, not far from her home, was greeted with unwonted hilarity by the rest of us, and was the subject of weak jokes thereafter: 'Nan's porcine employment', 'How's the wallowing, Nan?' and similar examples, until the novelty wore off. I, as another working girl, became quite inordinately involved in the Pig Market Association's monthly balance. Everyone in the place including Nan, at the bottom of the ladder, writhed and anguished for days and sometimes nights, until it was 'out', and some of this anxiety rubbed off on me. I had no idea what a balance *was* and Nan's attempts at illumination confused me even more (I had the distinct impression that she didn't know either). But the Pig Marketing Association, long-gone casualty of the open market, remains ominously in my memory.

I liked university from the start, though I had no real 'university life', as bona fide students lived it. While they were pursuing this life (which seemed, as recounted by Betty, to consist mainly of long, soul-searching encounters in the university 'caf' or at various coffee bars in the city) I was hanging out teatowels, issuing ingredients, checking supplies in the dark pantry, and helping to straighten the hems of the colourful 'dirndl' skirts that Rachel had arranged for the third form homecraft girls to make. All this was very cheerful and not arduous, and at lunchtime, once Rachel had departed to commune with her colleagues in the staff common room, I could read or study.

Both Bro, and my cousin Irma, who was also at Training College, contrived to get a 'section' posting at Beresford Street Primary School, just over the fence from Grammar, this year. In turn, they would join me in the deserted cookery room for lunch, where I would make tea or cocoa, and we would regale one another with tales of hilarity or catastrophe as they occurred in our respective teaching lives. Beresford Street School, in the heart of the city, served families that would now be described as socially and economically disadvantaged, but were then simply called poor.

'Morning talk', famous throughout the teaching world for its revelation of the seamier side of family life, was a great source of joy to us.

'Dad came home drunk last night and fell down the front steps and Mum said serve him right he can stay there and locked the door and it rained all night but he was still there in the morning.'

And Irma's proscribed, polite enquiry about a piece of five-year-old artwork. (No longer did one set up a flower or a bottle and instruct the class to 'Draw that'. The days of educational enlightenment had arrived.)

Irma (formulaically): 'It's lovely. Tell me about it, Jimmy.'

Jimmy (scathingly; didn't the stupid woman have any eyes?): 'It's Mum in bed with Uncle Charlie.'

Getting to four o'clock lectures *was* difficult. At school, it was my job to make sure that everything was finished, and the rooms neat and tidy for the next day. I would keep my eye on the clock from two-thirty onwards; I simply could not get to my lecture on time unless I was out the door by three-thirty, and this was near impossible, no matter how hard I tried to organise things. I became a familiar figure sprinting up the Howe Street Hill to the tram, which would transport me (so *slowly*) along Karangahape Road and down Queen Street, to the Victoria Street corner. In those days you could see the university clock tower from this point, and if it was only ten-to-four, I knew I could make it, by running all the way: up Victoria Street, then several flights of steep steps into Albert Park, and then upwards still, and across the park, to Princes Street and the university. I was never alone in this marathon; a throng of part-time students (and, I have no doubt, quite a few dilatory full-time students as well) made the trip from Queen Street every day, but none of us had any breath with which to converse. The exercise must have been very strengthening to our hearts, though anyone whose heart was already weak might easily have died in their tracks. I never saw this happen.

The first ten minutes of every four-o'clock lecture were spent trying to control one's stertorous breathing, to persuade one's heart to stop hammering at one's ribs and to covertly wiping away sweat from one's face. Hardly an ideal state for the absorption of distilled wisdom, but adequate for the maintenance of one's 'place'. In those days, rolls were kept. Only a few absences were allowed every year. Any more, and you simply did not get 'terms', and so could not sit your final exams.

Getting back to the homeward tram in Queen Street, usually after eight o'clock, had its perils too, but these were different in kind from those deriving from the breakneck race to get there in the late afternoon. We were disgorged into either inky blackness, or mysterious moonlight, street and house illumination having been blotted out by wartime regulation. We were all advised to 'take care in the park, and walk in groups'. The hazards, while not actually specified, certainly involved lurking and predatory *men* (American or indigenous), and we observed the rules, on the whole. If you happened to be separated from your friends, you simply and sensibly waited for the next group of park-crossers, and attached yourself to it. There were rumours of unfortunate encounters, but neither I, nor any of my friends met any hazard greater than missing our footing on the totally invisible steps down to Victoria Street.

Later in the year, I managed to buy a secondhand bike, a monstrous, black 'lady's cycle', which I replaced ultimately with a lighter, more sporting machine. This solved my 'getting there' problem, as I could desert the tram route and ride downhill most of the way to the Symonds Street university entrance. Getting home after lectures was harder: uphill, all the way to Karangahape Road, but then flat until Richmond Road, which was blessedly downhill. By this time, it was winter. I have vivid memories of pedalling stoically up Symonds Street, buffeted by wind and rain, my obligatory fawn gaberdine raincoat, my hair, and my legs and shoes drenched. Ross found me, from somewhere, an ancient nautical 'slicker' which, made of oilskin, was wonderfully rainproof. I made a canvas bag to hold this treasure rolled up, and lashed it to my bike's carrier. I would don my oilskin, fortunately in near total darkness, as I left university. I must have looked like some great looming bat on wheels, but of course I was as difficult to discern as the rest of the traffic. We all passed like ships in the night.

My mother would greet my arrival home, always, with cries of relief and delight, as if I had just made a crossing from the South Pole; and indeed, it often seemed like that to me. My dinner would be steaming away on the stove, between two plates on top of a saucepan of boiling water. Several hours old, it still tasted wonderful to me.

I soon discovered that I would have to work during any time I could snatch, if I were to manage even the minimum amount of work for 'terms', and only the absolute minimum was all I ever did accomplish. I was obliged to go into the university library as early as possible every Saturday morning in this first year, largely in the hope of securing the assistance of a huge *Idiomatic French Dictionary*, without which production of my weekly 'prose' would have been impossible. My own *Concise Oxford French Dictionary*, which I had 'gone without' to buy, was no match for this ferocious piece of English-to-French translation. In company with all the other French I part-timers, I would fall in when the library doors opened. In time, we worked out an equitable arrangement for 'turns'. We also made it very clear to full-timers that, with the whole of the week available for *their* work, Saturday was not to be regarded as a time of access to the vital dictionary. On the whole, the ban was observed.

In 1943 there was a distinct shortage of men at the university; almost all men of fighting age were doing just that. But there was a sprinkling — as well as the very clever very young, and the much-older part-timers who, in the main, were teachers — and before the year was out I was seeing a lot of a Law student called Ted. He was a few years older than I, had been in the army since school, and was now discharged. Our social life was greatly restricted by lack of time, wartime restrictions and sheer, shared penury, but I liked Ted, who was generous and genial, and occasionally able to borrow a very small, bucketing car from somewhere. The relationship wound down in the following year when I realised that I didn't care for having my life organised by someone else — even likeable Ted. I was starting to realise that Mum's early prediction that 'Dorothy will always do exactly what she *wants* to do' was true. Falling in agreeably with Ted's plans was *not* what I wanted to do.

Managing — just — to meet deadlines for assignments in my six 'papers' (two per subject) was possible, but time for any serious study was simply not available. I took to spending Sundays, once I was desperate, in the Auckland Public Library (since transformed into the Auckland Art Gallery). Only the Reading Room was open on a Sunday, and here a bevy of dilapidated old men sought refuge from the weather, and read newspapers and magazines. The well-heated room had most of them steaming away gently, if somewhat odiferously, and like as not snoring, as the comfort engulfed them, but I liked it there, and used to smile cheerfully at any old man who met my eye. There was always plenty of room on a table for me to spread my books around; no one else needed any space. And next door was Albert Park where I would eat my sandwiches, if it were fine, or at least walk, for a breath of fresh air, if it were not.

This year my friendship with Betty O'Dowd developed; by year's end I was occasionally visiting her home, where her parents and younger sister, Pat, made me so welcome that I could only assume that they enjoyed these visits, too. In fact, they became loved lifelong friends. Mr O'Dowd, a serious, conservative man otherwise, had what one could only describe as a comic genius, leaving no doubt as to the source of Betty's virtuosity, and Mrs O'Dowd seemed to devote her life to dispensing comfort and down-to-earth sense to all who swam within her orbit.

✿

Advice that my father was coming home, part of a huge contingent of battle-weary men who had been away for over three years, came, without warning, from the government. 'This is to advise you that Sergeant William Victor Norgrove . . .' No suspicion of this coming event had reached us by way of Dad's letters, or even rumour, which was always rife at that time. It was almost unbelievable.

Officially, the men were 'on furlough'; those without wives and children were to have three months' leave, and then return. The rush on the part of these single men to acquire wives and at least one child was said to be frantic; there was near rebellion in the ranks as the time for return approached. Publicity material was issued in pamphlet form: 'We have fought for your rights, now we are fighting for ours. You supported us then. Support us now . . .' Only a tiny proportion of the men in this first, big homecoming force actually returned, and public sympathy was with them. Many of their mates were dead; sending the survivors back for more seemed heartless and unnecessary.

There was no question of my father's return to the fields of war; not only had he 'wife and children', but he was older than the average soldier. In addition, he had been ill and in hospital for some weeks, before leaving Egypt, with an undiagnosed 'bug' of some sort. Dad was coming home to stay.

I remember vividly the night the men of the returning force arrived by train at the Auckland Railway Station, from which they had left more than three years before. The train was due to arrive at seven o'clock in the evening. It was July, and by that time the blackness was almost certain to be intense. I was horrified to realise that, in English I, I had a compulsory 'terms' test from six to seven o'clock. 'You can do it,' said my friend Val Parker, also sitting. 'If you tear out on time and dash down Anzac Avenue and then down the steps by the Railway Hotel . . .' I must have looked blank, for Val said, 'I'll come with you. I'm *sure* we can do it.' And do it we did; or rather Val did, with me sticking like glue. I had not been aware of this short-cut and have always suffered from intense night blindness anyway.

There seemed to be a thousand steps, and we ran all the way. (I have never been up or down these steps since, but two of my grandchildren who live at Kare Kare, and are third generation University of Auckland students, travel to the city by train daily, running up them every morning and down every night. They assure me that they are, as ever, a daunting flight, but excellent, when taken at speed, for the heart and lungs. These days, the young seem concerned about such things.) Val almost shoved me into the station, and left, to walk to Queen Street for her tram home.

The troop train was already in, as I pushed my way onto the platform, but I found our family party at almost the same time as Dad and they found one another. Everyone in the vast throng seemed to be shouting and laughing and hugging and crying with joy; a very different scene from that of three years ago. Later, I thought about the families who were not there because their son or father or brother was not coming home ever, but at the time, joy flowed like water. Shyness, reticence and false heartiness might come later, once families were alone; the tone of this dense crowd was one of shared delight.

Several of Dad's brothers and their wives, and some of our cousins had come to meet the train, and Uncle Harold took us home in his car. The others, and their families, joined us for a cup of tea; Mum had made cakes and scones, and there was much chatter, mainly about how everyone had, or had not, changed. Dad could not take his eyes off us. Ross was now taller and heavier than his father, and I had changed from child to young woman. Val had developed from a skinny nine-year-old to a plumpish twelve-year-old. Her hair had, to Mum's great joy, started to curl of its own accord (no more 'putting it up in rags' for special occasions), and our little sister was undeniably pretty. Dad later took to saying that between his three children he had 'the beauty, the brains and the brawn'. I had no doubt as to which category I had been assigned.

Mum had made herself a new dress for Dad's homecoming. She had a slim, neat figure and did not look her fifty-two years, I think now. Her smile that night was sincere, but I sensed some apprehension. There was no doubt that the years of my father's absence had been good ones for the rest of us, despite the worry, and the restrictions of wartime. With less likelihood of the sort of disruption we had all suffered in the preceding years, our lives had been more settled. Dad looked older, I thought — his hair was thinning — but bronzed and fit after the sea voyage home. It was clear that he had done well in the army, but we couldn't blame our mother for harbouring some apprehension about his transition to civilian life.

All that was in the future; tonight, relief and joy abounded. Our father had come home from the war. We were a family again.

TWENTY-EIGHT

This was the first year, since I had determinedly spelled out 'John ran down the road . . .' that reading declined as my most avidly pursued occupation. Not that books lessened in importance; when not occupied in domestic chores in the cookery room, I was almost always involved with books, but they were not novels of my own choosing. The required reading for English was, on the whole, to my taste, and introduced me to new authors such as Virginia Woolf, but my divergent habits could not be indulged. There was simply no time. My early morning reading habit stood me in good stead, but the book must always be a 'set' one, otherwise I should just fall hopelessly behind.

As I banged away in the cookery room (in those pre-plastic days all the washing-up basins, and many other utensils, were enamel or aluminium, and clatter was unavoidable) I was hardly conscious of my former friends and classmates who were now cloaked in glory in the Upper Sixth, and who would begin their university careers as real, well-prepared students, in the following year. In exactly the same way as I felt that I just wouldn't 'fit' in the staff common room, so I felt that the Upper Sixth Form sitting room was not for me either. I suppose, if I had thought about it, I'd have realised I was 'neither fish, nor flesh nor good red herring' this year, but I didn't think about it. I felt at home in both the cookery room and the university, and had put school behind me.

Rachel Woodward was, of course, almost solely responsible for my satisfaction in my job; she was not only patient but full of good humour. Disasters (of which there were quite a few) were always funny rather than catastrophic to Rachel, and she treated me as an equal. There could have been no greater encouragement to work well, than this.

At varsity (as it was generally called in those days) we were all totally enamoured, in English I, of Prof Sewell (Professor Arthur Sewell), a short, thickset, tweedy Englishman with a pipe and a wonderful voice. Quite apart from his charm, he introduced us for the first time to the work of several New Zealand poets and writers. I have never forgotten his reading of R. A. K. Mason's *On the Swag*:

> Bring him in cook
>   from the grey level sleet
>   put silk on his body
>   slippers on his feet,
>   give him fire
>   and bread and meat.
>
> Let the fruit be plucked
>   and the cake be iced,
>   and the bed be snug
>   and the wine be spiced
>   in the old cove's nightcap:
>   for this is Christ.

This must have been a favourite, for Prof Sewell read it to us more than once. I could have listened to his rich English voice reading aloud, forever, I thought.

Had we but known, we had quite a few lecturers who were to be remembered by posterity for their achievements and scholarship. Pip Ardern (Professor P. S. Ardern), whom Harry Orsman, compiler of the *Dictionary of New Zealand English* (Oxford, 1997) names as one of his academic mentors, was the other English professor: a fine scholar, we knew, but lacking Prof Sewell's glamour.

In the History Department was Willis Airey, known to have Marxist beliefs. A vague rather boring lecturer, he was nonetheless popular as a likeable man, with challenging views, if one could only discern them, and had been a Rhodes Scholar at Oxford. Bill Airey, as he was always called, must have raised several generations of historians, among them Keith Sinclair.

The History professor was James Rutherford, a tall, rather military Englishman with a very conventional approach to the subject. He always gave me better marks than I ever managed from Airey; a fact that produced considerable ribbing from my friends. In the French Department, both Professor Keyes and Doctor West struck fear to my heart. I knew — or hoped — that I could use my 'gift of the gab' as Ross called it, to enhance my performance in English and History, but French was a different matter. I and my friends discovered that AGGS had given us a better grounding in French pronunciation than most other schools provided, and this helped; but I knew that my French might well let me down. At the end of the year, we all had to submit to an individual, oral French exam, and I was terrified at the prospect. So was everyone else; Betty claimed that she was so over-come with panic that, being dismissed, she mistook the door and backed into a broom cupboard, from which she was obliged to reappear. (Betty seemed always to face exams in a state of rigid apprehension, which must have served her well, as she always got spectacular marks when it came to the point.)

Dad had been home for about six weeks, and was finally discharged from the army. Old family friends, Kath and Alf Hamlin, who ran the Atiamuri Fishing Lodge (today submerged beneath the waters of the Atiamuri dam and power station) wrote to invite Mum and Dad to stay at the Lodge as their guests, for a few weeks. Mum felt that she could not leave her children to care for themselves, though we three rather liked the idea, and tried to persuade her to change her mind. She was adamant, however, and it was ultimately arranged that I should accompany Dad. The August school holidays were imminent, and I could take my books with me. Atiamuri would be a wonderfully quiet and peaceful place for study.

It would have been, but in the event, I did little more than a bit of 'set' reading. Atiamuri, in its lovely setting on the banks of the Waikato, propelled me into holiday mood on sight. The Lodge itself was actually part of the Hamlin's dairy farm, which occupied Alf's working day while Kath, a wonderful 'old-fashioned' cook (huge roast dinners and cream sponge-cakes featured largely) ran the guest house. I loved the farm, and even rode a mild-mannered old horse, with pleasure that verged on ecstasy. I had never had such a holiday.

Dad enjoyed it as much as I did, working with his old friend Alf as often as he liked, resting for several hours every afternoon, and enjoying Kath's hearty meals. In two short weeks, his lean frame seemed to fill out, his face to glow with good health.

I loved being with Dad, as always. I could see that Kath and Alf, and several guests who were staying at the Lodge, liked his company enormously. But then, people always did. My father had a way of making other people's concerns his own, and a natural graciousness that was unconscious, but real. Mum would be thrilled to see him looking so well, I knew.

I found one incident disquieting, late in our stay. Alf had to go into Putaruru, the nearest township, to visit the bank and conduct mysterious farmers' business with supply companies, and suggested that Dad and I go too. Once there, Alf set about his business, and Dad and I inspected the small township, as it was then. Alf had arranged to meet Dad in the hotel for a drink before departing for the Lodge, and Dad finally made his way there, while I retreated to the warmth of the truck cab. Naturally, I had brought a book.

Alf was longer than he expected to be, and spent only a very short time in the pub before reappearing with Dad, who had clearly had far too much to drink. Alf was apologetic; he must have realised his old friend's weakness and obviously felt — wrongly, but understandably — that this was his fault. Dad went straight to bed once we arrived home, without the good meal Kath had prepared for us, and I felt a premonition of disaster which robbed me of my usual appetite.

Once back in Auckland, with school starting again and the last short university term upon me, I was too self-absorbed to notice what was going on in my family. Dad had applied for a 'Rehabilitation Loan', with the intention of buying a small butchery business, and everyone was delighted when news of his success arrived. He was out every day, looking at possible purchases, and seemed to be managing his life well. I could not help some apprehension, but did not mention the Putaruru incident to Mum. I think she was hoping that, after his good performance in the army, Dad might have managed to cast off his earlier drinking habits. It was a vain hope. I believe, now, that he was a true alcoholic. My father's only chance lay in total abstinence, and that was unlikely to occur.

Getting 'terms' in my three subjects was my preoccupation. My relief and delight when these came through banished any other consideration from my mind. I *must* pass the exams: six three-hour papers, altogether. French was still the bogie . . . The school automatically gave me 'time off' to sit — this was part of the contract — but no extra time to study. Why hadn't I worked harder in the August holidays? I asked myself despairingly, and futilely. I adopted a habit that stayed with me through my university years. In times of desperation (and there were many) I would get up before 4 am and spend almost four hours studying, before leaving for work. Mum's repeated assertion over the years that I needed very little sleep was demonstrated and proven; I was able to operate with even less sleep than usual.

My attitude to study at this time was of necessity utilitarian; I have often thought that I passed through the university without really touching either side. I have never been sure that I would have liked being a full-time student, anyway. I like to be up-and-doing much of the time, and would probably not have used the extra available hours profitably. In the circumstances, I was obliged to guess at topics we might be given in the exam, and prepare these, in the fervent hope that they would appear 'on the day'. Mostly, my luck held in English and History — but no such strategy would help with French. It would be touch-and-go, I knew.

And so I presented myself fatalistically — but still hopefully — when my first exam day arrived. Time would tell.

❄

On a morning in early December 1943, I walked down the old stone steps to the cookery room with my head in the clouds. The familiar room, with its benches and basins, was empty; Rachel would be in the staff common room, catching up on school news. There was a note on the desk with 'Miss D. Norgrove' on the outside. Inside were four words and a signature: 'Congratulations on degree results. E. M. Johnston'.

Perhaps she had always had faith in me, despite the rocky road of our relationship during the four years I had been at school. Obviously, she cared enough to search for my name, as well as those of all the other ex-Grammar girls, in the long columns that had been published in the *Auckland Star* the night before. I stood there for a long time, reading Johnny's note, over and over, and grinning. My future had not only arrived; it was, I suddenly felt, charging along in the right direction.

❧

'Remember,' says Ross, from the other side of the world, 'the time Pinky and I made home brew in the copper from Ginge's father's recipe and bottled it all with that special capping gadget and it brought on paralysing headaches and thunderous bowel reports and Mum asked in her puzzled way whatever happened to the bar of sandsoap she gave us to clean the copper with before we started — it couldn't just disappear . . .'

Ross is dissolving into laughter and I am grinning into the phone and thinking, I should get him to write that one up, he's better at it than I am . . .

'Still there, Dorothy?'

Yes, I'm still here. And I remember. I remember it all.